Causes and Deterrents of Transportation Accidents

Causes and Deterrents of Transportation Accidents

AN ANALYSIS BY MODE

Peter D. Loeb, Wayne K. Talley,
and Thomas J. Zlatoper

QUORUM BOOKS
Westport, Connecticut • London

363.12
L82a

Library of Congress Cataloging-in-Publication Data

Loeb, Peter D.
   Causes and deterrents of transportation accidents : an analysis by
mode / Peter D. Loeb, Wayne K. Talley, and Thomas J. Zlatoper.
      p.   cm.
   Includes bibliographical references and index.
   ISBN 0–89930–806–6 (alk. paper)
   1. Transportation accidents—United States. 2. Transportation—
Safety regulations—United States. I. Talley, Wayne Kenneth.
II. Zlatoper, Thomas John. III. Title.
HE194.5.U6L64   1994
363.12'07'0973—dc20   94–8541

British Library Cataloguing in Publication Data is available.

Library of Congress Catalog Card Number: 94–8541
ISBN 0–89930-806-6

First published in 1994

Quorum Books, 88 Post Road West, Westport, CT 06881
An imprint of Greenwood Publishing Group, Inc.

Printed in the United States of America

The paper used in this book complies with the
Permanent Paper Standard issued by the National
Information Standards Organization (Z39.48–1984).
10 9 8 7 6 5 4 3 2 1

In memory of my father, Erwin Loeb

PDL

To Dolly, Heather, Joseph, and Jason

WKT

To my parents, Joe and Ann Zlatoper

TJZ

Contents

Illustrations

Preface

Transportation safety issues have received a great deal of attention during the last few decades due to the impact transportation-related accidents have had on fatalities, injuries, and property damage. The costs to individuals, property, and society in general have been significant.

Given the increase in such accidents, various public policies and laws have been enacted and safety devices developed and made available to reduce the risks of accidents and their effects. Many of these policies, laws, and safety devices have been examined for their effectiveness in reducing accidents and/or the effects of accidents. The question of instituting policies and requiring the use of safety devices has been argued vehemently at both local and national levels.

Usually, studies examining the effectiveness of a particular safety policy have been conducted for a single transportation mode in isolation. For example, operator inexperience is a common factor contributing to accidents in all modes of transportation. Yet the inferences made on the impact of the experience factor and the possible policy actions suggested to address this issue for one mode of transportation are generally not extended to other modes. As such, researchers investigating the effects of the experience factor on airline accidents may not be aware of similar studies in the trucking industry. Another example concerns studies of the effects of alcohol consumption by automobile drivers on highway accidents. It is agreed that alcohol and driving automobiles do not mix. One could easily infer that alcohol consumption and operating a recreational boat also do not mix. However, while the policy of selecting a designated driver to reduce auto-related accidents is considered to be effective, a similar selection of a designated recreational boat operator may prove not as efficacious in preventing boating accidents. As such, absent from unimodal studies is an examination of why certain policies work for one mode of transportation but not necessarily for another.

Another example of possible similarities of policies across modes pertains to the deregulatory climate of the last decade and the impact of deregulation on safety across these transportation modes. While there have been numerous studies of the effects of deregulation on various modes of transportation, these are usually conducted without considering similar deregulatory effects on other modes. For example, studies of the effects of deregulation on safety within the airline industry are usually conducted independent of similar studies for other modes of transportation.

This book addresses these issues and such omissions by sequentially covering the topic of transportation safety across major modes of transportation (that is, automobiles, trucks, aircraft, recreational boats, commercial vessels, and railroads) in one volume. We examine the causes of accidents for each mode of transportation, drawing heavily on the recent literature. The deterrents of accidents and the reduction of the effects of accidents, be they due to safety devices or public policies and legislation, are examined by mode of transportation. Where applicable, accident deterrents and policies are compared across modes. In addition, where pertinent, we indicate that various modes of transportation may not be equally affected by the same types of contributing factors of accidents. Also, we address the issue that safety policies that are effective for one mode of transportation may not be necessarily as effective, if at all, in another mode. In any case, this volume presents a concise evaluation of factors and policies that contribute to transportation safety issues across various modes.

Acknowledgments

We are grateful to our editors, Eric Valentine and Ron Chambers, for their help, encouragement, and understanding throughout all stages of this enterprise. Thanks are also due to Tom Gannon, who assisted us in the early stages.

I am grateful to the Graduate School of Rutgers University, Newark, for a Graduate School Research Award, which was helpful with the completion of this book. Our departmental secretary, Marilyn L. Johnson, was most helpful with many of the tables, which always were needed at the last minute. I extend a special note of thanks to my wife, Marilyn, my son, Steven, and my daughter, Jennifer, who encouraged me to complete the tasks associated with this book. Their understanding during some trying times was of immense value. Without their love, this work would never have been completed.

Peter D. Loeb

I thank John Carroll University for a Grauel Faculty Fellowship, which enabled the completion of much research for this book. Michele McFarland and Barb Lovequist provided expert typing. Matthew Parish and Godfrey Chua provided excellent research assistance. A note of gratitude goes to Mike Fogarty, director of the Center for Regional Economic Issues, for encouraging my research on this and other projects.

I would especially like to thank Diane Hershberger and my parents for their moral support. Their constant encouragement helped me immensely on this project.

Tom Zlatoper

1

Introduction

THE CONCERN FOR TRANSPORTATION SAFETY

In the 1970s and 1980s, the United States and a number of other developed countries (for example, Australia, Canada, and the United Kingdom) deregulated a number of their transportation modes. In the United States, for example, airlines were deregulated with passage of the Airline Deregulation Act of 1978; railroads were deregulated with passage of the Railroad Revitalization and Regulatory Reform Act of 1976 and the Staggers Rail Act of 1980; truck carriers were deregulated with passage of the Motor Carrier Act of 1980; and ocean carriers were deregulated with passage of the Shipping Act of 1984. These laws allowed the modes to compete in a market environment, resulting in benefits (for example, lower prices) to transportation users and cost savings to modes. One concern of economic deregulation is the possible adverse effect on transportation safety — the adverse financial conditions expected in the market environment may result in modes cutting back on safety expenditures, thus resulting in a deterioration in safety.

The concern for transportation safety has not only intensified because of the public's heightened awareness of the possible adverse effect of deregulation on safety but also by the public's heightened awareness of the costs of transportation accidents. The latter costs, representing the value of resources that are lost or diminished as a result of accidents, are substantial. They include productivity loss and accident-generated activity costs (Bureau of Transport and Communications Economics,

1992). The former represent costs related to the loss of the productive efforts of accident victims and other individuals affected by accidents. The latter represent costs related to property damage and loss; medical, hospital, and rehabilitation; insurance administration; accident investigation; ambulance, search, and rescue; and legal proceedings. The monetary cost of U.S. motor vehicle accidents in 1986, for example, was estimated to be $74.2 billion; property losses, insurance expenses and productivity losses represented 36.9 percent, 28.1 percent, and 22.1 percent, respectively, of this total (National Highway Traffic Safety Administration, 1987). It is worth noting that motor vehicle fatalities for the period 1977–88 exceeded all U.S. battlefield fatalities in all wars from the revolutionary war through the Vietnam War (Evans, 1991, p. 1).

What are the causes of transportation accidents? In order to develop public policy for improving transportation safety or deterrents to accidents an understanding of the causes of accidents is needed. Once deterrents are in place, we further need an understanding of the effectiveness of these deterrents. By knowing which deterrents are effective and which are not, a more effective public policy can be developed.

This book examines transportation safety from the perspective of the causes of and deterrents to transportation accidents. The investigation is across transportation modes, both commercial and private. The focus of the discussion is U.S. transportation modes. Public policy for improving transportation safety is generally developed unimodally — the safety of one mode is examined in isolation from that of other modes. The investigation of accident causes and deterrents across modes will enhance our understanding for developing effective multimodal public policies for improving transportation safety. Our discussion will reveal that an effective deterrent for improving safety in one mode may not be an effective deterrent for another mode. The primary cause of accidents in one mode may not be the primary cause in other modes. Thus, policy makers should take caution in applying the public policy for improving transportation safety of one mode to that of other modes.

MODAL ACCIDENTS AND FATALITIES

Among U.S. transportation modes, motor vehicle accidents rank first (see Table 1.1). Motor vehicle accidents include private (for example, auto) as well as commercial (for example, truck carrier) motor vehicles. Prior to 1982, railroad accidents ranked second behind motor vehicle accidents. Since 1981, recreational boating accidents rank second. However, the number of motor vehicle accidents greatly exceeds that for recreational boating. In 1982, the ratio of the former to the latter was 3,366 to one; in 1987, this ratio was slightly lower at 3,083 to one. Since 1984, commercial vessel accidents rank third behind motor vehicle and recreational boating accidents. In 1987, the ratio of motor vehicle accidents to commercial vessel accidents was 6,650 to one.

Among U.S. transportation modes, Table 1.2 reveals that motor vehicle fatalities rank first. Fatalities of recreational boating rank second except for the years 1981 and 1982, when general aviation fatalities were slightly higher. General aviation fatalities rank third. In 1987, the ratio of motor vehicle fatalities to those for recreational boating was 45 to one, which is substantially less than the accident ratio; the ratio of motor vehicle to general aviation fatalities was 56 to one.

It is worth noting that, among U.S. transportation modes, accidents and fatalities of air carriers (that is, airlines) rank relatively low. In Table 1.1, air carrier accidents rank last; in Table 1.2, air carrier fatalities vary with those of commercial vessels in ranking last. Because air travel is a low risk activity, one wonders why the news media has devoted so much attention to air accidents. A recent survey (October 1988 through September 1989) of the New York *Times* front page coverage revealed more stories about the dangers of flying than about either homicide or AIDS (Barnett, 1990).

TERMS

The term "accident" encompasses conceptual ambiguities notwithstanding its near universal use in transportation safety literature. An accident in general refers to an unexpected event. Therefore, it would appear that accidents are unsuitable for scientific study, since they are apparently subject to random fluctuation. However, accident risk (that is, accidents per unit of transportation activity such as number of departures) contains a deterministic as well as a random component. Within the deterministic component, there are determinants, such as inexperienced operators, that increase risk (that is, causes) and determinants, such as vehicle or aircraft safety equipment, that decrease risk (that is, deterrents).

Transportation accidents are also heterogeneous — that is, they are heterogeneous in severity. For example, aircraft accidents may involve fatalities without damage to the aircraft or aircraft damage without fatalities. The more heterogeneous a group of accidents, the greater the

TABLE 1.1
U.S. Transportation Accidents by Mode

Year	Motor Vehicle (1,000)	Railroad	Air Carriers[a]	General Aviation	Recreational Boating	Commercial Vessel[b]
1970	16,000	8,095	NA	NA	3,803	2,582
1975	16,500	8,041	237	3,995	6,308	3,306
1980	17,900	8,451	228	3,590	5,513	5,738
1981	18,000	5,781	214	3,500	5,208	3,858
1982	18,100	4,589	178	3,233	5,377	3,198
1983	18,300	3,906	182	3,075	5,569	3,727
1984	18,800	3,900	185	3,010	5,700	3,151
1985	19,300	3,275	195	2,741	6,237	3,387
1986	17,700	2,260	155	2,581	6,407	3,026
1987	20,800	2,512	171	2,471	6,746	3,128
1988	NA	2,854	147	2,332	6,718	3,786
1989	NA	2,898	155	2,202	6,063	3,693

NA (Not Available)
[a]Includes scheduled and non-scheduled air carriers.
[b]For U.S. flagged vessels in U.S. waters.

Sources: U.S. Department of Commerce. (1990). *Statistical Abstract of the United States 1990*. Washington, DC: U.S. Government Printing Office. p. 598; U.S. Department of Commerce. (1991). *Statistical Abstract of the United States 1991*. Washington, DC: U.S. Government Printing Office. p. 604. U.S. Coast Guard annual reports for various years.

4

TABLE 1.2
U.S. Transportation Fatalities by Mode

Year	Motor Vehicle (1,000)	Railroad	Air Carriers[a]	General Aviation	Recreational Boating	Commercial Vessel[b]
1970	52.6	785	NA	NA	1,418	178
1975	44.5	575	221	1,252	1,466	190
1980	51.1	584	143	1,239	1,360	147
1981	49.3	556	132	1,282	1,206	99
1982	43.9	512	321	1,187	1,178	227
1983	42.6	498	88	1,064	1,241	262
1984	44.3	598	104	1,039	1,063	507
1985	43.8	454	639	950	1,116	146
1986	46.1	475	77	961	1,066	162
1987	46.4	541	357	830	1,036	154
1988	47.1	510	363	782	946	92
1989	45.5	523	NA	753	896	82

NA (Not Available)
[a]Includes scheduled and nonscheduled air carriers.
[b]For U.S. flagged vessels in U.S. waters.

Sources: U.S. Department of Commerce. (1990). *Statistical Abstract of the United States 1990*. Washington, DC: U.S. Government Printing Office. p. 598; U.S. Department of Commerce. (1991). *Statistical Abstract of the United States 1991*. Washington, DC: U.S. Government Printing Office. p. 604. U.S. Coast Guard annual reports for various years.

difficulty in discerning determinants (that is, causes and deterrents). One approach to addressing this heterogeneous problem is to investigate determinants of more homogeneous subgroups of accidents such as fatal and nonfatal accidents. Another approach is to investigate accident severity — that is, determinants of accident severity risk, such as the risk of a fatal accident, or the extent of accident severity damage, such as vehicle or aircraft damage severity.

The term "cause" refers to an at-fault determinant of an accident or a determinant that increases accident risk or severity. Investigating causes of accidents is complicated by the fact that a given accident seldom has a single unambiguous cause. Accident causes are often a sequence of causes. For example, the initial cause of an aircraft accident may be engine failure just after take off. If the pilot subsequently fails to land the aircraft safely, both equipment failure and pilot error will likely be listed as causes of the accident. In addition, there may be circumstances well in advance of the accident that may have contributed to its occurrence. For example, the equipment failure may have been attributable to improper maintenance prior to take off, which in turn may have been influenced by deficient regulatory inspection procedures.

The term "deterrent" refers to a preventive determinant of an accident or a determinant that decreases accident risk or severity. Deterrents may be legislated, or they may be safety investments of transportation manufacturers and providers (that is, private and commercial providers). An example of a legislated deterrent to highway accident severity is to require occupants of automobiles to wear seat belts. Whether this legislation will, in fact, be a deterrent will depend upon whether the wearing of seat belts reduces the severity of highway accidents and, if so, whether the legislation affects the conduct of occupants so that seat belts are worn. The latter will be affected by the extent of the enforcement of the legislation (for example, police inspection) and the effectiveness of the punishment (for example, fines) for noncompliance.

Safety investments consist of actions by transportation manufacturers in the manufacture of transportation equipment (for example, vehicles and aircraft) and actions by providers to improve safety. Examples of safety investments by an air carrier (or airline) include utilizing larger and newer aircraft, hiring more experienced pilots, utilizing specific aircraft safety equipment, and increasing the frequency of aircraft mechanical and safety inspection (Phillips and Talley, 1992).

METHODOLOGY

Three general approaches are used to investigate determinants of accidents — inspection, descriptive statistics, and statistical inference. Inspection refers to the determination of the causes or deterrents of accidents, or accident severity, by inspectors at the scenes of accidents. Since highway patrol officers are the inspectors at highway accidents, inspection determinants for these accidents may be found in highway patrol reports. U.S. air accidents are inspected by the National Transportation Safety Board (NTSB) and U.S. water accidents are inspected by the U.S. Coast Guard. Inspection determinants for these accidents may be found in NTSB and U.S. Coast Guard reports, respectively.

Descriptive statistics are various indices such as percentages and averages of data. An example of an accident descriptive statistic that may be used to investigate accident causes is the percentage of total accidents, for a given mode, for which a possible accident cause (for example, alcohol consumption, operator fatigue, or mechanical defect) was involved. A relatively high percentage may suggest that the possible cause is, in fact, a cause of the modal accidents. However, it should be noted that a high percentage, that is, the positive correlation between the presence of a particular factor or possible cause and the occurrence of accidents, does not necessarily imply that a causal relationship exists.

Statistical inference refers to analyzing data of a sample of accidents in order to infer determinants of all corresponding accidents. Determinants will be those hypothesized determinants that are statistically significant, that is, having a probability less than some specified low level (for example, at the 5 percent level) to have occurred by chance. Since data of many accidents are analyzed collectively for inferring determinants, the results of the statistical inference approach are often used to develop or evaluate public policy to promote transportation safety. However, this approach has certain limitations. A discussion of these limitations is found in Chapter 2.

OUTLINE OF BOOK

In Chapter 2, causes of highway accidents are examined. The empirical literature is surveyed, considering such possible causes as driver, vehicle, and highway characteristics as well as economic and environmental factors. Chapter 3 discusses the effectiveness of various deterrent policies for auto accidents. These policies include motor vehicle inspection, minimum legal drinking age, speed limit, and seat belt laws. The effectiveness of deterrent policies is investigated from a critique of the empirical literature. Chapter 4 addresses truck accidents. Causes related to the driver, the vehicle, the highway, and the environment are investigated. Truck safety under economic deregulation is discussed (that is, profitability-safety, new entrants-safety, and modal shift-safety relationships).

Chapter 5 considers air accidents. Measures of unsafe air travel are presented as well as a discussion of the role of economic deregulation in air safety and air accident costs. Determinants of air accidents from inspection and the empirical literature are presented; a distinction is made among types of air carriers. In addition, determinants of the severity of aircraft damage are examined. Chapter 6 addresses recreational boating accidents with particular attention being given to alcohol involvement. Determinants of operator at fault and the severity of boating accidents are also investigated. Chapter 7 examines commercial vessel accidents. Safety standards and enforcement are addressed. Further, determinants of the vessel damage severity of tankship and oil barge accidents are investigated. Chapter 8 considers rail accidents with particular attention being given to deterrent policies.

The final chapter, Chapter 9, summarizes lessons learned from the previous chapters for improving transportation safety (that is, for reducing transportation accidents, accident risk, and accident severity). Lessons learned in general as well as for particular transportation modes are discussed. Such lessons may be used as a basis for developing effective public policies for improving transportation safety.

REFERENCES

Barnett, A. (1990). "Air Safety: End of the Golden Age." *Chance: New Directions for Statistics and Computing* 3: 8-12.

Bureau of Transport and Communications Economics. (1992). *Social Cost of Transport Accidents in Australia.* Canberra: Australian Government Publishing Service.

Evans, L. (1991). *Traffic Safety and the Driver.* New York: Van Nostrand Reinhold.

National Highway Traffic Safety Administration. (1987). *The Economic Cost to Society of Motor Vehicle Accidents.* (1986 addendum) Washington, DC: U.S. Government Printing Office.

Phillips, R. A., and W. K. Talley. (1992). "Airline Safety Investments and Operating Conditions: Determinants of Aircraft Damage Severity." *Southern Economic Journal* 59: 157-164.

2

Highway Accidents: Causation

INTRODUCTION

As was noted in Chapter 1, among U.S. transportation modes motor vehicles rank first by a wide margin in both accidents and fatalities. In this chapter, we focus on the causes of accidents involving motor vehicles. We begin by providing a statistical profile of highway accidents and fatalities in the United States. Then we present an overview of selected empirical studies of U.S. highway accidents. Next, we summarize the collective findings of these studies on the determinants of motor vehicle accidents. We also discuss some of the limitations of this empirical research.

ACCIDENT AND FATALITY STATISTICS
FOR MOTOR VEHICLES

Table 2.1 provides a breakdown according to crash severity of U.S. motor vehicle accidents reported by police in 1990.[1] As can be seen, there were more than 6 million highway accidents in 1990, two-thirds involving property damage only. Of the more than 2 million crashes that resulted in human injury or death, greater than 80 percent were minor- or moderate-injury accidents. In 1990, there were 39,779 fatal highway crashes that resulted in 44,529 deaths (National Highway Traffic Safety Administration [hereafter NHTSA], 1991a).

TABLE 2.1
U.S. Motor Vehicle Crashes by Crash Severity, 1990

	Crashes	
Crash Severity	*Number*	*Percent*
Property Damage Only	4,255,000	66
Minor or Moderate Injury	1,825,000	28
Severe or Fatal Injury	382,000	6
Total	6,462,000	100

Source: National Highway Traffic Safety Administration. (1991b). *General Estimates System 1990*. DOT HS 807 781. Washington, DC: U.S. Department of Transportation. p. 15, Table C1.

Table 2.2 categorizes total U.S. motor vehicle fatalities in 1990 by vehicle type and person type. It indicates that more than 80 percent of those killed on highways were vehicle occupants. Among those who died in vehicles, about two-thirds were passenger car occupants and almost one-fourth were occupants of light trucks. In all vehicle types except buses, the majority of the occupants killed were drivers. Nonmotorists accounted for 17 percent of all motor vehicle deaths in 1990. More than 86 percent of the nonmotorists killed were pedestrians.

Until the early 1970s, the annual U.S. highway death toll generally followed an upward trend. According to National Safety Council (NSC) estimates (see Figure 2.1), it grew from a total of about 18,000 in 1923 to a maximum of more than 56,000 in 1972. Highway fatalities dropped noticeably during World War II and increased sizeably during the 1960s.

Since the early 1970s, the annual motor vehicle death count has trended downward, falling by nearly 17 percent between 1972 and 1990 (National Safety Council [hereafter NSC], 1992, pp. 74–75). The energy crisis and implementation of the 55 mph maximum speed limit contributed to a large fall in fatalities in 1974; the recession of 1981–83 along with increased efforts to deter drunk driving were reasons for another decline in the death toll during the early 1980s (Graham, 1988, p. 3).

The travel-adjusted U.S. motor vehicle death rate has fallen over time (see Figure 2.2). Highway deaths per 100 million vehicle miles decreased from a high of 21.65 in 1923 to a low of 2.18 in 1990 (NSC, 1992, pp. 72–73). Possible reasons for this decrease include: a fall in the

TABLE 2.2
U.S. Motor Vehicle Fatalities by Vehicle Type and Person Type, 1990

Fatalities	Driver	Passenger	Unknown	Total
Occupant Fatalities:				
Passenger Cars	16,047	7,909	69	24,025
Light Trucks	5,876	2,684	33	8,593
Motorcycles	2,890	345	3	3,238
Medium/Heavy Trucks	585	118	1	704
Buses	8	24	0	32
Other Vehicles	212	81	2	295
Unknown	109	85	0	194
Sub Total	25,727	11,246	108	37,081
Nonmotorist Fatalities:				
Pedestrians				6,468
Pedalcyclists				856
Other				124
Sub Total				7,448
Total				44,529

Source: National Highway Traffic Safety Administration. (1991a). *Fatal Accident Reporting System 1990*. DOT HS 807 794. Washington, DC: U.S. Department of Transportation. p. 129, Table 1.

ratio of occupants to motor vehicles, an increase in the ratio of urban to rural travel, safety improvements in vehicles and highways, and more-educated drivers (Graham, 1988, p. 3). Prior to the 1970s, the population-adjusted highway death rate did not generally follow the declining pattern of the travel-adjusted rate. However, it appears that since the early 1970s, the per capita rate has trended downward, just like the travel-adjusted rate and the overall death toll.[2] The post–World War II high and low in highway deaths per 100,000 population were 27.7 in 1969 and 18.8 in 1990, respectively (NSC, 1992, pp. 72–73).

FIGURE 2.1
U.S. Motor Vehicle Deaths, 1923–90

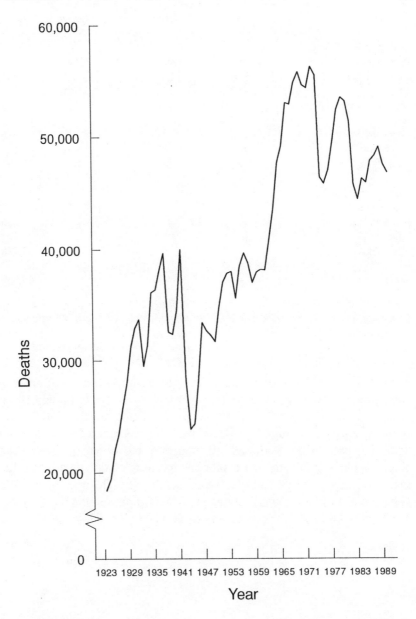

Source: National Safety Council. (1992). *Accident Facts*. 1992 Edition. Chicago: National Safety Council.

FIGURE 2.2
U.S. Motor Vehicle Death Rates, 1923–90

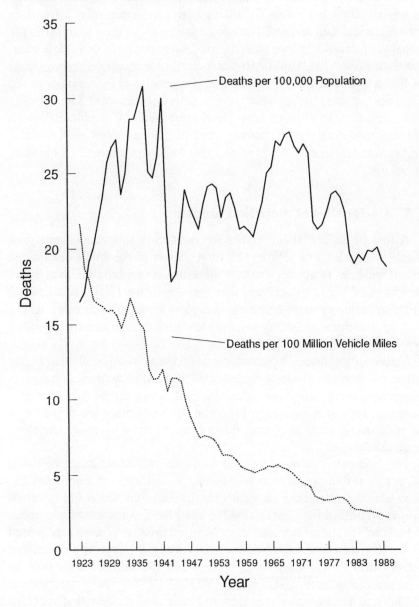

Source: National Safety Council. (1992). *Accident Facts*. 1992 Edition. Chicago: National Safety Council.

OVERVIEW OF PREVIOUS RESEARCH

In this chapter, we survey studies from the scientific research tradition in traffic safety known as field data analysis. This research approach uses historical data and multivariate statistical techniques to quantify the impacts of various independent factors, such as driver or vehicle characteristics (Graham, 1988).[3] Before reporting findings on determinants of highway crashes, we note some of the general characteristics of the statistical studies from which the results are drawn.[4] The specific characteristics we discuss here are the measures of accident damage studied, modeling considerations, types of data analyzed, data sources, and estimation issues. We also describe Peltzman's model of highway accidents.

Characteristics of Statistical Studies

A few of the statistical studies we refer to in this chapter analyzed highway accidents or injuries. However, most of the studies examined motor vehicle fatalities. Fatality data are more reliable than other measures of highway accident damage. As Evans (1991, p. 2) states: "Fatality data are more complete than data on injuries at other levels, and the definition of fatality involves less uncertainty than for any other type of loss."

Various categories of motor vehicle deaths were analyzed in the surveyed studies. These included total deaths as well as component subgroups such as vehicle occupant and nonoccupant fatalities (for example, pedestrian and bicyclist). The deaths of other specific subsets of road users, such as young drivers or interstate-highway travelers, were also studied.

For their outcome measures, the surveyed studies utilized two forms of accident-damage information: counts and rates. Counts are the numbers of deaths, injuries, or accidents. Rates are the count information standardized for (that is, divided by) a factor such as vehicle miles, vehicle registrations, population, or licensed drivers. When a rate is used as the dependent variable in a statistical study, a linear or proportional relationship is assumed to exist between the count value and the standardization factor (Hakim et al., 1991).

The statistical studies specified and estimated models that included factors thought to be important determinants of the accident-damage measures of interest. There were often differences across studies for which specific factors the models accounted. This was true even across studies that analyzed the same measures. The surveyed studies typically specified single-equation models, although multi-equation formulations were employed in a few instances.

The data used in the surveyed studies were of three types: time-series; cross-sectional; and pooled, also referred to as longitudinal or panel data. The time-series data were annual in nature and usually pertained to the entire United States, although in a few cases they corresponded to individual states. The units of observation in the cross-sectional data were individual states. The pooled data consisted of either annual information across states or annual information across vehicle model years. Regardless of type, the data were usually macrolevel in nature. That is, they consisted of aggregate or average values on the observational units.

Two noteworthy sources of accident-damage data used by many of the surveyed studies are NSC, a public service organization, and NHTSA, an agency of the U.S. Department of Transportation. In its annual publication, *Accident Facts*, NSC reports various information pertaining to motor vehicle accidents in the United States. This information includes death counts and rates.

The National Center for Statistics and Analysis (NCSA) of NHTSA maintains the Fatal Accident Reporting System (FARS). This system is a computerized file of data on each fatal crash reported since 1975 in the United States. A FARS annual report provides information on selected characteristics of fatal crashes, including death counts and rates. Computer tapes that contain more detailed FARS information are also available from NHTSA. In addition, NCSA maintains the National Accident Sampling System General Estimates System (GES), a probability sample of police-reported motor vehicle crashes of all types. A GES annual report provides estimates of various national crash characteristics.

NSC reports deaths that occur within one year of an accident, while fatalities accounted for in FARS occur within 30 days of a crash. Due primarily to these alternative post-crash time limits on fatalities, the death counts provided by the two data sources differ. For example, NSC (1992) reported that there were 46,800 motor vehicle deaths in the United States in 1990. This total is 5 percent higher than the 44,529 fatalities reported for the same year by NHTSA (1991a).

The statistical technique that most of the surveyed studies used to estimate their models was regression analysis. This technique can calculate the impact of a single factor on a dependent variable while controlling for the influence of other explanatory variables. For this reason, it is a useful method for determining causation. Regression analysis is discussed at greater length in the appendix at the end of this chapter. The studies referred to typically estimated either linear or double-log forms of their models.[5]

The Peltzman Model of Highway Accidents

Peltzman (1975) specified a model of the demand for auto accidents. The model is noteworthy because it was based on a particular theory of driver behavior; it incorporated many potential determinants of motor vehicle accidents; and it has been adapted for use in several other statistical studies. We refer to components of the model throughout this chapter and, therefore, feel that it would be informative to summarize the formulation here.

Peltzman's model had a rationalist's theoretical perspective.[6] It incorporated the possibility raised by Lave and Weber (1970) that placing safety devices in motor vehicles might cause drivers to take more risks. In other words, there is a certain amount of risk individuals are willing to accept. As safety devices and regulations provide possibly greater safety, individuals may compensate by engaging in riskier behavior to achieve their acceptable levels of risk. In his model, Peltzman assumed that a typical driver faces a choice between the probability of death from accident and a consumption activity called driving intensity. According to Peltzman, more driving intensity (for example, increased speed and thrills) can be obtained only by giving up some safety. He viewed auto accidents as the by-product of driving intensity and, therefore, maintained that accident rates were determined by factors that shift the demand for risky driving or modify the cost of having an accident.

In his study, Peltzman conducted separate time-series and cross-sectional statistical analyses. He estimated the following model for accident rates in his time-series study:

$$\text{RATE} = f(\text{PRICE, INCOME, ALCOHOL, SPEED, AGE, TREND, } u) \quad (1)$$

where

RATE = an accident rate (per vehicle mile)
PRICE = the cost of an accident
INCOME = income
ALCOHOL = alcoholic intoxication among the population at risk
SPEED = driving speed
AGE = driver age

TREND = secular trend
  u = random factors.

The first five variables on the right side of the above equation were specific factors that Peltzman identified as having a likely impact on the accident rate. TREND was included to account for the combined impact of other influences that could contribute to a decline in the accident rate over time.[7]

In the model that he estimated in his cross-sectional analysis, Peltzman specified that the accident rate per capita depended on all of the variables on the right side of Equation 1 except for TREND — a time-dependent variable. The following potential determinants of the accident rate were also included in the model: volume of driving, type of driving (urban versus rural), and urban and rural driving densities.

DETERMINANTS OF HIGHWAY ACCIDENTS: FINDINGS FROM STATISTICAL STUDIES

Several potential determinants of motor vehicle accidents in the United States have been accounted for in statistical studies. The intent here is to note what can be inferred collectively from selected studies about the effects of various factors on accidents. In our discussion, these factors will be organized into the following categories: economic, driver, vehicle, highway, environmental (traffic and climatological), and others. When referring to a specific factor, we indicate studies in which it was found to have a significant relationship with accident-damage measures.[8] Peltzman's (1975) study serves as the chronological starting point in our survey of statistical studies.[9] In addition to reporting findings from statistical research, in many instances we report descriptive statistics on factor involvement in U.S. highway accidents. While not necessarily implying causation, this descriptive information identifies the relative presence of certain factors in accidents.

Economic Factors

Accident Cost

Peltzman (1975) noted that most of the cost of having an accident is usually covered by insurance. Assuming that a driver incurs some percentage of insured expenses associated with his or her risky driving, Peltzman hypothesized that the number and severity of accidents should decline if the cost of an accident increases. To approximate this cost in his time-series statistical analysis, he used a measure of explicit accident costs (approximated by price indexes for medical expenses and property damage) multiplied by an insurance loading factor (premiums divided by benefits paid). He found that the measure had a significant negative relationship with total and nonoccupant motor vehicle death rates. Other time-series studies employing a comparable accident-cost variable reported similar significant results for total, occupant, or nonoccupant death counts or rates (Peltzman, 1976; Crandall and Graham, 1984; Garbacz, 1985; Crandall et al., 1986; Garbacz and Kelly, 1987; McCarthy, 1992; Chirinko and Harper, 1993). These findings are consistent with the expectation that an increase in the cost of an accident leads to less accident damage.[10]

Income

Assuming that safety and driving intensity are both normal goods, the demand for each should increase with income.[11] Because of the offsetting effects of these two factors, Peltzman (1975) maintained that income has an ambiguous impact a priori on accident rates. The increased demand for safety would lessen the likelihood of death from an accident, but the probability of an accident would increase both because of the increased demand for driving intensity and because of the reduced likelihood of death. The overall impact of income on accident rates would depend on the relative strengths of these offsetting effects. Peltzman also noted that the source of income influences the relative strengths of these effects. For instance, he claimed that an increase in some types of income (for example, wages, transitory income) should have less of a lifesaving effect than an equal increase in other forms of income (for example, property income, permanent income), since the former types increase the demand for driving intensity for production purposes. For example, when wages rise, workers place a higher value on their time and may drive with greater intensity.

The income measure used in statistical studies of motor vehicle accidents has typically been some proxy for earned or disposable income. Several of the surveyed time-series studies (Peltzman, 1975, 1976; Robertson, 1977; Crandall and Graham, 1984, 1989; Forester, McNown, and Singell, 1984; Graham and Garber, 1984; Loeb and Gilad, 1984; Zlatoper, 1984b, 1987b; Garbacz, 1985, 1990a; Crandall et al., 1986; Loeb, 1990; McCarthy, 1992) found such a proxy to have a significant positive relationship with the accident-damage measure analyzed.[12] In contrast, the income variable was reported to have a significant inverse effect in many cross-sectional studies (Peltzman, 1975; Loeb, 1985; Crandall et al., 1986; Zlatoper, 1987a, 1991; Fowles and Loeb, 1989; Garbacz, 1990a, 1990b, 1992) and in two pooled studies (Saffer and Grossman, 1987a, 1987b). These seemingly conflicting findings can be reconciled if it is assumed that time-series estimates measure short-run effects while cross-sectional and longitudinal estimates approximate long-run impacts.[13] The results then imply that when short-run income increases, the value-of-time effect dominates the safety effect; and the opposite is true when long-run income grows.

Fuel Price

The net impact on highway safety of changes in the price of fuel is uncertain a priori. Other things remaining constant, higher fuel prices would lead to less highway travel and consequently fewer accidents and fatalities. However, they would also encourage motorists to purchase smaller, more fuel-efficient cars that would place occupants at greater risk in the event of an accident.

Time-series studies have reported conflicting results on the linkage between fuel prices and total highway deaths per vehicle mile. Crandall and Graham (1989) found the relationship to be significant and negative, while Garbacz (1990a) found it to be significant and positive. Garbacz (1990a) also found that fuel price had a significant positive association with occupant deaths per vehicle mile. In another time-series study, Crandall and others (1986) reported a significant negative linkage between fuel price and nonoccupant deaths.

Economic Activity

There is evidence that motor vehicle fatalities increase with the level of economic activity. For example, in a longitudinal study, Robertson (1984) reported a significant positive relationship between the Index of Industrial Production and various death rates associated with car crashes. In a time-series regression, Partyka (1991) found that total motor vehicle fatalities had a significant negative linkage with unemployed workers and a significant positive relationship with employed workers.

Driver Factors

Alcohol Use

Alcohol consumption affects traffic safety through its impact on survivability and crash risk. Evans (1991) cited recent evidence that, other things remaining constant, the severity of injury from a particular physical impact is directly related to the amount of alcohol consumed; and the likelihood of a traffic accident increases substantially at high levels of driver inebriation. He attributed the latter to alcohol's effect on driver performance (for example, skills such as reaction time) and driver behavior (for example, choices such as vehicle speed).

Alcohol involvement increases with accident severity. Based on police reports for U.S. highway accidents in 1990, the alcohol involvement rate for severe- or fatal-injury crashes was 20 percent — four times the rate for property-damage-only crashes, and more than twice the rate for minor- or moderate-injury crashes[14] (NHTSA, 1991b, p. 44). The presence of alcohol is especially high in fatal crashes. Of the people killed in motor vehicle accidents in 1990, 39.7 percent died when a driver or nonmotorist was intoxicated — Blood Alcohol Concentration (BAC) of 0.10 or more — and an additional 9.9 percent perished when a driver or nonmotorist had a positive BAC less than 0.10 (NHTSA, 1991a, p. 24).

Several statistical studies of highway fatalities have accounted for the influence of alcohol in their estimations. Since data on the level of inebriation among the general driving population are unavailable, the studies have typically used reported figures on adult consumption of one or more alcoholic beverages (beer, distilled spirits, and wine) to approximate driver drunkenness. In using such measures, the studies have assumed that there is a positive correlation between alcohol consumption in general and alcohol consumption by drivers. A significant direct relationship between highway fatality measures and proxies for driver intoxication has been found in time-series studies (Peltzman, 1975, 1976; Joksch, 1976; Crandall and Graham, 1984; Graham and Garber, 1984; Garbacz, 1985, 1990a; Crandall et al., 1986; Zlatoper, 1987b; Loeb, 1990; McCarthy, 1992; Chirinko and Harper, 1993), cross-sectional studies (Peltzman, 1975, Zlatoper, 1984a, 1987a, 1991; Loeb, 1985, 1987, 1988; Sommers, 1985; Crandall et al., 1986; Asch and Levy, 1987; Fowles and Loeb, 1989; Garbacz, 1990a, 1990b, 1992), and panel studies (Wilkinson, 1987; Sass and Leigh, 1991). Asch and Levy (1987) also reported cross-sectional evidence that drinking inexperience had a significant direct relationship with death rates for young drivers. There is further discussion of research findings on the relationship between alcohol consumption and motor vehicle fatalities in Chapter 3.

Speed

Vehicle speed is believed to be an important consideration in highway safety. It directly affects the likelihood of a crash through its impact on stopping distance and other considerations in accident avoidance. In the event of a crash, vehicle speed directly influences the energy released and, hence, the extent of property damage and injury.

More than half of all police-reported U.S. crashes in 1990 occurred on roadways with posted speed limits of 35 mph or less (NHTSA, 1991b, p. 28). However, the most severe accidents typically involved higher speeds. Half of all fatal crashes during 1990 were on highways with posted speed limits of 55 mph or more (NHTSA, 1991a, p. 78).

There is evidence that speed is a contributing factor in highway accidents. For example, police determined that "driving too fast for conditions or in excess of posted speed limit" was a factor in 22 percent of the fatal crashes in 1990 (NHTSA, 1991a, p. 154).[15] In addition, several statistical studies have investigated the influence of the level of speed on highway accidents. They typically used as their measure for speed some estimate of average vehicle speed on either all highways or some particular type of roadway (for example, main rural roads, rural interstates, or urban interstates). Time-series studies (Peltzman, 1975, 1976; Joksch, 1976; Robertson, 1977; Zlatoper, 1984b; McCarthy, 1992), cross-sectional studies (Peltzman, 1975; Koshal, 1976; Zlatoper, 1984a, 1991; Sommers, 1985; Asch and Levy, 1987; Loeb, 1987, 1988; Fowles and Loeb, 1989), and longitudinal studies (Wilkinson, 1987; Snyder, 1989; Leigh and Wilkinson, 1991; Sass and Leigh, 1991) reported that speed has a significant direct relationship with various motor vehicle fatality measures. Rodriguez (1990) found evidence of a significant negative connection between average speed and a total fatality rate, but he claimed that his findings were consistent with the theory that speed kills at the individual level.

In modeling the relationship between accident damage and speed, a relevant issue is whether speed is exogenous (that is, determined outside the model) or endogenous (that is, determined within the model). The statistical studies cited in the preceding paragraph made the former assumption. Other studies have allowed for the possibility that speed is endogenous. For example, Forester, McNown, and Singell (1984) estimated a recursive model of traffic fatalities that included separate equations for fatalities, speed concentration, and average speed. The fatality equation included both speed concentration and average speed as explanatory factors. Additional studies (Crandall and Graham, 1984, 1989; Crandall et al., 1986; Garbacz, 1990a, 1990b) estimated reduced-form models of highway death measures that did not include endogenous speed as an independent variable.

Speed Variance

Lave (1985) asserted that lack of speed coordination (that is, speed variance) might be more important than the level of speed in the determination of accident risk. He reasoned that vehicles moving at similar speeds are less likely to collide, regardless of the speed level. Various statistical studies have investigated the relationship between accident damage and speed variance. The measures used to represent the latter concept have included the standard deviation of speed (approximated by eighty-fifth-percentile speed minus average speed) and speed concentration (approximated by the percentage of vehicles travelling within some range of speeds). A larger standard deviation represents greater dispersion, while increased concentration corresponds to less dispersion.

Cross-sectional studies (Lave, 1985, 1989; Fowles and Loeb, 1989; Levy and Asch, 1989) and pooled studies (Wilkinson, 1987; Rodriguez, 1990; Leigh and Wilkinson, 1991) have found a significant positive relationship between the standard deviation of speed and various motor vehicle fatality measures.[16] Forester, McNown, and Singell (1984) and Garbacz (1990b, 1992) reported a significant inverse linkage between speed concentration and highway death measures. Taken together, the statistical results suggest that accident risk increases with speed variance. Chapter 3 discusses additional research findings on the effects of both vehicle speed and speed variance on motor vehicle fatalities.

Gender

In 1990, the male share of all crash-involved U.S. drivers (62 percent) was considerably higher than the male share of all licensed drivers (51 percent) (NHTSA, 1991b, p. 92). At 76 percent, male driver involvement was even greater in fatal crashes during 1990 (NHTSA, 1991a, p. 8). Male drivers are overrepresented in accidents because of exposure. According to preliminary data from the 1990 National Personal Transportation Study (NPTS), males drove on average 74 percent more miles than females (Federal Highway Administration [hereafter FHWA], 1991, p. 220). Other reasons for male overinvolvement in crashes may include gender differences in the circumstances, time, and location of driving (NSC, 1992, p. 59). Greater risk-taking on the part of male drivers, particularly those who are younger, could be another relevant consideration. A few cross-sectional studies (Koshal, 1976; Lave, 1989; Levy and Asch, 1989) have found that the percentage of licensed drivers who are male has a significant direct relationship with motor vehicle death measures.

Age

As can be seen in Table 2.3, the fatal accident involvement rate (number of drivers involved in fatal crashes per 100,000 licensed drivers) in 1990 was highest for U.S. drivers under the age of 21. The rate declined with age except for drivers aged 70 and over. Interestingly, the involvement rate of 24.92 for drivers aged 45–54 was almost three times smaller than the rate for the youngest drivers (70.82) and was somewhat less than the oldest group's rate (27.27). NPTS estimates suggest that during 1990 drivers aged 45–54 travelled on average more than 50 percent farther than those aged 16–19 and more than twice as many miles as those aged 70 and over (FHWA, 1991, p. 220). Thus, factors other than exposure apparently account for the age differences in accident involvement rates.

TABLE 2.3
Driver Involvement in Fatal U.S. Crashes by Age, 1990

Age (Years)	Driver Involvement Rate[a]
16-20	70.82
21-24	52.51
25-34	38.85
35-44	28.25
45-54	24.92
55-64	21.74
65-69	20.30
70 and over	27.27

[a]Drivers involved in fatal crashes per 100,000 licensed drivers.

Source: National Highway Traffic Safety Administration. (1991a). *Fatal Accident Reporting System 1990*. DOT HS 807 794. Washington, DC: U.S. Department of Transportation, p. 150, Table 18.

As with the gender results discussed above, differences among age groups in the time, location, and circumstances of driving may help to explain the pattern of crash involvement rates in Table 2.3. Skill may be another explanatory factor. However, Evans (1991) noted that while an increase in driving skills, such as more efficient information processing, may lead to a lower accident involvement rate with age, this effect is probably minimal. He concluded that higher rates for younger drivers are more likely the result of how these individuals drive, especially their inclination to take risks. Deterioration in eyesight, reflexes, and other factors that directly affect driving performance may contribute to the higher rate for the oldest drivers. The inability of an older body to withstand shocks that a younger one might successfully endure could be another contributing factor.

Stamatiadis, Taylor, and McKelvey (1991) used exposure-based accident rates derived from data for 1983–85 on intersection accidents in Michigan to determine the accident risk of elderly drivers (60 years old and over). They found that the Relative Accident Involvement Ratio (RAIR) equalled 1.20 for drivers under 25 years old, 0.85 for drivers 25–59 years old, 1.01 for young-old drivers (60–69 years old), 1.33 for middle-old drivers (70–74 years old), and 1.91 for old-old drivers (75 years old and over).[17] Given that a RAIR greater (less) than 1.0 indicates overinvolvement (underinvolvement) in accidents, the findings suggest that young-old drivers are slightly overrepresented in crashes, but middle-old and old-old drivers are overinvolved to a much greater extent.

Several statistical studies have estimated the relationship between highway death measures and youthful driving. The latter factor has been approximated by either driving-age data (for example, the percentage of drivers aged 16–24) or population data (for example, the ratio of the 15–25-year-old population to those older). Time-series studies (Peltzman, 1975, 1976; Joksch, 1976; Crandall and Graham, 1984; Crandall et al., 1986; Garbacz and Kelly, 1987; Garbacz, 1990a; Loeb, 1990; Chirinko and Harper, 1993), cross-sectional studies (Crandall et al., 1986; Asch and Levy, 1987), and panel studies (Saffer and Grossman, 1987a, 1987b) have found significant positive associations between highway fatality measures and proxies for youthful driving. A significant positive association between fatality measures and the percentage of drivers who are young males has also been found in panel studies (Wilkinson, 1987; Leigh and Wilkinson, 1991). In contrast, one time-series study (McCarthy, 1992) and two cross-sectional studies (Garbacz, 1990b and Loeb, 1985) reported that variables representing the extent of youthful driving had significant negative associations with death or injury measures.

Some statistical studies have examined the linkage between accident-damage measures and proxies for driving by individuals other than the youngest motorists. For example, in cross-sectional studies, Loeb has analyzed the relationship of motor vehicle death measures to the percentages of the population aged 25–44, 45–64, and 65 or older. He found that total motor vehicle fatalities had a significant inverse relationship with the percentage aged 45–64 and a significant direct association with the percentage aged 65 or older; but the percentage aged 65 or older had a significant negative association with fatalities per capita in one set of estimates (Loeb, 1985). Loeb (1987) also found that the percentages of the population aged 25–44 and 65 or older had significant negative relationships with deaths per vehicle mile.

Amount of Travel

Exposure to dangerous driving situations increases with the volume of travel. Therefore, accident risk is expected to increase with the amount of driving. If an empirical study of accident causation uses as its dependent variable some count measure standardized by a measure of travel volume (for example, motor vehicle deaths divided by vehicle miles), it assumes that a proportional relationship exists between the two mea-sures. Rather than make this assumption, several statistical studies have estimated the relationship between the two measures by employing amount of travel as an independent variable and not as a standardizing factor. Empirical variables used to approximate travel volume include: vehicle miles, fuel consumption, registered vehicles, and population.

Many studies have reported significant positive relationships between travel volume variables and measures of total and/or vehicle-occupant deaths. These include time-series studies (Loeb and Gilad, 1984; Crandall et al., 1986), cross-sectional studies (Peltzman, 1975; Zlatoper, 1984a, 1987a, 1991; Loeb, 1985; Crandall et al., 1986; Levy and Asch, 1989; Fowles and Loeb, 1989; Garbacz, 1990a, 1990b, 1992), and panel studies (Saffer and Grossman, 1987a, 1987b; Wilkinson, 1987). Direct linkages between the amount of travel and other measures of accident damage have also been reported. For example, Vitaliano and Held (1991) found that the average daily traffic vehicle count flow had a significant positive association with the number of accidents on New York roadways. Also, Graham and Lee (1986) and Sass and Leigh (1991) reported that measures of motorcycle deaths were directly and significantly related to motorcycle registrations.[18]

Evidence pertaining to the linkage between travel volume and nonoccupant fatalities varies depending on the type of data analyzed. Two time-series studies (Zlatoper, 1984b; Crandall et al., 1986) reported a significant negative relationship between vehicle mileage and these deaths; but three cross-sectional studies (Crandall et al., 1986; Garbacz, 1990b, 1992) found the relationship to be positive and significant.

Vehicle Factors

Vehicle Type

Table 2.4 provides registration, travel, and crash information for 1990 on the various types of motor vehicles in the United States. As can be seen, passenger cars and light trucks accounted for more than 90 percent of the registrations, vehicle miles, and crash involvements. Medium/heavy trucks had the lowest crash-involvement rate (285 crashes per 100 million vehicle miles). In comparison, the rate for passenger cars was almost twice as large, while the rates for motorcycles and buses were more than three times greater.

Table 2.4 reveals that, based on travel share, passenger cars were underinvolved in fatal crashes in 1990. Although they accounted for more than 70 percent of travel, cars comprised less than 60 percent of the vehicles involved in these crashes. In contrast, trucks of all kinds accounted for 29 percent of vehicle miles, but they were 35 percent of the vehicles involved in fatal crashes. The passenger car fatal crash-involvement rate (2.2 fatal crashes per 100 million vehicle miles) was the lowest among the vehicle types. The rates for both light and medium/ heavy trucks were about 50 percent higher, while the motorcycle rate was more than 15 times the car rate. Vehicle characteristics contribute to the differences in the fatal crash-involvement rates. For example, large trucks place the occupants of other vehicles at greater risk when there is an accident. Also, the small size and lack of protection provided by motorcycles endanger their riders in the event of a crash. Later in this section we report findings on the relationships of selected vehicle characteristics (for example, size, safety features, and age) with highway safety.

Some time-series statistical studies have analyzed the effect of truck and/or motorcycle activity on accident-damage measures. They typically approximated this activity by the proportion of registrations or vehicle miles accounted for by these vehicle types. A number of studies found a significant direct relationship between truck activity and

TABLE 2.4
Registration, Travel, and Crash-Involvement Information for U.S. Motor Vehicles, 1990

Vehicle Type	Registered Vehicles (Percent)	Vehicle Miles (Percent)	Vehicles Involved in Crashes (Percent)[a]	Crash-Involvement Rate[b]	Vehicles Involved in Fatal Crashes (Percent)[c]	Fatal Crash-Involvement Rate[d]
Passenger Car	74	71	74	551	59	2.2
Light Truck[e]	20	22	21	501	27	3.3
Medium/Heavy Truck	3	7	4	285	8	3.2
Motorcycle	2	*	1	1,097	6	34.2
Bus	*	*	1	1,117	*	5.0
Total	100	100	100	525	100	2.8

[a]Vehicles of other types (for example, all-terrain vehicles and farm equipment) are not accounted for in these percentages.
[b]Vehicles involved in crashes per 100 million vehicle miles.
[c]Vehicles of other types and unknown vehicles are not accounted for in these percentages.
[d]Vehicles involved in fatal crashes per 100 million vehicle miles.
[e]Includes light trucks, vans, and utility vehicles.
*Less than 0.5 percent.

Sources: National Highway Traffic Safety Administration. (1991b). *General Estimates System 1990*. DOT HS 807 781. Washington, DC: U.S. Department of Transportation. p. 55, Table V1; National Highway Traffic Safety Administration. (1991a). *Fatal Accident Reporting System 1990*. DOT HS 807 794. Washington, DC: U.S. Department of Transportation. p. 103.

measures of total, vehicle-occupant, or nonoccupant deaths (Crandall and Graham, 1984, 1989; Graham and Garber, 1984; Crandall et al., 1986; Chirinko and Harper, 1993). Robertson (1977) reported that non-occupant deaths per vehicle mile increased significantly with motorcycle activity. Unexpectedly, Chirinko and Harper (1993) found that vehicle occupant deaths, both per mile and per accident, declined with motorcycle activity.

Size

If there is an accident, the protection a motor vehicle affords its occupants, and the risk it poses to occupants of other involved vehicles, should vary directly with its size. Statistical evidence suggests that, on balance, vehicle size has a lifesaving effect. Some time-series studies (Crandall and Graham, 1984, 1989; Zlatoper, 1984b; Crandall et al., 1986) and a panel study (Graham, 1984) found significant negative associations between size — measured by average vehicle weight — and various motor vehicle fatality measures. Consistent with these findings, another time-series study (Garbacz, 1990a) reported a significant positive linkage between a proxy for small vehicle size — average miles per gallon of the vehicle stock — and highway death measures. In contrast, the time-series results of Forester, McNown, and Singell (1984) revealed a significant inverse relationship between total highway fatalities and small size; but the authors noted that they may have used an inappropriate proxy for small size: percentage of purchased cars that are imported.

In time-series multiple regression models of motor vehicle fatality rates, McCarthy (1992) included both car and truck size among his explanatory variables. He approximated size by the inverse of the average miles per gallon for cars and trucks. As expected, his regression results revealed that car size had significant inverse relationships with both total and urban fatalities per vehicle mile; truck size had significant positive associations with total, urban, and rural deaths per vehicle mile.

Evans and Frick (1992) examined the safety effects of two aspects of vehicle size: weight and dimensions. Specifically, they used FARS data for two-car crashes to analyze the linkages between car mass (measured by weight), car size (measured by wheelbase), and driver fatality risk. They found that when cars with similar wheelbases but different masses collide, driver fatality risk is lower in the heavier car. They also found that in accidents involving cars of comparable masses but dissimilar wheelbases, driver fatality risk does not vary with wheelbase. Based on these results, Evans and Frick (1992, p. 1111) concluded that "mass is the dominant causative factor in the large dependence of driver fatality risk on mass in two-car crashes, with size playing at most a secondary role."

Mandated Vehicle Safety Features

Federal motor vehicle safety regulation in the United States began with the passage of the National Traffic and Motor Vehicle Safety Act of 1966. This act created NHTSA and directed the new agency to determine design standards for motor vehicles sold in the United States. The first set of standards became effective in 1968. They included 19 requirements, some directed toward accident avoidance (for example, hydraulic brakes in passenger cars) and others directed toward crash protection and survivability (for example, padded dashboards).[19]

Technological studies concluded that the mandated safety devices had dramatic lifesaving effects. Peltzman (1975) criticized these studies for disregarding the offsetting influences of the private demand for safety and the response of drivers to the required safety features. He utilized the model discussed earlier to analyze the impact of the federally mandated safety regulation. Using results from his time-series estimates, he predicted highway death rates that could have been expected without safety regulation. Comparing these rates with actual rates, Peltzman concluded that automobile safety regulation did not affect the total motor vehicle fatality rate and may have brought about a shift in the burden of accident risk toward nonoccupants. The results of his cross-sectional statistical analysis also led Peltzman to conclude that safety regulation did not decrease highway deaths.

Subsequent to Peltzman's analysis, several statistical studies of traffic fatalities, which account for the impact of federal safety regulation, have been conducted.[20] Unlike Peltzman, many of these studies have employed direct measures of the federal safety standards as independent factors in their regression estimations. In time-series and cross-sectional studies, the measures have been continuous in nature (for example, the proportion of cars subject to safety standards or the proportion of miles driven by safety-regulated cars), while pooled studies have typically employed discrete measures (for example, dummy variables for safety-regulated car model years). Evidence of some offsetting driver behavior (that is, a significant direct relationship between the extent of safety regulation and deaths of pedestrians and other nonoccupants) has been reported (Zlatoper, 1984b; Crandall et al., 1986; Garbacz, 1990a). The consensus among this research is that mandated safety regulation has led to reductions in measures of total highway and vehicle-occupant fatalities. Statistically significant results supporting this conclusion have been reported in time-series studies (Crandall and Graham, 1984, 1989; Graham and Garber, 1984; Zlatoper, 1984b, 1987b; Garbacz, 1985, 1990a; Crandall et al., 1986; Garbacz and Kelly, 1987; Loeb, 1990), cross-sectional studies (Zlatoper, 1984a, 1987a; Crandall et al., 1986), and longitudinal studies (Robertson, 1981, 1984; Orr, 1984; Graham, 1984).

Drawing upon the economics and cognition literature, Chirinko and Harper (1993) recently provided a new assessment of the effect of automobile safety regulation. In order to have a reference point, they conducted a conventional econometric analysis of this regulation by using annual U.S. data to estimate separate equations for occupant and nonoccupant fatality rates. In multiple regression estimates of their preferred functional form (logarithmic first differences), an index of occupant safety standards had a significant inverse relationship with occupant deaths per vehicle mile and an insignificant positive association with nonoccupant deaths per vehicle mile.

Chirinko and Harper noted that conventional analyses of automobile safety regulation focused on the probability of death. Pursuing an alternative approach, they specified a component model which decomposed the likelihood of death into the probability of death in an accident and the probability of an accident. Again using annual U.S. data, they estimated separate multiple regression equations for both component probabilities, representing the former probability by a vulnerability rate (occupant deaths divided by motor vehicle accidents) and the latter by an accident rate (motor vehicle accidents divided by vehicle miles). In estimates of the preferred functional form, the occupant safety index had a significant negative association with the vulnerability rate and an insignificant positive linkage with the accident rate. Chirinko and Harper also performed simulations that revealed that the number of occupant deaths averted by the safety standards exceeded the nonoccupant fatalities attributable to the standards. Their findings supported the consensus opinion that automobile safety regulation has had an overall lifesaving effect.

Age

Due to wear and tear, an older vehicle should be less safe than a newer vehicle, other things being equal. Interestingly, accident-involved vehicles tend to be newer models. For example, 53 percent of the U.S. vehicles involved in crashes in 1990 were model year 1985 or newer (NHTSA, 1991b, p. 56). This reflects newer vehicles' share of the vehicle fleet. In 1990, 46 percent of U.S. cars had been in use five years or less (U.S. Department of Commerce, 1992, p. 605). It can also be attributed to the fact that newer cars are driven more miles annually than older cars (Crandall et al., 1986, p. 61). There is evidence from statistical studies that older vehicles are less safe. A few pooled studies (Robertson, 1981; Orr, 1984; Graham, 1984) found that vehicle age has a significant direct relationship with various motor vehicle death rates.

Highway Factors

Type of Roadway

Table 2.5 provides a breakdown for the United States in 1990 of fatal-crash and vehicle-mileage information by roadway function class. Its contents reveal the relative safety of interstate highways. Although 22.3 percent of motor vehicle travel occurred on interstates, only 10.6 percent of fatal accidents were on these roadways. The fatal crash rate (per 100

TABLE 2.5
Fatal Crashes and Vehicle Mileage in the United States
by Roadway Function Class, 1990

Roadway Function Class	Fatal Crashes (Percent)	Vehicle Miles (Percent)	Rate[a]
Interstate	10.6	22.3	0.9
Other Freeways and Expressways	4.1	5.9	1.3
Other Principal Arterial	23.6	23.8	1.8
Minor Arterial	20.7	18.2	2.1
Major Collector	15.6	8.9	3.3
Minor Collector	4.0	2.3	3.2
Collector	3.3	4.8	1.3
Local	17.5	13.7	2.4
Unknown	0.4		
Total	99.8[b]	99.9[b]	1.9

[a]Fatal crashes per 100 million vehicle miles.
[b]Total does not equal 100.0 due to rounding.

Source: National Highway Traffic Safety Administration. (1991a). *Fatal Accident Reporting System 1990*. DOT HS 807 794. Washington, DC: U.S. Department of Transportation. p. 70, Table 3.

million vehicle miles) of 0.9 on interstates was the lowest among all highway types; it was more than three times smaller than the rates for major and minor collectors. Certain features of interstate roadways (for example, wide shoulders, limited access, divided highways) are credited with making them safer than other types of highways.

Statistical studies have provided additional evidence of the safety benefits of interstate highways. Time-series studies (Garbacz, 1985; Crandall et al., 1986; Garbacz and Kelly, 1987; Crandall and Graham, 1989; Loeb, 1990) reported that variables approximating interstate travel (for example, percentage of miles driven on limited access highways, miles of interstate highways) have significant negative associations with measures of total or vehicle-occupant deaths. A cross-sectional study (Loeb, 1985) found that the share of highway miles built with federal aid was negatively related to injuries per vehicle mile.

Location

While most traffic accidents occur in urban locations, the majority of fatal crashes happen in rural settings. In 1990, 76 percent of all police-reported traffic crashes in the United States were in urban areas (NHTSA, 1991b, p. 26). However, 56 percent of the fatal crashes were in rural locations; and the rural fatal crash rate (per 100 million vehicle miles) of 2.6 was almost twice as large as the urban rate of 1.4 (NHTSA, 1991a, p. 67). Although only about one-third of all motor vehicle deaths are in urban areas, the majority of pedestrian and bicyclist fatalities occur in these settings (NSC, 1992, p. 62).

Varying travel patterns probably contribute to the differences in locational crash rates. For instance, there are relatively more commuting trips in urban travel than in rural travel. On these trips, speed is limited due to congestion, and alcohol consumption is highly unlikely (Evans, 1991, p. 84).

Statistical studies have examined the relationship between travel location and measures of accident damage. Time-series studies (Crandall and Graham, 1984; Zlatoper, 1984b) and cross-sectional studies (Peltzman, 1975; Koshal, 1976; Zlatoper, 1984a; 1987a, 1991; Crandall et al., 1986; Levy and Asch, 1989; Garbacz, 1990a) reported that total and/or occupant motor vehicle fatality measures have significant inverse relationships with variables that approximate the proportion of travel on urban highways. Cross-sectional studies by Crandall and others (1986) and Garbacz (1990b, 1992) found a significant direct association between nonoccupant deaths and measures of the relative amount of urban travel.

Other Highway Factors

In a cross-sectional analysis of accidents on road segments in New York, Vitaliano and Held (1991) accounted for the following highway characteristics: limited access, number of intersections, number of lanes, and length of road segment. They found the number of accidents to be significantly lower on road segments having limited access. They also found accident frequency to be significantly higher on segments having more intersections, more lanes, and longer lengths. In another cross-sectional study, Koshal (1976) reported that an index measuring the quantity and quality of highways had a significant inverse relationship with total highway death rates. This result implies that increases in highway capacity or quality have lifesaving effects, other things remaining constant.

Environmental Factors

Density

According to Peltzman (1975), driving density has a complicated effect on highway death rates. Other things being constant, the likelihood of an accident, and hence death, should increase with density. However, as traffic becomes more congested, certain types of risky driving behavior (for example, speeding) may be discouraged, thereby reducing deaths. Because of these offsetting considerations, the expected impact of density on motor vehicle death rates is unclear.

Some cross-sectional studies have estimated the relationship between traffic density and highway death measures. In his analysis, Peltzman (1975) distinguished between urban and rural driving densities, measuring both by the ratio of vehicle miles to highway miles. He found that the former density measure had a significant direct effect on total, vehicle-occupant, and nonoccupant fatality rates. The latter measure had an inverse, and sometimes significant, impact on total and vehicle-occupant death rates, but it had a significant direct effect on nonoccupant rates. Statistically significant results reported by Zlatoper (1984a) corroborated Peltzman's findings that urban and rural driving densities had positive and negative associations, respectively, with total highway death rates. Thus, there is evidence that greater density discourages risky driving behavior in rural areas.

There have been varying cross-sectional results on the effect of overall density on measures of total motor vehicle deaths. Loeb (1988) and Fowles and Loeb (1989) found that population density (population per square mile) had a significant negative relationship with total deaths per vehicle mile and total deaths, respectively. However, Zlatoper (1991) reported a significant positive association between driving density (the ratio of vehicle miles to highway miles) and total fatalities per capita.

Weather

Relatively few motor vehicle accidents occur in adverse weather conditions. Among all police-reported crashes in the United States during 1990, 81 percent occurred under normal conditions; 15 percent were in rain; 3 percent were in snow or sleet; and 1 percent were in fog, smog, or other adverse conditions (NHTSA, 1991b, p. 22). An even higher share (87 percent) of fatal crashes occurred under normal conditions; and 9 percent of fatal accidents were in the rain (NHTSA, 1991a, p. 72).

There is evidence that unfavorable weather conditions may have a lifesaving effect on highways. A time-series study (Zlatoper, 1987b) found a significant inverse relationship between snowfall and motor vehicle deaths per vehicle mile; a cross-sectional study (Loeb, 1985) reported a significant inverse association between precipitation and highway deaths per capita. It may be that motorists drive more cautiously or less frequently when there are adverse conditions.

In 1990, the fatal crash rate per vehicle mile was lower during January through May than during the rest of the year (NHTSA, 1991a, p. 67). Thus, fatal accident risk is greater during the period that includes the warmest months. Evidence from statistical studies confirms that fatality rates are higher in warmer conditions. Cross-sectional studies (Koshal, 1976; Zlatoper, 1984a, 1987a, 1991) reported a significant positive relationship between total highway death rates and average temperature. Similarly, a panel study (Sass and Leigh, 1991) found motorcycle deaths per capita to be significantly lower in colder conditions.

Lighting

Two-thirds of all police-reported accidents in the United States in 1990 were in daylight (NHTSA, 1991b, p. 22). However, among fatal accidents, only 45 percent were in daylight (NHTSA, 1991a, p. 72). Thus, fatal crashes are more likely to occur in nondaylight conditions than are the less severe types of accidents. Furthermore, there is greater fatal accident risk in darker circumstances. In 1991, the death rate per vehicle mile was more than three times larger at night than during the day (NSC, 1992, p. 60). Lighting may contribute to these differing rates;

however, there may be other relevant explanatory factors as well. For example, there is more commuting, which leads to greater congestion and lower speeds, during the day. Also, alcohol consumption is more likely to occur at night.

Altitude

There is evidence that altitude intensifies the adverse impact of alcohol use on highway safety. In a cross-sectional study, Fowles and Loeb (1992) found that elevation and alcohol consumption have a significant positive interaction effect on motor vehicle fatalities. This reflects the fact that at higher altitudes oxygen intake is lower and, therefore, alcohol has a more deleterious effect on reaction time (Newman, 1949; Mazess et al., 1968).

Other Considerations

Hospital Access

The likelihood of death due to injury in a motor vehicle accident should be lower when medical care is more accessible. Two cross-sectional studies (Lave, 1985; Fowles and Loeb, 1989) have provided evidence consistent with this expectation. They reported a significant inverse relationship between highway deaths and a measure of hospital access.

Geographical Area and Time Factors

In a cross-sectional study of U.S. highway fatality rates, Sommers (1985) reported that the estimated coefficients for dummy variables representing Bureau of Economic Analysis regions of the United States were jointly significant and varied in sign. This suggests that there are differences in regional fatality rates. For instance, Sommers' results indicated that Southern and Rocky Mountain states had above-average death rates. He offered the following possible reasons for the higher rates: noncompliance with and nonenforcement of speed laws, ineffective or nonexistent motor vehicle inspection programs, higher proportions of young drivers, higher proportions of recreational driving, and highways conducive to faster speeds. In other cross-sectional studies, Fowles and Loeb (1989) and Zlatoper (1991) reported evidence of higher fatality rates in western states. Findings of Fowles and Loeb (1992) indicate that these higher rates may be at least partly attributable to the interaction between altitude and alcohol consumption.

As noted previously, Peltzman (1975) included a trend variable in his time-series model to account for the combined impact of omitted factors that could improve safety over time. Consistent with Peltzman's expectation, several time-series studies reported that such a variable had significant inverse relationships with measures of total, vehicle-occupant, and/or nonoccupant highway deaths (Peltzman, 1975, 1976; Joksch, 1976; Robertson, 1977; Crandall and Graham, 1984; Graham and Garber, 1984; Loeb and Gilad, 1984; Zlatoper, 1987b; Garbacz, 1990a; McCarthy, 1992). Loeb and Gilad (1984) also reported a significant inverse association between a trend variable and total accidents.

Many longitudinal studies of highway accident damage have employed dummy variables for years and states. This method of analysis is called the fixed-effects model.[21] The year-dummies represent the influence of omitted factors (for example, economic conditions) that change over time but are the same across states. The state-dummies account for excluded factors (for example, highway characteristics) that vary across states but are constant over time. Some panel studies have reported significant relationships between motor vehicle death measures and year- and/or state-dummy variables (Cook and Tauchen, 1984; Graham and Lee, 1986; Snyder, 1989; Asch and Levy, 1990). These results indicate that highway deaths are influenced by time- and state-related factors, although they do not identify the specific determinants.

Another time-related consideration in motor vehicle crashes is day of the week. In 1990, 74 percent of all crashes occurred during the week; while one-fourth of property-damage-only crashes were on Saturday or Sunday, almost one-third of severe- or fatal-injury crashes were on these two days (NHTSA, 1991b, p. 18). Thus, most accidents occur during the week, but the likelihood of an accident happening on the weekend increases with accident severity.

Airline Deregulation

U.S. airline deregulation reduced air fares and increased the number of flights. Bylow and Savage (1991) calculated the decrease in highway travel due to these changes and the consequent impact on motor vehicle fatalities. Their calculations indicated that there were between 2,300 and 3,300 fewer automobile deaths during 1978–88 because of airline deregulation.

LIMITATIONS OF STATISTICAL STUDIES

In this section, we focus on certain shortcomings of the statistical studies surveyed in this chapter.[22] We do not critique specific studies. Rather, we point out limitations often present in regression analyses, which can affect estimation results. Each shortcoming is described briefly, and its consequences and possible remedies are noted. The specific limitations considered here are: omitted variables, errors in variables, multicollinearity, incorrect functional form, and simultaneous equations bias. We hope that the discussion of these limitations will aid the reader in assessing the quality of published statistical studies and in conducting future empirical research.

Omitted Variables

When a statistical study excludes important explanatory factors, there is an omitted-variable problem. This exclusion may bias the estimated effects of the explanatory variables included in the analysis. Practical considerations, such as unavailable data or too few degrees of freedom, may preclude accounting for certain important determinants. Still, the omitted-variable problem can be minimized by incorporating as many important factors as possible in an analysis. In our survey of statistical studies, we identified many factors thought to be significant accident determinants.

Errors in Variables

An error-in-variables problem occurs when independent variables are measured incorrectly. The incorrect measurements can result when there are errors in data collection or when an empirical measure is a poor approximation of its theoretical counterpart. The latter would occur, for example, if an empirical measure used by many of the surveyed studies — consumption of alcoholic beverages among the population at large — is not correlated sufficiently with the theoretical concept it represents — alcoholic intoxication among the driving population. If errors in variables exist, regression estimates may be biased. Two estimation techniques that are used to remedy this problem are weighted regression and instrumental variables.[23] Alternatively, a better data set could be obtained, but this may not be a feasible option.

Multicollinearity

Multicollinearity exists when independent variables are highly correlated. The estimated regression coefficients of highly correlated variables are unbiased, but they have high variances and are, therefore, often statistically insignificant. A few studies referred to previously stated that some of their insignificant results may have been attributable to multicollinearity (Graham and Garber, 1984; Zlatoper, 1984b, 1991). A researcher might be able to address a multicollinearity problem by using more information.[24]

Incorrect Functional Form

Estimation results may differ depending on the form of the equation utilized in a regression analysis. For example, Graham and Garber (1982) used two alternative specifications — linear and double log — to estimate a single-equation model of motor vehicle fatality rates; they found that the estimated impact of vehicle safety regulation varied with the functional form. If an incorrect functional form is employed, estimates may be biased.

Theory can provide direction on which functional form to employ. For instance, if it is theorized that accident determinants have interactive effects, a double-log specification is warranted. Such a form has often been utilized in regression studies of highway deaths. The linear form, which presumes no interaction among independent factors, has also been employed in many studies. In some situations, specifications other than the double-log and linear forms have been found to be appropriate in estimating single-equation models of motor vehicle fatalities (Zlatoper, 1984a, 1987a; Chirinko and Harper, 1993).

Simultaneous Equations Bias

Many of the surveyed statistical studies assumed that accident damage was endogenous and the determinants of this damage were exogenous. As a result, they estimated single-equation models, regressing their measures of accident damage on the determinants accounted for in the analyses. MacAvoy (1976) pointed out that some of the causes of accidents may be endogenous in nature.

Problems can arise if the endogeneity of causal factors is not accounted for in model estimation. Specifically, biased estimates may result if a single-equation model that has endogenous explanatory variables is estimated by ordinary least squares. A remedy to this problem is to specify a model consisting of a system of equations within which all endogenous variables can be determined jointly. There are methods available to estimate the equations in a simultaneous system either individually or jointly.[25] Some of the studies surveyed in this chapter accounted for the potential endogeneity of causal factors in their estimation procedures (Crandall and Graham, 1984; Crandall et al., 1986; Saffer and Grossman, 1987b; Garbacz, 1990a, 1990b; Sass and Leigh, 1991).

Methods have been suggested for the detection of many of the above-mentioned specification errors. Chapter 3 refers to some of these methods.

SUMMARY

Several statistical studies have investigated the impact of various factors on highway accidents in the United States. In this chapter, we reported the collective findings of some of this research. The types of accident damage analyzed were fatalities, injuries, and accidents. Among these three damage types, fatalities were examined most often. The surveyed studies specified models that included factors thought to be important determinants of accident-damage measures expressed either as counts or rates (that is, standardized counts). Typically, the models were estimated by regression analysis, using one or more of the following types of data: time-series; cross-sectional; and pooled.

Statistical findings indicate that various economic factors affect highway safety. For example, some studies found that explicit accident costs, such as medical expenses and property damage, have a statistically significant inverse relationship with highway death measures. This suggests that increases in these costs lead to fewer motor vehicle deaths. The relationship between income and measures of highway accident damage was found to be significant in many analyses, although its nature varied depending on the type of data used. In time-series studies, the relationship was direct, while it was inverse in cross-sectional and pooled analyses. The time-series results suggest that when short-run income increases, the desire to save time outweighs the desire to consume more safety. The cross-sectional and pooled findings imply that the safety effect dominates when long-run income increases. Another consideration in highway safety is the level of economic activity. Evidence suggests that motor vehicle deaths increase when the economy is improving.

The impact of many driver-related factors on highway safety has been examined. Statistically significant results indicate that highway death measures increase with alcohol consumption, the level of speed, speed variance, and the amount of travel. There is also evidence that the measures are directly related to the percentage of male drivers. On the matter of driver age, findings suggest that motorists from the youngest and oldest age categories are overrepresented in highway accidents.

Research results imply that certain vehicle factors have a bearing on highway safety. Some studies reported that highway death measures are significantly and inversely related to weight-based proxies for vehicle size, indicating that heavier vehicles provide more crash protection. Several analyses found that federally mandated vehicle safety features have had an overall lifesaving effect. There is also evidence that motor vehicle death measures are directly linked to vehicle age and the relative amount of truck activity.

The functional class and location of roadways appear to be relevant considerations in highway safety. Researchers have found that highway death measures are significantly lower on interstate roadways, which have special design features, than on other types of highways. Studies have reported a direct relationship between motor vehicle death measures and the relative amount of driving in rural settings, where vehicle speed tends to be higher. There is also evidence that the number of accidents that occur on a road segment is directly related to the number of intersections, the number of lanes, and the length of the segment.

Features of the driving environment comprise another category of factors that influence highway safety. For example, there is statistical evidence that total highway death rates increase with urban traffic density and decrease with rural traffic density. Also, studies have reported that motor vehicle death measures increase with average temperature and decrease with the amount of precipitation. In other words, there are fewer fatalities in adverse weather conditions. Distance-adjusted motor vehicle death rates are substantially higher at night than during the day, indicating that there are reasons (for example, less commuting, more alcohol use) why driving is more dangerous at night than during the day. There is also evidence that the harmful effect of alcohol use on highway safety increases with altitude.

Studies have reported significant relationships between highway death measures and proxies for factors that vary by time, state, or region. This probably reflects the importance of aforementioned determinants that the analyses did not explicitly account for. There is evidence that highway fatality measures are lower when there is better access to medical care. Also, researchers estimate that U.S. airline deregulation has reduced the number of automobile deaths.

Certain shortcomings characterize statistical studies that we referred to in this chapter. They include the problems of omitted variables, errors in variables, multicollinearity, incorrect functional form, and simultaneous equations bias.

APPENDIX: ORDINARY LEAST SQUARES

Consider a model of the form:

$$Y_i = \beta_1 + \beta_2 X_{2i} + \beta_3 X_{3i} + \dots + \beta_k X_{ki} + \varepsilon_i \tag{A1}$$

where:

$$
\begin{aligned}
Y_i &= \text{ith value of the dependent variable} \\
X_{2i} &= \text{ith value of the independent variable } X_2 \\
X_{ki} &= \text{ith value of the independent variable } X_k \\
\varepsilon_i &= \text{ith value of a random error term} \\
\beta_1, \beta_2, \dots, \beta_k &= \text{k parameters to be estimated.}
\end{aligned}
$$

Ordinary Least Squares (OLS) is a statistical procedure which estimates the values of the parameters of Equation A1. The parameters provide a measure of the independent effect of the independent variables on the dependent variable, all else equal. For example, β_2 is the effect of a unit change in X_2 on Y when all other independent variables are held constant. As such, β_2 corresponds to the partial derivative of Y with respect to X_2. OLS is a procedure which fits data to the linear specification suggested above by minimizing the sum of squared deviations about the estimated regression surface. To do this, a set of assumptions are usually entertained. These assumptions comprise the Classical Linear Regression Model. Specifically, the following is assumed:

1. A linear relation exists between Y and the Xs as specified in Equation A1.
2. The Xs are nonstochastic.
3. The Xs are not correlated, (that is, no multicollinearity).
4. $E(\varepsilon_i) = 0$.
5. $E(\varepsilon_i^2) = $ Variance of the error term = a constant.
6. $E(\varepsilon_i \varepsilon_j) = 0$ for $i \neq j$.
7. The error term is uncorrelated with the Xs.

The above comprise the assumptions of the Classical Linear Regression Model. In addition, it is often assumed that:

8. ε_i has a normal distribution.

If the assumptions underlying the Classical Linear Regression Model are upheld, OLS provides estimates of the ß's in Equation A1, that is, $\hat{ß}_j$ (j = 1, 2, ..., k), which are best linear unbiased estimates (known as BLUE). Best means minimum variance (that is, the variances associated with the OLS estimates are less than that provided by any other linear unbiased estimators). Linear means that $\hat{ß}_j$ (j = 1, ..., k) is a linear function of Y. Unbiased means that $E(\hat{ß}_j) = ß_j$ (j = 1, ..., k).

OLS applied to Equation A1 results in:

$$\hat{Y}_i = \hat{ß}_1 + \hat{ß}_2 X_{2i} + \hat{ß}_3 X_{3i} + ... + \hat{ß}_k X_{ki} \tag{A2}$$

$\hat{ß}_2$ is an estimate of the change in Y due to a unit change in X_2, all else equal. This type of interpretation of the estimated coefficient associated with each variable can be made for the entire equation. $\hat{ß}_1$ indicates the estimate of Y when $X_2 = X_3 = ... = X_k = 0$.

If the error term is normally distributed, t-tests can be applied to evaluate the null hypothesis (H_0: $ß_j$ equals zero) versus the alternative hypothesis (H_A: $ß_j$ does not equal zero). In addition, goodness-of-fit measures (for example, R^2) can be calculated, and various statistical tests (for example, F-tests) can be performed to evaluate the model. Pindyck and Rubinfeld (1991) provide further discussion of OLS.

NOTES

1. Some highway safety researchers prefer to use the term "crash" instead of the more widely employed term "accident." They feel that the latter word conveys the notion of an unpredictable, chance occurrence (Evans, 1991, p. 8). In this chapter, we use these terms interchangeably.

2. Haight (1984) provided a possible explanation for the decline in the per capita fatality rate during the late 1970s and the early 1980s. He hypothesized that along with safer travel over a fixed distance (that is, a decline in fatalities per vehicle mile), there may have occurred travel saturation (that is, a cessation in the annual increase in travel per capita).

3. See Graham (1988, pp. 6-12) for further discussion of field data analysis as well as descriptions of four other scientific research traditions in traffic safety: accident investigation, injury epidemiology, human factors, and biomechanics.

4. In this chapter, statistical studies will refer to analyses that employ the techniques of statistical inference. These will typically be multiple regression studies.

5. In the estimation of linear models, data are used in their original form. In the estimation of double-log models, logarithmic transformations of the data are utilized.

6. According to Graham and Garber (1984, p. 207): "A rationalist predicts human behavior by assuming that well-informed people make optimal decisions." See Graham and Garber (1984, pp. 207–210) and Chirinko and Harper (1993, pp. 276–281) for discussions of alternative theoretical perspectives on driver behavior.

7. By using the trend variable instead of the individual factors it accounted for, Peltzman increased the number of degrees of freedom in his statistical analysis. He asserted that the variable represented the impact of potential determinants such as driver skill, highway quality, vehicle design and maintenance, and health care.

8. In this chapter, a significant relationship is one that is statistically significant at a level of 10 percent or less in a two-tail hypothesis test.

9. Other surveys of research on motor vehicle accidents include Zlatoper (1989) and Hakim et al. (1991).

10. It should be noted that several studies found an insignificant relationship between highway death measures and variables approximating the price of an accident. Time-series studies reporting such findings include: Joksch (1976), Graham and Garber (1984), Zlatoper (1984b, 1987b), Crandall and Graham (1989), Garbacz (1990a), and Loeb (1990). Cross-sectional studies reporting insignificant results include Peltzman (1975) and Zlatoper (1984a, 1987a).

11. A normal good is one that consumers buy more (less) of at each price when incomes increase (decrease).

12. Contrary to other time-series findings, Loeb (1990) reported that real disposable income per driver had a significant negative relationship with both total and vehicle-occupant deaths per vehicle mile. In their time-series study, Chirinko and Harper (1993) found that a proxy for permanent income had a significant positive association with a vulnerability rate (the ratio of occupant deaths to motor vehicle accidents), and a significant negative linkage with an accident rate (the ratio of motor vehicle accidents to vehicle miles).

13. Saffer and Grossman (1987a, 1987b) had many more cross-sectional units (48) than time periods (7) in their pooled data set.

14. According to NHTSA (1991b, p. 125), alcohol involvement is noted by the police when there is evidence of alcohol. It does not necessarily indicate that any individuals were tested for alcohol.

15. The only factor related to driver behavior cited more frequently (in 28 percent of fatal crashes during 1990) was "failure to keep in proper lane or running off road" (NHTSA, 1991a, p. 154).

16. Snyder (1989) and Lave (1989) distinguished between speed variance attributable to fast drivers (measured by eighty-fifth–percentile speed minus median speed) and speed variance attributable to slow drivers (measured by median speed minus fifteenth-percentile speed). Snyder found the fast driver measure of variance to be positively and significantly related to a fatality rate, while Lave reported a significant direct association between the slow driver measure of variance and a fatality rate.

17. For a given age group, Stamatiadis, Taylor, and McKelvey (1991) computed RAIR by the following ratio: the percentage of multivehicle accidents in which the

driver at fault was from the age group, divided by the percentage of multivehicle accidents in which the driver not at fault was from the age group.

18.   Evidence refuting the existence of a direct relationship between accident-damage measures and the amount of travel has been reported in a few cases. For example, Forester, McNown, and Singell (1984) found that total highway deaths had a significant inverse relationship with vehicle miles; a significant negative association between these deaths and population was reported by Fowles and Loeb (1989). Loeb (1985) found a significant negative association between fuel consumption and injuries per vehicle mile.

19.   See Crandall et al. (1986, p. 48) for an itemized list of the initial 19 standards along with subsequent NHTSA requirements.

20.   See Blomquist (1988, Chapter 3) for a survey of Peltzman's study and several subsequent analyses of the effects of federal safety regulation.

21.   See Kennedy (1992, pp. 222–223, 225–226) for a discussion of the fixed-effects model and other models that can be applied to panel data.

22.   The discussion in this section is similar to that in Zlatoper (1989, pp. 146–147).

23.   See Kennedy (1992, Chapter 9) for a discussion of these procedures.

24.   Kennedy (1992, Chapter 11) identifies and describes the following ways of using more information: obtain more data, formalize relationships among regressors, specify a relationship among some parameters, drop a variable, incorporate estimates from other studies, form a principal component, and shrink the ordinary least-squares estimates. As Kennedy notes, another option when there is multicollinearity is to do nothing.

25.   See Kennedy (1992, Chapter 10) for a discussion of these methods.

REFERENCES

Asch, P., and D. T. Levy. (1990). "Young Driver Fatalities: The Roles of Drinking Age and Drinking Experience." *Southern Economic Journal* 57: 512–520.

____. (1987). "Does the Minimum Drinking Age Affect Traffic Fatalities?" *Journal of Policy Analysis and Management* 6: 180–192.

Blomquist, G. C. (1988). *The Regulation of Motor Vehicle and Traffic Safety*. Boston: Kluwer Academic Publishers.

Bylow, L. F., and I. Savage. (1991). "The Effect of Airline Deregulation on Automobile Fatalities." *Accident Analysis and Prevention* 23: 443–452.

Chirinko, R. S., and E. P. Harper, Jr. (1993). "Buckle-Up or Slow-Down?: New Estimates of Offsetting Behavior and Their Implications for Automobile Safety Regulation." *Journal of Policy Analysis and Management* 12: 270–296.

Cook, P. J., and G. Tauchen. (1984). "The Effect of Minimum Drinking Age Legislation on Youthful Auto Fatalities, 1970–1977." *Journal of Legal Studies* 13: 169–190.

Crandall, R. W., and J. D. Graham. (1989). "The Effect of Fuel Economy Standards on Automobile Safety." *Journal of Law & Economics* 32: 97–118.

____. (1984). "Automobile Safety Regulation and Offsetting Behavior: Some New Empirical Estimates." *American Economic Review* 74: 328–331.

Crandall, R. W., H. K. Gruenspecht, T. E. Keeler, and L. B. Lave. (1986). "The Effects of Regulation on Automobile Safety." In *Regulating the Automobile* (pp. 45–84). Washington, DC: The Brookings Institution.

Evans, L. E. (1991). *Traffic Safety and the Driver*. New York: Van Nostrand Reinhold.

Evans, L., and M. C. Frick. (1992). "Car Size or Car Mass: Which Has Greater Influence on Fatality Risk?" *American Journal of Public Health* 82: 1105–1112.

Federal Highway Administration. (1991). *Highway Statistics 1990*. FHWA-PL-91-003. Washington, DC: U.S. Department of Transportation.

Forester, T. H., R. F. McNown, and L. D. Singell. (1984). "A Cost-Benefit Analysis of the 55 MPH Limit." *Southern Economic Journal* 50: 631–641.

Fowles, R., and P. D. Loeb. (1992). "The Interactive Effect of Alcohol and Altitude on Traffic Fatalities." *Southern Economic Journal* 59: 108–112.

_____. (1989). "Speed, Coordination, and the 55-MPH Limit: Comment." *American Economic Review* 79: 916–921.

Garbacz, C. (1992). "More Evidence on the Effectiveness of Seat Belt Laws." *Applied Economics* 24: 313–315.

_____. (1990a). "How Effective is Automobile Safety Regulation?" *Applied Economics* 22: 1705–1714.

_____. (1990b). "Estimating Seat Belt Effectiveness with Seat Belt Usage Data from the Centers for Disease Control." *Economics Letters* 34: 83–88.

_____. (1985). "A Note on Peltzman's Theory of Offsetting Consumer Behavior." *Economics Letters* 19: 183–187.

Garbacz, C., and J. G. Kelly. (1987). "Automobile Safety Inspection: New Econometric and Benefit/Cost Estimates." *Applied Economics* 19: 763–771.

Graham, J. D. (1988). "Injury Control, Traffic Safety, and Evaluation Research." In Graham, J. D. (Ed.), *Preventing Automobile Injury: New Findings from Evaluation Research* (pp. 1–23). Dover, MA: Auburn House Publishing Company.

_____. (1984). "Technology, Behavior, and Safety: An Empirical Study of Automobile Occupant-Protection Regulation." *Policy Sciences* 17: 141–151.

Graham, J. D., and S. Garber. (1984). "Evaluating the Effects of Automobile Safety Regulation." *Journal of Policy Analysis and Management* 3: 206–224.

_____. 1982. "The Lifesaving Effects of U.S. Auto Safety Standards: New Estimates." Working Paper, School of Urban and Public Affairs, Carnegie-Mellon University.

Graham, J. D., and Y. Lee. (1986). "Behavioral Response to Safety Regulation." *Policy Sciences* 19: 253–273.

Haight, F. A. (1984). "Why the Per Capita Traffic Fatality Rate is Falling." *Journal of Safety Research* 15: 137–140.

Hakim, S., D. Shefer, A. S. Hakkert, and I. Hocherman. (1991). "A Critical Review of Macro Models for Road Accidents." *Accident Analysis and Prevention* 23: 379–400.

Joksch, H. C. (1976). "Critique of Sam Peltzman's Study." *Accident Analysis and Prevention* 8: 129–137.

Kennedy, P. K. (1992). *A Guide to Econometrics*. 3rd ed. Cambridge, MA: The MIT Press.

Koshal, R. (1976). "Deaths from Road Accidents in the United States." *Journal of Transport Economics and Policy* 10: 219–226.

Lave, C. A. (1989). "Speeding, Coordination, and the 55-MPH Limit: Reply." *American Economic Review* 79: 926–931.

____. (1985). "Speeding, Coordination, and the 55 MPH Limit." *American Economic Review* 75: 1159–1164.

Lave, L. B., and W. E. Weber. (1970). "A Benefit-Cost Analysis of Auto Safety Features." *Applied Economics* 2: 265–275.

Leigh, J. P., and J. T. Wilkinson. (1991). "The Effect of Gasoline Taxes on Highway Fatalities." *Journal of Policy Analysis and Management* 10: 474–481.

Levy, D. T., and P. Asch. (1989). "Speeding, Coordination, and the 55-MPH Limit: Comment." *American Economic Review* 79: 913–915.

Loeb, P. D. (1990). "Automobile Safety Inspection: Further Econometric Evidence." *Applied Economics* 22: 1697–1704.

____. (1988). "The Determinants of Motor Vehicle Accidents — A Specification Error Analysis." *Logistics and Transportation Review* 24: 33–48.

____. (1987). "The Determinants of Automobile Fatalities: With Special Consideration to Policy Variables." *Journal of Transport Economics and Policy* 21: 279–287.

____. (1985). "The Efficacy and Cost-Effectiveness of Motor Vehicle Inspection Using Cross-Sectional Data — An Econometric Analysis." *Southern Economic Journal* 52: 500–509.

Loeb, P. D., and B. Gilad. (1984). "The Efficacy and Cost Effectiveness of Vehicle Inspection." *Journal of Transport Economics and Policy* 18: 145–164.

MacAvoy, P. W. (1976). "The Regulation of Accidents." In Manne, H. G., and R. L. Miller (Eds.), *Auto Safety Regulation: The Cure or the Problem?* (pp. 83–88). Glen Ridge, NJ: Thomas Horton and Daughters.

Mazess, R. B., E. Picon-Reategui, R. B. Thomas, and M. A. Little. (1968). "Effects of Alcohol and Altitude on Man During Rest and Work." *Aerospace Medicine* 39: 403–406.

McCarthy, P. (1992). "Highway Safety Implications of Expanded Use of Longer Combination Vehicles (LCVs)." Paper presented at the 6th World Conference on Transport Research, Lyon, France, June 29–July 3, 1992.

National Highway Traffic Safety Administration. (1991a). *Fatal Accident Reporting System 1990.* DOT HS 807 794. Washington, DC: U.S. Department of Transportation.

____. (1991b). *General Estimates System 1990.* DOT HS 807 781. Washington, DC: U.S. Department of Transportation.

National Safety Council. (1992). *Accident Facts.* 1992 Edition. Chicago: National Safety Council.

Newman, H. W. (1949). "The Effect of Altitude on Alcohol Tolerance." *Quarterly Journal of Studies on Alcohol* 10: 398–403.

Orr, L. D. (1984). "The Effectiveness of Automobile Safety Regulation: Evidence from the FARS Data." *American Journal of Public Health* 74: 1384–1389.

Partyka, S. C. (1991). "Simple Models of Fatality Trends Revisited Seven Years Later." *Accident Analysis and Prevention* 23: 423–430.

Peltzman, S. (1976). "The Effects of Automobile Safety Regulation: A Reply." *Accident Analysis and Prevention* 8: 139–142.

____. (1975). "The Effects of Automobile Safety Regulation." *Journal of Political Economy* 83: 677–725.

Pindyck, R. S., and D. L. Rubinfeld. (1991). *Econometric Models and Economic Forecasts*. 3rd ed.. New York: McGraw-Hill.

Robertson, L. S. (1984). "Automobile Safety Regulation: Rebuttal and New Data." *American Journal of Public Health* 74: 1390–1394.

____. (1981). "Automobile Safety Regulations and Death Reductions in the United States." *American Journal of Public Health* 71: 818–822.

____. (1977). "A Critical Analysis of Peltzman's 'The Effects of Automobile Safety Regulation.'" *Journal of Economic Issues* 11: 587–600.

Rodriguez, R. J. (1990). "Speed, Speed Dispersion, and the Highway Fatality Rate." *Southern Economic Journal* 57: 349–356.

Saffer, H., and M. Grossman. (1987a). "Beer Taxes, the Legal Drinking Age, and Youth Motor Vehicle Fatalities." *Journal of Legal Studies* 16: 351–374.

____. (1987b). "Drinking Age Laws and Highway Mortality Rates: Cause and Effect." *Economic Inquiry* 25: 403–417.

Sass, T. R., and J. P. Leigh. (1991). "The Market for Safety Regulation and the Effect of Regulation on Fatalities: The Case of Motorcycle Helmet Laws." *Review of Economics and Statistics* 73: 167–172.

Snyder, D. (1989). "Speeding, Coordination, and the 55-MPH Limit: Comment." *American Economic Review* 79: 922–925.

Sommers, P. M. (1985). "Drinking Age and the 55 MPH Speed Limit." *Atlantic Economic Journal* 13: 43–48.

Stamatiadis, N., W. C. Taylor, and F. X. McKelvey. (1991). "Elderly Drivers and Intersection Accidents." *Transportation Quarterly* 45: 377–390.

U.S. Department of Commerce. (1992). *Statistical Abstract of the United States 1992*. Washington, DC: U.S. Government Printing Office.

Vitaliano, D. F., and J. Held. (1991). "Road Accident External Effects: An Empirical Assessment." *Applied Economics* 23: 373–378.

Wilkinson, J. T. (1987). "Reducing Drunken Driving: Which Policies Are Most Effective?" *Southern Economic Journal* 54: 322–334.

Zlatoper, T. J. (1991). "Determinants of Motor Vehicle Deaths in the United States: A Cross-Sectional Analysis." *Accident Analysis and Prevention* 23: 431–436.

____. (1989). "Models Explaining Motor Vehicle Death Rates in the United States." *Accident Analysis and Prevention* 21: 125–154.

____. (1987a). "Factors Affecting Motor Vehicle Deaths in the USA: Some Cross-Sectional Evidence." *Applied Economics* 19: 753–761.

____. (1987b). "Testing for Functional Form and Autocorrelation in the Analysis of Motor Vehicle Deaths." *Quarterly Review of Economics and Business* 27: 6–17.

____. (1984a). "Analyzing Cross-Sectional Motor Vehicle Death Rates: The Issue of Functional Form." In *Modeling and Simulation*, Proceedings of the Fifteenth Annual Pittsburgh Conference, Part 1: Geography-Regional Science (pp. 523–527). Research Triangle Park, NC: Instrument Society of America.

____. (1984b). "Regression Analysis of Time-Series Data on Motor Vehicle Deaths in the United States." *Journal of Transport Economics and Policy* 18: 263–274.

3

Auto Accidents: Effectiveness of Deterrent Policies

INTRODUCTION

The use of high speed vehicle transportation has progressed rapidly with the arrival of the industrial and technological ages. Needless to say, such transportation systems have provided great benefits to all sectors of society. A trip from the east coast to California, which used to take weeks via covered wagon during the 1800s, can now be completed in about one week by passenger car. However, the massive benefits that accompany modern transportation systems are not without costs. Associated with the benefits are increases in accidents, air, water, and noise pollution, and a hastier life style that may impinge on the quality and quantity of life, along with other factors. The increase in accidents has been of particular concern because of the impact such accidents have on the loss of lives and the losses due to additional injuries and property damage.

In this chapter, we consider the effects of policy measures that might be initiated to reduce the impact of auto accidents on individuals and society. The basis of the material is centered on experiences in the United States. These matters have become of major interest to policy makers, health professionals, economists, and statisticians. The benefits and costs of such potential and actual policies have generated much discussion. This is particularly relevant in light of the approximately 50,000 lives lost per year just in auto accidents. This is about 80 percent of the number of fatalities the United States incurred during the entire Vietnam War. Many of these fatalities affect young individuals, and many of them have been associated with alcohol consumption, speeding, and avoidance of seat belt usage. What can be done and what should be done is debated not only in Congress but also in local newspapers and among neighbors in most communities. The costs to society due to auto accidents are significantly exacerbated when increases in the number of injuries and morbidity along with property damage are considered. For example, in 1980, there were 47,400 fatal auto accidents resulting in 52,600 fatalities and 2 million injuries along with 16.5 million property damage accidents (see National Safety Council [hereafter NSC], 1981, p. 45). Nonetheless, policies aimed to reduce auto accidents, or the effects of accidents, are not costless even when they are effective. Furthermore, some may argue that certain policy measures suggested by Congress and others are not even efficacious. It is to these issues that we direct our attention.

The Safety Legislation of 1966

Accidents are a major cause of death in the United States. In 1984, accidents ranked fourth as a cause of death. Automobile accidents were the major type of accident in the United States, accounting for over 46,000 fatalities. Traffic related fatalities rose from approximately 32,000 in the late 1940s to over 50,000 in the 1960s (see Blomquist, 1988). The carnage on the roadway resulted in congressional action. Most notably, in 1966, the National Traffic and Motor Vehicle Safety Act of 1966 and the Highway Safety Act of 1966 were enacted. These acts were envisioned to reduce accidents and the effects of accidents. In addition, the concerns with safety at that time led to the establishment of the U.S. Department of Transportation (U.S.D.O.T.) and the National Highway Traffic Safety Administration (NHTSA).

With the establishment of NHTSA and other safety agencies, a great deal of effort was expended in developing safety standards that were expected to impinge on the safety of the motoring public. These included safety standards pertaining to seat belts, rearview mirrors, windshields, braking systems, and so forth. In addition, the legislative climate led to proposals regarding motor vehicle inspection, driver education, highway design, and so forth. As time progressed, the number of proposals envisioned to reduce accidents and the effects of accidents blossomed. The relevant question then became whether these safety proposals were indeed effective and, if efficacious, whether they were cost-effective. As the previous chapter demonstrated, theoretical constructs were developed to argue either for or against regulations.

Peltzman's classic article (1975), discussed in Chapter 2, provides the reference base for many of the theoretical and empirical studies done to date. Peltzman makes use of an economic model to examine the effects of regulation. His empirical results have been defended and assaulted by various researchers. Similarly, others have suggested alternative models and empirical results that have also been defended and attacked. As previously mentioned, this chapter is concerned with the empirical evaluation of many of the important policy issues suggested.

Statistical and Econometric Modeling of Safety Issues

A host of statistical and econometric procedures have been applied to determine the effects of safety devices and policies. These include, among others: comparison of accident rates prior to and after a safety regulation was initiated in a given area; comparison of safety records between two geographical areas, one with, and the other without, a safety policy in effect; the use of regression techniques to model the effects of policies on safety, which allow for the normalization of other factors (for example, technology, income, and so forth); and time-series techniques (Box-Jenkins/ARIMA) used to forecast, for example, anticipated fatalities based on a time series prior to the initiation of a policy, which can then be compared to actual fatalities — the difference being ascribed to the policy effect.

The particulars for the above statistical procedures are well documented in standard texts in statistics, econometrics, and experimental design. The regression, or econometric procedures, are perhaps the most important of these techniques because of their concern with causality and prediction and their relationship with Box-Jenkins/ARIMA techniques. They are discussed in Chapter 2 and the appendix to that chapter. To summarize, the regression techniques allow researchers to examine the independent effect or influence of a set of independent variables (or causal factors) on a variable of interest, that is, the dependent variable. As such, models may be posited to measure the influence, if any, of various policy issues on fatality rates, fatality levels, and so forth, as well as comparable influences on injuries and degrees of morbidity.

Policy and Safety Factors — Their Influence on Accidents

Numerous policy issues, such as the minimum legal drinking age and mandatory seat belt usage, have been suggested over the years. The influence of these factors on avoiding or minimizing the effects of auto accidents, fatalities, injuries, and property damage has been debated with fervor. In what follows, we address the empirical results associated with several of these policy actions. Specifically, we investigate the impact on auto accidents of: motor vehicle inspection, the minimum legal drinking age, alcohol consumption, speed limits, vehicle speed versus speed variance, and mandatory seat belt laws.

MOTOR VEHICLE INSPECTION

Motor vehicle inspection has been employed in most states at one time or another. A major catalyst for the initiation of inspection was the Highway Safety Act of 1966, which set criteria and standards for periodic safety inspection of motor vehicles. The possible withholding of federal highway funds was used to induce compliance with the standards. Hence, it might be argued that some states initiated inspection procedures to satisfy the federal requirements instead of to reduce accidents. As such, the quality and type of inspection procedures imposed varied across states. In 1976, Congress relaxed its position with regard to imposing inspection on the states. In any case, as of 1980 only 21 states imposed periodic inspection upon vehicles registered in those states.

The effectiveness of motor vehicle inspection in reducing accidents, fatalities, injuries, and property damage has been of concern to policy makers for many years. Quite often, the question and its solution becomes embroiled in politics and value judgments. To provide a more scientific approach to the question, empirical studies have examined the impact of inspection laws on accidents after adjusting for other factors that could also have influenced the rise and fall of such accidents.

Early Empirical Results

Numerous studies were conducted regarding the effectiveness of periodic motor vehicle inspection. Some studies, such as the one commonly referred to as the Indiana Study, examined the relationship between vehicle defects and accidents (see, for example, Treat and Stansifer, 1977). More specific to the relationship between inspection and accidents were the early studies by Mayer and Hoult (1963) and Buxbaum and Colton (1966). Mayer and Hoult, using data from 1948 through 1959 and grouping states into four categories of inspection (states having state-owned and operated inspection; states with licensed garages conducting inspection; states where only parts of the state had inspection; and states having no inspection), evaluated motor vehicle related death rates, measured as deaths per 100 million vehicle miles. Death rates were found to be related to the degree of inspection (that is, states with a greater degree of inspection were found to have the lowest death rates). A major weakness of the study was that it did not consider (or normalize for) other factors that could have contributed to the results, for example, the degree of urbanization, age of drivers, and number of registered vehicles in the states.

Buxbaum and Colton, using data for 1960, extended the work of Mayer and Hoult in their evaluation of the effect of inspection on death rates by normalizing for other factors. They looked at the death rate (measured as deaths per 100,000 population) for males aged 45–54 in states with no inspection, annual inspection, and biannual inspection. States with inspection programs had lower fatality rates than states without such programs.[1] Multiple regression techniques allowed other researchers, more recently, to examine the influence of inspection on fatality and other accident rates while normalizing for the influence of a host of additional factors.

Fuchs and Leveson (1967), using regression techniques, found that, on average, states requiring inspection had a 29.8 percent lower age-adjusted fatality rate than states without such a requirement. This statistically significant result, however, was based upon a very elementary model in which inspection was the only predictor. The influence of inspection was found to be insignificant when the model was extended to include the influence of other possible factors.[2] In this case, the influence of inspection was a reduction in age-adjusted fatality rates by 9.6 percent, which, as mentioned above, was not statistically significant.[3]

Recent Statistical Results

Crain (1980) investigated the impact of motor vehicle inspection on auto accidents using data by states for 1974. In addition to inspection as an explanatory variable, a host of socioeconomic factors were considered as well. Five different measures of inspection were examined for their impact on death rates, accident rates, and non-fatal injury rates.[4] These measures of inspection include the presence or absence of state-wide inspection; statewide or local inspection; twice-yearly inspection; state owned and operated inspection facilities; and spot inspection. The presence or absence of inspection is accounted for with dummy variables, where the variable is assigned a value of 1 when inspection is in effect and 0 otherwise. In general, Crain does not find his measures for inspection to have a significant influence on fatality rates except for the case of spot inspection, which is found to have a significant negative effect at the 10 percent significance level. A caveat with regard to interpreting results associated with the dummy variables in Crain's models is warranted. For example, in the model accounting for the effect of spot inspection, a dummy variable equal to 0 does not necessarily mean that the state in question has no inspection. It could, for example, have annual or biannual inspection.

More recently, Loeb and Gilad (1984) and Loeb (1985) evaluated the effects of motor vehicle inspection using a state specific time-series and a cross-sectional data set, respectively. Both studies were based on a study conducted by Jackson, Loeb, and Franck (1982). The time series study was based on data specific to New Jersey. Examining the levels of fatalities in New Jersey from 1929 to 1979 suggested a major decline in deaths in 1938 — the very year inspection was put into effect. To examine this more fully, an econometric model to determine the influence of inspection on fatalities and accidents was developed, normalizing for many socioeconomic and driving-related variables. In addition, the impact of technology was accounted for in the model using various functional forms of a measure of the calendar year, with which this variable could be associated.[5] A large set of possible specifications for the true relationship between fatalities and the inspection variable, as well as the other contributing factors, was estimated and the results showed significant negative effects of inspection on fatalities and accidents. These results were stable across the many specifications suggested. Loeb and Gilad also provide a benefit-cost analysis of inspection and calculate a benefit-cost ratio of 1.24. It can be argued that this estimate is conservative, because the estimates of benefits are based on Hartunian, Smart, and Thompson (1980). Benefits would be considerably greater if estimates of the value of a life were based on, for example, NHTSA (1976).[6]

Loeb (1985) evaluates the effect of motor vehicle inspection on various measures of automobile related fatalities and injuries using cross-sectional data and an econometric model normalized for many possible socioeconomic and driving-related variables that might impact on the statistical results. Once again, especially with the fatality models, nonfragile (robust) results are obtained regarding the effect of inspection, that is, inspection has a significant negative effect on fatalities. A benefit-cost analysis is also presented that finds inspection to be cost-effective (see Jackson, Loeb, and Franck, 1982, for alternative estimates as well as Miller, 1986).

In another paper, Loeb (1987) re-examines the effect of inspection on fatality rates using cross-sectional data and accounting for additional policy-related factors (for example, the minimum legal drinking age and speed of vehicles). Once again, inspection is found to have a statistically significant negative effect on fatality rates. The results are nonfragile across a host of potential specifications.

The models suggested above were generally evaluated in terms of the coefficient of determination (R^2), t-tests, and standard tests generally applied to regression results (see Pindyck and Rubinfeld, 1991, for a discussion of these). Additionally, Loeb emphasizes the necessity to consider stability of results among competing models. Nevertheless, no specific attempt was made in the prior mentioned studies to account for specification errors. Specification errors can arise due to several factors. These include, among others, the omission of an important variable in the model, misspecifying a model as a single-equation model when a simultaneous equation model is appropriate, misspecification of the structural form of the model, the presence of heteroscedasticity, the existence of serial correlation, the presence of multicollinearity, and nonnormality of the residuals. These errors, as discussed in Chapter 2, can impact on the regression results in a major manner. For example, omission of variables in the model, a misspecified structural form of the model, and the simultaneous equation problem may result in biased estimates of the parameters of the model. Because of the varying results claimed by various researchers, Loeb (1988a) employed a set of specification error tests developed by Ramsey (1969, 1970, 1974) to examine models similar to those he evaluated previously using cross-sectional data.[7] These tests examine the residuals of the estimated models for violations of statistical conditions, which if violated may lead to biased or inefficient regression results. Loeb (1988a) examines a selection of cross-sectional models incorporating inspection as an independent variable for specification errors. None of the models examined were rejected for the presence of specification errors lending additional support to the claim that inspection is a significant factor in reducing fatality rates. Loeb concludes this study with a benefit/cost analysis that finds that inspection is cost effective.

Loeb (1988b) examines a state specific time-series model (the New Jersey model) for specification errors and again finds that the model fails to be rejected. (Evidence of the effectiveness of inspection using cross-sectional models is also provided.) All in all, these results add credence to the findings that inspection is efficacious in reducing vehicle-related fatalities, given the power of the specification error tests employed. In addition, benefit/cost estimates are provided based on the willingness to pay criterion supplied by Miller (1986). These suggest that benefits outweigh costs.

More recently, Fowles and Loeb (1988) examine cross-sectional models for vehicle fatality rates using a Bayesian procedure. More specifically, extreme bounds analysis is applied to various cross-sectional models of fatality rates. The methodology of extreme bounds is suggested by Leamer (1978, 1983). In general, a host of possible specifications are suggested to explain fatality rates. Because the true model is not known for certain a priori, Fowles and Loeb examine the stability of the coefficients across a large set of alternative specifications. Should the estimates of a parameter in question (for example, the coefficient associated with the inspection variable) prove to be fragile (that is, vary in sign) then the effect of the variable would be questioned and one would not be inclined to accept a claim that the variable is important in the model. The results of the study find the effect of inspection to be robust and, as such, add additional support to the Loeb and Loeb and Gilad findings that inspection is an effective means to reduce auto fatality rates.

Additional support for the benefits of motor vehicle inspection is provided by Saffer and Grossman (1987). Using simultaneous equation econometric models to examine the relationship between auto-related mortality rates, taxes on beer, and drinking age, Saffer and Grossman account for the effects of motor vehicle inspection. Using a time-series of state cross-sections, they conclude that states requiring vehicle inspection have lower mortality than the other states.

Recently, Garbacz and Kelly (1987) argued that inspection is not effective in reducing vehicle-related fatalities. They question the results of Loeb and Gilad, claiming that the Loeb and Gilad model (for New Jersey) was misspecified because it did not include the impact of accident price, alcohol consumption, or the effects of youthful drivers. They then developed an aggregate U.S. model to examine automobile fatality rates for the time period 1952 to 1982. Using a multiplicative model, they concluded that inspection is not effective in reducing fatalities.

In response to Garbacz and Kelly, Loeb (1990) examines models similar to those suggested by Garbacz and Kelly using aggregate U.S. time-series data for the periods 1952–82 as well as 1952–85.[8] Loeb finds that inspection is effective in reducing fatalities and fatality rates.

Because of the disparity of results between Loeb (1990) and Garbacz and Kelly (1987), Loeb examines his models for specification errors using one of the Ramsey tests — the Regression Specification Error Test (RESET) — discussed above. This test is used for detecting specification errors of omission of variables, simultaneous equation problems, and misspecification of the structural form of the models. In addition, it is statistically powerful. None of the models estimated by Loeb can be rejected due to the above mentioned specification errors, adding credence to the general results he reports. Also, Loeb examines the New Jersey time-series model for specification errors, given Garbacz and Kelly's charge that the model is misspecified due to omission of variables. RESET, the appropriate test for errors of this type, is applied to the model, and, once again, no evidence is found that the model is misspecified. As such, significant evidence is presented to refute the Garbacz and Kelly claim and to support the statistical results of Loeb and others that vehicle inspection is effective in reducing fatalities.[9]

As such, a large number of statistical studies have been conducted that examined the effect of motor vehicle inspection on automobile fatalities and fatality rates. The statistical results have not been consistent with each other. In addition, many arguments posed on the advisability of inspection have centered on the political aspects associated with inspection. For example, should the federal government or individual states be the determining body regarding the imposition of inspection? In addition, questions regarding the type of inspection (spot, biannual, or annual) and the degree of inspection (for example, whether a wheel should be pulled in checking brakes) are still debated. Furthermore, the question regarding the preferability of state versus private inspection, or a combination of both, has yet to be settled in a definitive manner. Nevertheless, there seems to be statistical evidence in favor of inspection. In addition, the results in favor of inspection make use of not only standard descriptive statistics and traditional econometric models but also fairly powerful specification error tests and extreme bounds analysis. Finally, there is evidence indicating the cost-effectiveness of inspection as well. Yet, the definitive word with regard to the effectiveness of inspection may still be forthcoming.

Table 3.1 reviews selected statistical results of the effect of motor vehicle inspection on various measures of auto-related fatalities.

TABLE 3.1
Estimates of the Effect of Motor Vehicle Inspection on Auto Fatalities

Model	Effect of Inspection on the Dependent Variable[a]	Dependent Variable[b]	Type of Data[c]
Fuchs & Leveson (1967)	– in general/sig. & insig.	Age Adjusted Death Rate	CS for 1959–61
Crain (1980)	+/insig. & sig. & –/sig.	log (Fatalities/Registered Vehicle)	CS (1974)
Jackson, Loeb, & Franck (1982)	–/sig.	Fatalities	TS (1929–79 for NJ)
			CS (1979)
Loeb & Gilad (1984)	–/sig.	Fatalities	TS (1929–79 for NJ)
Loeb (1985)	–/sig.	Fatalities, Fatalities/Capita, ln (Fatalities/Capita)	CS (1979)
Loeb (1987)	–/sig.	Fatality Rate	CS (1979)
Saffer & Grossman (1987)	–/sig.	Death/100,000 Population	TS/CS (1975–81)
Garbacz & Kelly (1987)	±/insig. (mostly +/insig.)	ln (Fatality Rate)	TS (1952–82 for the US)
Loeb (1988a)	–/sig.	Fatality Rate	CS (1979)
Loeb (1988b)	–/sig.	Fatalities, ln (Fatalities/Capita)	CS (1979)
Fowles & Loeb (1988)	–/sig.	Fatalities	TS (1929–79 for NJ)
	–/sig.	Fatality Rate	
	–/sig.	Fatalities/Capita	
	–/sig.	ln (Fatalities/Capita)	
	Negative & Nonfragile Using Extreme Bounds Analysis	ln (Fatality Rate)	CS (1979)

Loeb (1990)	−/sig.	Various measures of levels of Fatalities and Fatality Rates	TS (1952–82 for the US)
			TS (1952–85 for the US)
Garbacz (1990)	insig. for TS models*	Various measures of Fatalities and Fatality Rates	TS (1947–85)
	−/sig. & insig. for CS Models**		CS (1984)

[a]Significant coefficients at the 5–10 percent significance level or better are denoted as "sig." while insignificant coefficients are denoted as "insig."

[b]Fatality Rates are generally measured as fatalities/100 million vehicle miles.

[c]CS indicates cross-sectional data and TS indicates time-series data.

*Sign not reported.

**Sign not always reported.

Source: Compiled by the authors.

ALCOHOL CONSUMPTION AND THE MINIMUM LEGAL DRINKING AGE

The effects of alcohol consumption by drivers on motor vehicle accidents are well known. The consumption of alcohol by drivers (clearly beyond some threshold) increases the likelihood of motor vehicle accidents substantially. It is estimated that approximately half of all motor vehicle fatalities are alcohol-related (see NSC, 1989). As such, approximately 20,000–25,000 auto fatalities per year are associated with alcohol consumption. This is approximately equal to one-third of all the fatalities suffered by the United States during the entire Vietnam War. As such, it is not a negligible number. Of great importance is the possibility of preventing such fatalities as well as the injuries associated with this type of driving behavior.

Attempts to measure the impact of alcohol consumption on vehicle fatalities are numerous. Most studies have attempted to examine this issue by regression techniques where a measure of fatalities is regressed against alcohol consumption as well as other control variables. The danger is that the alcohol consumption variables generally used in such studies have been based on sales, or consumption of alcoholic beverages, on the part of the population at large. Implicit in this approach is the assumption that as the consumption of alcoholic beverages increases by the general population, so shall the consumption of alcoholic beverages by drivers increase. This is not necessarily true. If alcoholic consumption increases over time in the United States, it may be done primarily by the nondriving public. The use of designated drivers allegedly has become popular among those who might find themselves at an occasion where the consumption of alcoholic beverages is contemplated. Occupants of a vehicle might select a particular member of the group, who would agree not to drink at such an occasion, to act as the driver. The designated driver would be rewarded for this act of constraint by, among other possibilities, the psychic income of assuring the relative safety of his or her passengers as well as himself or herself. Nevertheless, it is most likely that there is an association between alcohol consumption of the population in general and drivers. This association might not be linear, or exactly proportional, but it does not seem unreasonable to assume that the relationship is positive. As such, the use of alcohol consumption on the part of the population at large may prove to be an acceptable measure of risk imposed on the driving public, because a better one does not seem readily available.

As mentioned above, a large number of statistical and econometric studies to date have found a positive and statistically significant relationship between alcohol consumption and various measures of auto-related fatalities. These results are common for both cross-sectional studies, such as in Sommers (1985), Asch and Levy (1987), some results of Peltzman (1975), Jackson, Loeb, and Franck (1982), and Loeb (1985, 1987, 1988a), as well as in time-series studies by Zlatoper (1988) and some models of Loeb (1990) and Peltzman (1975). Other studies have found the expected sign associated with the coefficient of the alcohol variable to be positive, but not statistically significant.[10] A few have found a negative coefficient associated with this variable (see, for example, Fuchs and Leveson, 1967) where the coefficients were statistically insignificant. Table 3.2 reviews selected studies on the effect of alcohol consumption on motor vehicle fatalities. By and large, the econometric models provide statistical results expected by conventional wisdom. Given a positive association between alcohol consumption by the population at large and drivers of automobiles, the results confirm a priori expectations regarding alcohol consumption.

Because of the enhanced risk attributes that alcohol places on potentially intoxicated drivers, their passengers, and those they may come into contact with, law enforcement agencies have vigorously attempted to find such drivers and remove them from the roadways. New Jersey, for example, has recently imposed sobriety check points. The efficacy of this procedure, especially with regard to its cost-effectiveness, is still being debated. Yet, the courts have upheld this method of searching for those drivers under the influence of alcohol.

The effect of official measures against drunk drivers has been evaluated by a few researchers to date. Loeb (1985), for example, has found that increases in the percentage of arrests for alcohol-related offenses (lagged two years) resulted in a significant reduction of the log of fatalities per capita based on cross-sectional data. Time-series studies by Jackson, Loeb, and Franck (1982) and Loeb and Gilad (1984) found, in one case, a significant and positive coefficient (one-tail) associated with license revocations due to drunk driving and fatalities. This unusual result might be explained by recognizing that arrests may have been increasing due to an increasing trend in alcohol consumption. As such, there may have been an increase in arrests due to increases in drunk driving as opposed to an increased fervor on the part of the police. Once again, these results should be considered with caution, because of the number of such findings and their statistical significance.

TABLE 3.2
Estimates of the Effect of Alcohol Consumption on Auto Fatalities

Model	Effect of Alcohol Consumption on the Dependent Variable	Measure of Alcohol Consumption	Dependent Variable	Type of Data
Fuchs & Leveson (1967)	−/mostly insig.	1	Age Adjusted Death Rate	CS (1959–61)
Peltzman (1975)	+/sig.	9	ln (Total Deaths/Vehicle Mile) & ln (Vehicle Occupant Deaths/Vehicle Mile)	TS (1947–65)
	+/sig. & insig. and −/insig.		ln (Total Deaths/Capita) & ln (Vehicle Occupant Deaths/Capita)	CS (1962, 1965, 1967, 1970)
Crain (1980)	+/insig.	1	log (Fatalities/Registered Vehicle)	CS (1974)
Jackson, Loeb, & Franck (1982)	+/sig.	3	Fatalities	CS (1979)
Zlatoper (1984)	+/insig.	6	ln (Deaths)	TS (1947–80 for the US)
Sommers (1985)	+/sig.	5	Fatality Rates	CS (1981)
Lobe (1985)	+/sig.	3	Fatalities Fatalities/Capita ln (Fatalities/Capita)	CS (1979)
Asch & Levy (1987)	+/sig. & insig.	8	log (Fatality Rates)	CS (1978)
Loeb (1987)	+/usually sig.	2	Fatality Rates	CS (1979)
Saffer & Grossman (1987)	−/sig.*	7	Deaths/100,000 Population	TS/CS (1975–81)
Garbacz & Kelly (1987)	+/insig.	4	ln (Fatality Rates)	TS (1952–82 for the US)
Loeb (1988a)	+/sig.	2	Fatality Rates	CS (1979)
Zlatoper (1988)	+/sig.	6	Measures of Fatality Rates	TS (1947–60 for the US)

		Interstate Fatalities Per Licensed Driver	Various Measures of Levels of Fatalities and Fatality Rates
		CS (1985)	TS (1952–82 & 1952–85 for the US)
Levy & Asch (1989)	+/insig.	11	
Loeb (1990)	+/sig. & insig.**		10

1 Per capita alcohol consumption.
2 Per capita consumption of malt beverages (in gallons).
3 Per capita consumption of distilled spirits.
4 Per capita consumption of spirits, wine, and beer adjusted for alcohol content (wine gallon).
5 Annual beer consumption (gallons) per person 18 and over.
6 Weighted sum of adult consumption of distilled spirits, wine, and beer per capita.
7 Real beer tax.
8 Absolute apparent alcohol consumption (in US gallons) per person age 14 and above.
9 Consumption of distilled spirits per person 15 years and older.
10 Per capita consumption of beer.
11 Apparent alcohol consumption per capita, ages 14 and above, in gallons.
* Alcohol variable is in terms of Real Beer Tax.
**Coefficients were always positive and significant when evaluating death rates and positive and insignificant when evaluating measures of levels of fatalities.

Source: Compiled by the authors.

63

A more important debate regarding the potential control of alcohol-related accidents has centered on the effect of raising the minimum legal drinking age (MLDA). Advocates for this policy argue that raising the MLDA will result in a reduction of highway accidents, fatalities, and the like by reducing the availability or the likelihood of acquiring alcohol by youthful, immature drivers. It has been found that a major cause of death among the young is accidents, and the prominent accident is one involving motor vehicles. As such, raising the MLDA would reduce the probability of such accidents by making it more difficult for young adults to acquire alcoholic beverages legally as well as allowing for the punishment, with fines and jail sentences, of those youths who violate the law. Hence, the cost of drinking and driving by youths would increase (provided they are not killed in an accident) and the cost of search for alcoholic beverages by youthful drivers (and the risk involved) would increase. Opponents to this strategy argue that raising the MLDA in a state will merely induce youthful drivers who wish to drink to drive to neighboring states where they can acquire alcoholic beverages legally. Such individuals would then have longer distances to drive when returning from purchasing these beverages than if they had bought them locally. If they drink while driving, they may enhance the likelihood of an accident. In addition, some might argue that it is not the age of the driver alone that affects the mortality rate, but rather some learning experience in combination with the MLDA that must be controlled. More precisely, it may be argued that raising the minimum legal drinking age might merely transfer accidents from, for example, 18-year-olds to 21-year-olds if the MLDA is raised from 18 to 21. What is in effect here, is the lack of experience with alcoholic beverages that may be the modus operandi.

Literature exists supporting both arguments presented above. Cook and Tauchen (1984), using pooled time-series and cross-sectional data for the years 1970–77, find that the MLDA has a statistically significant impact on youthful fatality rates, that is, lowering the MLDA from 21 to 18 would result in an increase in youthful fatality rates. Fatality rate models using cross-sectional data by Sommers (1985) find the coefficient of the drinking age variables to be negative and statistically significant, adding support to those advocating the efficacy of raising the MLDA to reduce auto-related fatalities. Saffer and Grossman (1987) contribute some additional evidence. They find that in three of their four mortality rate models, covering two of three age categories, the coefficient associated with the MLDA is negative and statistically significant. (The coefficient is negative, but not significant in a statistical sense in the remaining fourth equation examining mortality rates for individuals aged 21–24.) Loeb (1987), however, does not find statistically significant coefficients associated with the MLDA variable. In addition, Asch and Levy (1987) do not find statistical support for the efficacy of the MLDA. Their model, using cross-sectional data, finds the coefficient associated with the MLDA to be statistically insignificant and positive. They are inclined to consider drinking experience to be a more important factor in explaining vehicle fatality rates. This position is further supported in Asch and Levy (1990) using pooled data across states for 1975–84. Table 3.3 reviews these results.

SPEED LIMITS, VEHICLE SPEED, AND SPEED VARIANCE

The speed limit became a policy issue in the United States in 1973 with the Arab Oil Embargo. It was felt that lowering the maximum speed limit to 55 mph would prove to be a useful means of reducing our dependency on foreign oil. With the emplacement of the reduced speed limit, traffic and public health officials noted a fall-off in automobile fatalities. This externality to the initial motivation for the reduced speed limit was lauded by many in the public safety area. However, as the supplies of oil increased and the price of gasoline at the pump declined, there were efforts made to increase the speed limit once again. Advocates for raising the speed limit argued that speed limits were state issues and not within the province of the federal government. In addition, arguments, especially by many western and mountain states, were presented that raising speed limits was both economically defendable and might even result in reducing, or at least stabilizing, vehicle-related fatalities. Notably, an argument by western states was suggested pointing out that drivers could be on the road for many miles without much change in scenery and without much traffic. This would result in fatigue of the driver that would increase the probability of an accident. Advocates of raising the speed limit would argue that by increasing the speed limit, drivers who adhered to the legal limit could reduce their travel time and thus reduce the potential for a fatigue-related accident. The defenders of the 55 mph speed limit would point out that driving at higher speeds would increase the stopping time required should a danger present itself and, in so doing, increase the probability of an accident. Furthermore, given the rural landscape with few passing vehicles and few towns and hospitals in many of these areas, the probability of deaths arising in such accidents would increase.

TABLE 3.3
Estimates of the Effect of the Minimum Legal Drinking Age on Auto Fatalities

Model	Effect of Minimum Legal Drinking Age on the Dependent Variable	Dependent Variable	Type of Data
Cook & Tauchen (1984)	−/sig.*	Log (Youthful Fatalities per 1000 State Resident Population)	Pooled Data (1970–77)
Sommers (1985)	−/sig.**	Fatality Rates	CS (1981)
Loeb (1987)	−/insig.	Fatality Ratse	CS (1979)
Asch & Levy (1987)	+/insig.	Log (Fatality Rates)	CS (1978)
Saffer & Grossman (1987)	−/sig. (for 2 of 3 age groups)	Death/100,000 Population	TS/CS (1975–81)
Loeb (1988a)	Always insig.	Fatality Rates	CS (1979)
Asch & Levy (1990)	Unclear†	Log (Alcohol Involved Single-Vehicle and Single-Vehicle-Nighttime Driver Fatality Rates‡)	Pooled Data (47 states for the period 1975–84)

*The actual coefficients reported in Cook & Tauchen are positive because Cook & Tauchen consider a reduction in minimum legal drinking age. We normalize signs to be consistent with other studies.
**Model considers changes in the law after July 1980 as well as the minimum legal drinking age for beer.
†Drinking experience affects the dependent variable and mitigates the effect of drinking age.
‡These rates are based on the number of licensed drivers in the appropriate age group.

Source: Compiled by the authors.

The problem of the advisability of raising speed limits is related to the speed of vehicles as well. A given distribution of speeds is associated with a given speed limit. For example, a certain percentage of free-moving vehicles will exceed the 55 mph speed limit by 5 mph, 8 mph, and so forth. Others will drive below the speed limit. Similarly, as the speed limit is increased, a different distribution of speeds about the speed limit may occur. In other words, it is not unusual to find a certain percentage of vehicles driving above or below the speed limit. Some argue that drivers seek out some optimal speed (see, for example, Graves, Lee, and Sexton, 1989, and Jondrow, Bowes, and Levy, 1983). In any case, it seems intuitively obvious that vehicle speed is associated with accident and fatality rates. In addition, there may indeed be a relationship between vehicle speed and speed limits (see Transportation Research Board, 1984).

These questions have been addressed by numerous researchers. Garbacz and Kelly (1987) model the determinants of vehicle-related fatality rates for the United States using time-series data for the period 1952–82. The effect of the national speed limit of 55 mph, which was imposed after the oil embargo, is included in the model. The coefficient associated with this variable is found to be negative and statistically significant. Loeb (1990), evaluating models similar to Garbacz and Kelly, but with a time-series data set covering the periods 1952–82 and 1952–85, finds, similarly, that the coefficient associated with the speed limit variable is negative and statistically significant. In addition, Loeb (1991, 1993) evaluates models for driver-involved injury rates in California for the time period 1982–87. Monthly data were employed and the effect of raising the speed limit to 65 mph on certain roadways was examined. Models for driver-involved injury rates (including fatalities and serious injuries known as K and A injuries, respectively) were estimated for single and multiple vehicle accidents. In both cases, the coefficient associated with raising the speed limit was positive and statistically significant, demonstrating that raising the speed limit was associated with a rise in these injury rates. (Less significant results were obtained when evaluating other combinations of injury severities.)

The effect of speed per se was modeled by many investigators. Quite commonly, speed is measured in these models as the average speed of free-moving vehicles on rural interstate highways. The empirical results generally find a positive relationship between vehicle speed and various measures of fatalities, or fatality rates. Cross-sectional studies of fatality rates were conducted by Peltzman (1975), Asch and Levy (1987), Sommers (1985), and Loeb (1987, 1988a). All of these studies found the coefficient associated with the speed variable to be positive and statistically significant. Time-series models of fatalities and fatality rates were developed by Peltzman (1975), Zlatoper (1984, 1988), and others. The coefficient associated with the speed variable is found to be positive and statistically significant here as well.

Forester, McNown, and Singell (1984) examine automobile fatalities using a three-equation recursive model. The authors find the effect of speed on fatalities to be positive and significant. They also find a positive relationship between speed variability and fatalities. In addition, they find a positive and significant coefficient associated with the speed limit variable. These findings are in their fatality equation. When the effect of speed limits on variability and average speed are accounted for, the net impact on fatalities is estimated to be negative.

As such, there is a large amount of evidence relating fatality rates with higher speeds — both average speed of free-moving vehicles and speed limits. However, Lave (1985) has recently argued that the major impact on fatality rates due to vehicle motion is not due so much to the speed of the vehicle as to the variance of speed. To test this hypothesis, Lave develops econometric models for vehicle fatality rates using cross-sectional data for six types of roadways for the years 1981 and 1982. As such, he estimates 12 regressions. In general, he finds the coefficients associated with the speed variable to be negative and insignificant, while the coefficients associated with speed variance are generally positive and both statistically significant and insignificant. As such, he argues that speed variance is a causal factor in fatality rates. However, he cannot find similar evidence linking speed to fatality rates.

The findings of Lave are disputed by several other researchers. Levy and Asch (1989), using cross-sectional data for 1985, develop a model for interstate fatality rates and conclude that "speed kills." Their results are dependent on whether an interaction term is included in their model. Fowles and Loeb (1989) use a Bayesian procedure referred to as extreme bounds analysis on models of the determinants of fatalities employing 1979 cross-sectional data. They conclude that both the effects of speed and speed variance on fatalities are positive and nonfragile. Snyder (1989), using models of fatality rates employing panel data, finds that the coefficient associated with speed is positive and significant and that the effect of speed variance is dependent upon whether one examines the fastest or the slowest moving vehicles. Only in the case of the fastest moving vehicles does he find speed variance to have a positive impact on fatality rates. Finally, Rodriguez (1990) finds a negative relationship between average speed and the fatality rate and a positive relationship between variance and the fatality rate. He concludes that a reasonable policy is to control individual driver speed. Table 3.4 reviews these results.

SEAT BELT LAWS

Seat belts are known for their life-saving attributes. Restricting the amount of force with which occupants strike a vehicle's interior during an accident results in a reduction of the number of fatalities and the severity of injuries. In addition, seat belts help prevent ejections from a vehicle involved in an accident. As such, the control of the potential projectile action that victims are subjected to in a crash results in life-saving and injury-reducing effects.[11] NHTSA has estimated that seat belts are effective in reducing fatalities in the neighborhood of 40–50 percent (see, for example, Partyka, 1988). Alternatively, Evans (1991, p. 244) has estimated the effectiveness of occupant safety restraints in preventing fatalities. His estimates indicate that a lap/shoulder belt has an effectiveness of 41 percent. This means that for every 100 nonusers of this device that are killed, 41 would have avoided death if they had worn the lap/shoulder belt. An airbag together with a lap/shoulder belt is estimated to have an effectiveness of 46 percent. In addition, Evans estimates the effectiveness of a shoulder belt to be 29 percent, of a lap belt (rear seats) to be 18 percent, and of an airbag only to be 17 percent.[12] The lap/shoulder belt in conjunction with the airbag saves the most lives.

The potential effect of seat belts is mitigated by the lack of use of seat belts by the motoring public. As such, seat belt laws have been instituted in many states. Usage rates generally increase with the advent of a seat belt law and decline after some initial period of time, but not to the prelaw rate. The question next becomes, are the seat belt laws effective? By and large, they are indeed capable of reducing fatality rates and various types of injury rates.

Basically, two different types of seat belts laws, otherwise referred to as mandatory usage laws, have been applied by the states initiating such laws. These are primary and secondary laws. Primary seat belt laws, such as employed in Texas, allow police officers to stop vehicles for noncompliance with the law. Secondary seat belt laws, as found in New Jersey, do not allow police officers to stop vehicles for noncompliance with the seat belt requirement alone. Rather, only when stopping a vehicle for some other reason may the police officer consider a violation of the seat belt law. In addition, the penalties for noncompliance, that is, the fine structures, vary among the states. As economic theory would

TABLE 3.4
Alternative Estimates of the Effect of Speed Limits, Speed, and Speed Variance on Auto Fatalities

Model	Effect on the Dependent Variable of			Dependent Variable	Type of Data
	Speed	Speed Limit	Speed Variance		
Peltzman (1975)	+/sig.			ln (Total Deaths/Vehicle Mile) ln (Vehicle Occupant Deaths/Vehicle Mile)	TS (1947–65)
	+/sig.[1]			ln (Total Deaths/Capita) ln (Vehicle Occupant Deaths/Capita)	CS (1962, 1965, 1967, 1970)
Forrester, McNown & Singell (1984)	+/sig.	+/sig.[3]	+/sig.[4]	Fatalities	TS (1952–79 for the US)
Zlatoper (1984)	+/sig.			ln (Deaths)	TS (1947–80 for the US)
Lave (1985)	generally –/insig.		generally +/sig. & insig.	Fatality Rate	CS (by 6 types of roadways for 1981 and 1982)
Sommers (1985)	+/sig.			Fatality Rates	CS (1981)
Asch & Levy (1987)	+/sig.	–/sig.		log (Fatality Rates)	CS (1978)
Garbacz & Kelly (1987)	+/sig.[2]			ln (Fatality Rates)	TS (1952–82 for the US)
Loeb (1987)	+/sig.			Fatality Rates	CS (1979)
Loeb (1988a)	+/sig.			Fatality Rates	CS (1979)
Zlatoper (1988)	+/sig.			Measures of Fatality Rates	TS (1947–80 for the US)
Fowles & Loeb (1989)	+ and non-fragile ****		+ and non-fragile ****	Fatalities	CS (1979)
Levy & Asch (1989)	+/sig.		+/sig. for fastest moving vehicles	Interstate Fatalities per Licensed Driver	CS (1985)
Snyder (1989)	+/sig.			Fatality Rate	Panel Data, that is, from 26 states (1972–74)
Loeb (1990)		–/sig.		Various measures of Levels of Fatalities and Fatality Rates	TS (1952–82 & 1952–85 for US data)
Loeb (1991)		+/sig.[5]		Driver Involved (A+K) Injury Rates, Single & Multiple Vehicle Accidents	TS (1982–87, monthly)

			CS (1981–85) and Pooled
Rodriguez (1990)	±/insig. for CS data[6]	+/sig. and insig. for CS data	Fatality Rate
	−/sig. for pooled data	+/sig. for pooled data[7]	

[1]Measured as speed limit on main rural roads.

[2]Speed is measured as average speed of free moving vehicles on rural interstate highways (in mph).

[3]Using a three-equation recursive model, the effect of speed limits on variability and average speed are accounted for and the net impact on fatalities is estimated to be negative.

[4]Actual coefficient is negative & significant. However, variability is measured as concentration of speed, that is, percentage of cars travelling between 45 and 65 mph. As such, as concentration increases, variability declines and we have adjusted the sign of the coefficient to reflect this and to be consistent with other studies.

[5]Reflects the increase of the speed limit on certain roads in California to 65 mph. As such, the result is not contrary to the other studies reported.

[6]Measured as $(\mu - c)$.

[7]Measured as $\mu^2 + \sigma^2$.

****Results are dependent on whether an interaction term is included in the model. Asch and Levy conclude that speed kills.

Source: Compiled by the authors.

suggest, seat belt usage is higher in states with primary enforcement than with secondary enforcement. Furthermore, usage is higher in states after a seat belt law is initiated than prior to the imposition of the law (see Campbell, Stewart, and Campbell, 1987, and Campbell and Campbell, 1986).[13]

A large number of statistical studies have been conducted to evaluate the effectiveness of seat belt laws on fatality and injury rates. These studies have varied both in the types of data used and the statistical techniques employed. The statistical techniques include: the comparison of injury rates in a given state prior to and after a seat belt law has gone into effect; the comparison of injury rates in a state with a seat belt law to a reference state without such a law; the use of Box-Jenkins/ARIMA techniques to forecast the effect of mandatory seat belt laws on injury rates; and the development of econometric models to evaluate the effects of mandatory seat belt laws on various types of injuries (see, for example, Campbell, Stewart, and Campbell, 1987; Hoxie and Skinner, 1987; Lund, Pollner, and Williams, 1987; Latimer and Lave, 1987; Streff, Schultz, and Wagenaar, 1989; Womble, 1989; and Loeb, 1991, 1993). By and large, the studies provide evidence that the seat belt laws generally help to reduce fatality and injury rates. However, the reported results vary across states and time periods as well as across the types of injuries.

Many of the studies employ the KABCO scale in ranking injuries. K represents fatalities, A represents serious injuries, B represents moderate injuries, C represents complaint(s) of injuries, and O represents no injuries. The evaluation as to the degree of injury is usually determined by the official at the scene of the accident — usually a police officer. Needless to say, one may anticipate measurement error in some of the statistics. Yet, it is a scale that is often used and probably has many more benefits than costs associated with it. Most researchers, when evaluating injuries, combine two or more injury levels. As such, it is quite common to see results with regard to the evaluation of K+A, A+B, and K+A+B injuries.

Womble (1989) evaluates the effect of seat belt laws by comparing four states with seat belt laws to three states without such laws when examining accidents involving vehicles that were towed. The seat belt law states examined were Maryland, Michigan, Texas, and Washington. The reference states were Pennsylvania, Arizona, and Oregon. Womble estimates that seat belt laws result in reductions in the driver involved injury rate for A+B injuries between 6.41 and 12.21 percent. Results regarding K+A injuries were less stable across states, with Maryland having an 8.46 percent increase and Washington a 12.97 percent decrease.

Lund, Pollner, and Williams (1987) examine the effect of the seat belt law in New York. Their preliminary estimate of the effect of the law using regression analysis is a reduction in fatalities of about 9 percent during the first nine months the law was in effect.

Campbell, Stewart, and Campbell (1987) examine the effects of seat belt laws using ARIMA methods where forecasts are made on fatalities using data prior to the implementation of a seat belt law and comparing the forthcoming forecasts of fatalities with actual fatalities during the time period when seat belt laws are in effect in various states. The authors, using the data from the Fatal Accident Reporting System, find a reduction of 6.6 percent in covered fatalities. More precisely, the authors (Campbell, Stewart, and Campbell, 1987, p. 24) find, "In terms of overall results, observed fatalities among Covered occupants are 6.6% less than the number forecast from pre-law experience in the belt law states, and concurrent trends in the non-law states." They translate this to a savings of 1,300 lives in the covered states for the time period considered.

Campbell and Campbell (1986) examine the effects of the seat belt law on injuries for North Carolina using time-series analysis (Box-Jenkins). They estimate that the seat belt law results in an 8.7 percent reduction in A+K injuries and an 8.5 percent reduction in A+B+K injuries.

Campbell, Stewart, and Campbell (1986) report the effects of seat belt laws in eight states using time-series techniques (ARIMA). They report reductions in front seat occupant fatalities for the eight states of 9.9 percent. However, the effects of the law, as measured by this technique for the period under investigation, vary from 4.6 percent for Missouri to −17.6 percent for Texas.

Reinfurt, Campbell, Stewart, and Stutts (1988) use time-series analysis to show that the effect of the seat belt law on various levels of injuries (on covered occupants) is greater when citations are issued than when only warnings are issued in North Carolina.

Hatfield and Hinshaw (1987), using Box-Jenkins analysis on Texas data, find that the mandatory seat belt law results in a 10 percent reduction in fatalities. However, the authors do not attribute this entire reduction to the seat belt law in that fatalities were falling prior to the initiation of the law.

Hoxie and Skinner (1987) develop econometric models to examine the impact of seat belt laws on fatalities. They evaluate both a national model and a set of state models. Their national model suggests a 6.7 percent reduction in fatality rates due to the seat belt law. They note that the first quarter effect of the law is larger than subsequent quarter effects, −11.6 percent versus −2.4 percent. When examining state models, they find results vary across the states. The coefficient associated with the seat belt law variable ranges from −0.02 and insignificant for New Jersey to −0.191 and significant for Texas. Skinner and Hoxie (1988) update their earlier study with additional data. The general result for the national model remains intact with a seat belt effect of −7.5 percent. The state models often give different results. Of the original states examined, only Texas has a significant negative coefficient associated with the seat belt law variable.

Streff, Schultz, and Wagenaar (1989) examine the effect of the Michigan seat belt law using time-series data on injured occupants and control for crash severity damage along with other factors. The authors find an overall effect of the law to be −6.2 percent on all injuries which is statistically significant. However, at a more micro level, they find that the effect of the law is dependent upon crash severity and the type of injury inflicted. For example, the seat belt law has a −16.8 percent reduction, which is statistically significant, on A-level injuries associated with moderate crash severity accidents and only a −3.9 percent reduction, which is not statistically significant, on A-level injuries associated with minor crash severity accidents.

Finally, Loeb (1991) evaluates the effects of seat belt laws in three states, Texas, Maryland, and California, using time-series data for the period 1982–87 and econometric modeling techniques. Texas is a primary enforcement state while Maryland and California are secondary enforcement states. Loeb adjusts for damage severity (towed away vehicle accidents) in the cases of Texas and Maryland. He examines the effects of the seat belt laws on various levels of driver involved injury rates and for single-vehicle, multiple-vehicle and combined single + multiple vehicle accidents. He finds that the effects of the seat belt laws vary across states. The models accounted for the general effects of the laws as well as the dynamic effects, that is, first quarter versus subsequent quarter effects. With regard to the general seat belt law effect, the Texas results were quite robust. The coefficients associated with the seat belt law variable were always negative and significant for all driver involved injury rates examined (A+B, A+K, and A+B+K) for single, multiple and single + multiple vehicle accidents. The Maryland results were more fragile. Significant negative coefficients associated with the seat belt variable occurred for A+B and A+B+K injuries associated with single vehicle accidents and single + multiple vehicle accidents.[14] In the case of the California models, negative and significant coefficients associated with the seat belt law were found for A+B and A+B+K injury rates for both single and multiple vehicle accidents. However, generally, insignificant statistical results (often with positive signs) were found when evaluating the A+K models (see Loeb, 1991, for a further discussion).

An interesting observation forthcoming from the Loeb study is that negative and significant coefficients associated with the seat belt variable are found for A+B injury rates involving single-vehicle accidents for *all three* states. The coefficients range in magnitude from –0.057 to –0.087. This, indeed, provides strong evidence of the potential effectiveness of seat belt laws. Table 3.5 reviews these results.

SUMMARY

Chapter 2 provided a discussion of the determinants of highway accidents. The present chapter considered the effectiveness of specific policy actions on fatality rates using statistical methods.[15] The most general, and perhaps illuminating, procedures used were based on regression/econometric models, including time-series (Box-Jenkins/ARIMA) procedures. Results were often found to vary across states and time periods. However, a rather strong statistical argument can be made for initiating or maintaining many of the safety policies investigated.

Motor vehicle inspection seems to be a highly political issue. Empirical results vary among the studies. Yet, there seems to be some overall statistical evidence that vehicle inspection results in a reduction in fatalities. Benefit/cost studies have also provided some evidence that inspection is cost-effective.[16]

Alcohol consumption on the part of vehicle drivers is a major factor in accidents. Approximately half of all fatal accidents are associated with the use of alcohol. The empirical studies reported are in agreement with this general statement. In addition, many studies have investigated the effect of raising the MLDA on fatality rates. Some studies, indeed, show that raising the MLDA will result in a reduction of fatalities. Others suggest that raising the MLDA will not impact significantly on fatalities. These latter studies suggest that the experience factor, that is, experience with the use of alcoholic beverages, may be an important element in such accidents. In any case, they may argue that raising the MLDA alone

TABLE 3.5
Estimates of the Effect of Seat Belt Laws on Auto Fatalities and Injuries

Model	Effect of Seat Belt Law on the Dependent Variable	Dependent Variable	Statistical Technique Employed
Campbell and Campbell (1986)	−8.7% in (A+K) Injuries −8.5% in (A+B+K) Injuries	Percent of (A+K) and (A+B+K) Injuries for North Carolina	Box-Jenkins/ARIMA
Campbell, Stewart, and Campbell (1986)	−9.9% in Front-seat Occupant Fatalities for 8 States	Fatality Rates* for 8 States	ARIMA
Campbell, Stewart, and Campbell (1987)	−6.6% in Fatalities	Fatality Rate*	ARIMA
Hatfield and Hinshaw (1987)	−10% (in Fatalities)	Fatalities in Texas	Box-Jenkins
Hoxie and Skinner (1987)	−6.7% (in Fatalities) for National Model −0.02/insig. to −0.19/sig. for State Models	Front-seat Occupant Fatalities Per Capita Covered Fatalities	Regression
Lund, Pollner, and Williams (1987)	−9%	Fatalities (NY)	Regression
Reinfurt, Campbell, Stewart, and Stutts (1988)	Greater Effect when Citations are in Effect than when Only Warnings Used	Injuries of Covered Occupants in North Carolina	Time-series Analysis
Skinner and Hoxie (1988)	−7.5% (National Model) −/sig. for Texas	See Hoxie and Skinner (1987)	Regression
Streff, Schultz, and Wagenaar (1989)	−6.2%/sig.	Injuries of Various Levels	Box-Jenkins and Intervention Models

Study	Results	Outcome Measure	Method
Womble (1989)	−6.41% to −12.21% for (A+B) Injury Rates +8.46% to −12.97% for (A+K) Injury Rates	(A+B) and (A+K) Driver-involved Injury Rates for 4 States	Comparison of Law State with a Reference State
Loeb (1991)	−/sig. for (A+B) Injury Rates in Single-vehicle Accidents for All States Examined. Other Results Vary.	Various Driver-involved Injury Rates	Regression

*Fatalities among crash-involved occupants in a given law state(s)/fatalities in all non-seat belt law states.

Source: Compiled by the authors.

may not be sufficient to gain the major reduction in fatalities sought from a policy regarding the use of alcoholic beverages.

The effects of speed limits, vehicle speed, and speed variance on fatal accidents have recently been of great interest to the media and to Congress. Once again, the issue was highly politicized as to whether speed limits should be under the jurisdiction of the states or the federal government. In addition, some argued that raising speed limits would result in a reduction of fatalities as travel time on sparsely travelled roads is reduced due to higher speeds. Nonetheless, most statistical studies associate higher speed limits and higher vehicle speeds with higher fatalities. The question of whether it is the speed of vehicles or the variance of vehicle speed that is the major factor in vehicle accidents is the most recent topic of interest in this area. Statistical results have found that fatality rates and fatalities may be related to speed variance. However, this is not to say that the speed of the vehicles is unimportant. Indeed, there is evidence associating speed and speed variance with fatalities. In addition, it has been argued that only the variability of speed at the high end of the speed distribution may be important in this relationship. In general, statistical evidence is found that suggests that raising speed limits and the average speed of free-moving traffic are associated with increases in motor vehicle fatalities.

Seat belts have been effective in preventing fatalities in vehicle accidents. Numerous studies, using various statistical techniques, have found that seat belt laws reduce fatalities and injuries by enhancing the probability of seat belt use. That is, belt usage is higher in a state after a belt law is initiated than prior to the imposition of the law. In addition, seat belt use is higher in states with primary enforcement than in states with secondary enforcement laws.[17]

NOTES

1.   Nevertheless, the normalization process employed was rather elementary in that factors that could influence the death rate, other than inspection, were introduced only one at a time.

2.   These additional factors include: fuel consumption per capita, population density, the percentage of the population aged 18–24, mortality rate for other accidents, percentage nonwhites, alcohol consumption per capita, percentage of motor vehicles more than nine years old, indication of vision inspection for license renewal, median level of education, and median level of income.

3.   The interested reader may review State of Nebraska (1974) and State of Alaska (1974) for additional early evidence of the effects of inspection.

4.   The death rate was measured as yearly deaths per registered vehicle; the nonfatal injury rate as yearly nonfatal injuries per 1,000 vehicle miles; and the nonfatal accident rate as yearly nonfatal accidents per 1,000 vehicle miles. See Crain (1980) for further discussion.

5.   See Loeb (1988b) for further evidence of the effects of modeling technology differently on the relationship between inspection and fatalities.

6.   See Miller (1986) for alternative estimates of the value of life based on the willingness to pay method. See also, Atkinson and Halvorsen (1990), who estimate the value of a statistical life at $3.357 million 1986 dollars.

7.   See, in addition, Ramsey and Gilbert (1972), Ramsey and Schmidt (1976), Ramsey and Zarembka (1971), Loeb (1976, 1986), and Loeb and Lin (1977).

8.   Loeb (1990) makes use of linear models incorporating the general characteristics of the models of Garbacz and Kelly (1987) in terms of variables and similar data included in the models.

9.   Garbacz (1990) reports additional time-series and cross-sectional regression results. He reports mostly statistically insignificant coefficients associated with the inspection variable. However, he reports negative and statistically significant coefficients associated with biannual inspection in his cross-sectional regressions when evaluating occupant deaths and occupant death rates. In addition, he finds a significant and negative coefficient associated with a general inspection variable using a linear regression and cross-sectional data.

10.   See, for example, Levy and Asch (1989), Crain (1980), Garbacz and Kelly (1987), and Zlatoper (1984). An alternative modeling approach is suggested by Saffer and Grossman (1987), who consider the effect of a beer tax on fatality rates. Saffer and Grossman find a negative and significant coefficient associated with a real beer tax and fatalities per 100,000 population after accounting for additional factors in their model.

11.   It should be noted that a potential cascading effect may be present. That is, to the extent that seat belts reduce fatalities, they may be instrumental in the increase of various levels of injuries. More precisely, as fatalities are reduced, type A (severe) injuries may be increased. To confuse matters, seat belts may result in a reduction of what otherwise would have been type A injuries. However, there may be an increase in type A injuries due to the transference of fatal accidents to type A accidents. The net effect has not been evaluated with precision as of yet. In addition, there is a possible interaction not only between potentially fatal and type A accidents but also types B (moderate), C (complaints), and O (no) injuries. The cascading and interacting effects may be quite important. For example, a reduction in fatal accidents with a rise in type A injuries (for example, head and spinal column trauma) may be more costly from a societal point of view than the original fatalities. Nevertheless, much of research to date suggests that the effect of seat belts on (Fatal+A+B) injuries is a significant reduction.

12.   The lap belt estimate is for the right-rear and lef-rear passengers. All other estimates are for drivers and right-front passengers.

13.   As of 1992, 10 states had primary laws and 31 states and the District of Columbia had secondary laws. Nine states did not have seat belt laws (see NSC, 1992).

14.   Some coefficients associated with A+B and A+B+K injury rate models for multiple-vehicle accidents were negative and significant (at the one-tail level). Positive

and significant results were obtained when examining several A+K injury rate models (see Loeb, 1991, for a discussion).

15.   In addition to the policies discussed, one can also consider the effects of highway law enforcement on highway safety. Programs that increase the highway police efforts should prevent highway deaths by discouraging risky driving behavior (see Zlatoper, 1991).

16.   An exception is provided by Garbacz and Kelly (1987), who do not find inspection to be cost-effective.

17.   Research indicating the possible offsetting effects of seat belt usage and seat belt laws on fatalities has been provided by some investigators (see, for example, Garbacz, 1992).

REFERENCES

Asch, P., and D. T. Levy. (1990). "Young Driver Fatalities: The Roles of Drinking Age and Driving Experience." *Southern Economic Journal* 57: 512–520.

____. (1987). "Does the Minimum Drinking Age Affect Traffic Fatalities?" *Journal of Policy Analysis and Management* 6: 180–192.

Atkinson, S. E., and R. Halvorsen. (1990). "The Valuation of Risks to Life: Evidence from the Market for Automobiles." *Review of Economics and Statistics* 72: 133–136.

Blomquist, G. C. (1988). *The Regulation of Motor Vehicle and Traffic Safety*. Boston: Kluwer Academic Publishers.

Buxbaum, R. G., and T. Colton. (1966). "Relationship of Motor Vehicle Inspection to Accident Mortality." *Journal of the American Medical Association* 197: 101–106.

Campbell, B. J., and F. A. Campbell. (1986, December). *Seat Belt Law Experience in Four Foreign Countries Compared to the United States*. Falls Church, VA: AAA Foundation for Traffic Safety.

Campbell, B. J., J. R. Stewart, and F. A. Campbell. (1987, September). *1985–1986 Experience with Belt Laws in the United States*. Chapel Hill, NC: University of North Carolina Highway Safety Research Center.

____. (1986, July). *Early Results of Seat Belt Legislation in the United States of America*. Chapel Hill, NC: University of North Carolina Highway Research Safety Center.

Cook, Ph. J., and G. Tauchen. (1984). "The Effect of Minimum Drinking Age Legislation on Youthful Auto Fatalities, 1970-1977." *Journal of Legal Studies* 13: 160–190.

Crain, W. M. (1980). *Vehicle Safety Inspection Systems*. Washington, DC: American Enterprise Institute for Public Policy Research.

Evans, L. E. (1991). *Traffic Safety and the Driver*. New York: Van Nostrand Reinhold.

Forester, T., R. F. McNown, and L. D. Singell. (1984). "A Cost Benefit Analysis of the 55 mph Speed Limit." *Southern Economic Journal* 50: 631–641.

Fowles, R., and P. D. Loeb. (1989). "Speeding, Coordination, and the 55-MPH Limit: Comment." *American Economic Review 79: 916–921.*

____. (1988, March 10). "The Determinants of Traffic Fatalities with Considerations of the Effects of Speed and Speed Variance." Paper presented at the Eastern

Economic Association Meetings, Boston, MA.

Fuchs, V. R., and I. Leveson. (1967). "Motor Accident Mortality and Compulsory Inspection of Vehicles." *Journal of the American Medical Association* 201: 87–91.

Garbacz, C. (1992). "More Evidence on the Effectiveness of Seat Belt Laws." *Applied Economics* 24: 313–315.

_____. (1990). "How Effective is Automobile Safety Regulation?" *Applied Economics* 22: 1705–1714.

Garbacz, C., and J. G. Kelly. (1987). "Automobile Safety Inspection: New Econometric and Benefit/Cost Estimates." *Applied Economics* 19: 763–771.

Graves, P. E., D. R. Lee, and R. L. Sexton. (1989). "Statutes Versus Enforcement: The Case of the Optimal Speed Limit." *American Economic Review* 79: 932–936.

Hartunian, N., C. Smart, and M. Thompson. (1980). "The Incidence and Economic Cost of Cancer, Motor Vehicle Injuries, Coronary Heart Disease, and Strokes: A Comparative Analysis." *American Journal of Public Health* 70: 1249–1260.

Hatfield, N. J., and W. M. Hinshaw. (1987, September). *Evaluation of the Fatality Reduction Effectiveness of the Texas Mandatory Safety Belt Law.* The Texas A&M University System, Texas Transportation Institute.

Hoxie, P., and D. Skinner. (1987, April). *Effects of Mandatory Seatbelt Use Laws on Highway Fatalities in 1985.* Cambridge, MA: U.S. Department of Transportation, Research and Special Programs Administration, Transportation Systems Center.

Jackson, B., P. D. Loeb, and K. A. Franck. (1982, November). *Comprehensive Analysis of New Jersey Motor Vehicle Inspection System.* A report submitted to the Department of Law and Public Safety, Division of Motor Vehicles, by New Jersey Institute of Technology.

Jondrow, J., M. Bowes, and R. Levy. (1983). "The Optimal Speed Limit." *Economic Inquiry* 21: 325–336.

Latimer, E. A., and L. B. Lave. (1987). "Initial Effects of the New York Auto Safety Belt Law." *American Journal of Public Health* 77: 183–186.

Lave, C. A. (1985). "Speeding, Coordination, and the 55 MPH Limit." *American Economic Review* 75: 1159–1164.

Leamer, E. E. (1983). "Let's Take the Con Out of Econometrics." *American Economic Review* 73: 31–43.

_____. (1978). *Specification Searches: Ad Hoc Inference with Non-Experimental Data.* New York: Wiley & Sons.

Levy, D. T., and P. Asch. (1989). "Speeding, Coordination, and the 55-MPH Limit: Comment." *American Economic Review* 79: 913–915.

Loeb, P. D. (1993). "The Effectiveness of Seat Belt Legislation in Reducing Various Driver-Involved Injury Rates in California." *Accident Analysis and Prevention* 25: 189–197.

_____. (1991, January 16). *The Effectiveness of Seat Belt Legislation in Reducing Driver Involved Injury and Fatality Rates in Texas, Maryland, and California.* Final Report. Report submitted to U.S.D.O.T./NHTSA.

_____. (1990). "Automobile Safety Inspection: Further Econometric Evidence." *Applied Economics* 22: 1697–1704.

____. (1988a). "The Determinants of Motor Vehicle Accidents — A Specification Error Analysis." *Logistics and Transportation Review* 24: 33–48.

____. (1988b, April). "An Evaluation of the Determinants of Motor Vehicle Accidents with Special Consideration to Vehicle Inspection Using Residual Based Specification Error Tests." Mimeograph.

____. (1987). "The Determinants of Automobile Fatalities with Special Consideration to Policy Variables." *Journal of Transport Economics and Policy* 21: 279–287.

____. (1986). "Specification Error Tests and the Jorgenson-Stephenson Investment Function." *Applied Economics* 18: 851–861.

____. (1985). "The Efficacy and Cost-Effectiveness of Motor Vehicle Inspection Using Cross-Sectional Data — An Econometric Analysis." *Southern Economic Journal* 52: 500–509.

____. (1976). "Specification Error Tests and Investment Functions." *Econometrica* 44: 185–194.

Loeb, P. D., and B. Gilad. (1984). "The Efficacy and Cost-Effectiveness of Vehicle Inspection — A State Specific Analysis Using Time Series Data." *Journal of Transport Economics and Policy* 18: 145–164.

Loeb, P. D., and V. Lin. (1977). "Research and Development in the Pharmaceutical Industry — A Specification Error Approach." *Journal of Industrial Economics* 26: 45–51.

Lund, A. K., J. Pollner, and A. F. Williams. (1987). "Preliminary Estimates of the Effects of Mandatory Seat Belt Use Laws." *Accident Analysis and Prevention* 17: 219–223.

Mayer, A. J., and T. F. Hoult. (1963). *Motor Vehicle Inspection: A Report on Current Information, Measurement and Research.* Institute for Regional and Urban Studies, Wayne State University.

Miller, T. R. (1986, December). "Benefit-Cost Analysis of Health and Safety: Conceptual and Empirical Issues." Working Paper, The Urban Institute, Washington, DC.

National Highway Traffic Safety Administration. (1976). *1975 Societal Costs of Motor Vehicle Accidents.* Washington, DC: U.S. Department of Transportation.

National Safety Council. (1992). *Accident Facts.* 1992 Edition. Chicago: National Safety Council.

____. (1989). *Accident Facts.* 1989 Edition. Chicago: National Safety Council.

____. (1981). *Accident Facts.* 1981 Edition. Chicago: National Safety Council.

Partyka, S. C. (1988, June). *Lives Saved By Seat Belts from 1983 through 1987.* U.S. Department of Transportation, NHTSA.

Peltzman, S. (1975). "The Effects of Automobile Safety Regulation." *Journal of Political Economy* 83: 677–725.

Pindyck, R. S., and D. L. Rubinfeld. (1991). *Econometric Models and Economic Forecasts.* 3rd ed. New York: McGraw-Hill.

Ramsey, J. B. (1974). "Classical Model Selection Through Specification Error Tests." In Zarembka, Paul (Ed.), *Frontiers in Econometrics* (pp. 13–47). New York: Academic Press.

____. (1970). "Models, Specification Error, and Inference: A Discussion of Some Problems in Econometric Methodology." *Bulletin of the Oxford Institute of Economics and Statistics* 32: 301–318.

____. (1969). "Tests for Specification Error in Classical Linear Least-Squares Regression Analysis." *Journal of the Royal Statistical Society* 31 (Ser. B): 350–371.

Ramsey, J. B., and R. Gilbert. (1972). "A Monte Carlo Study of Some Small Sample Properties of Tests for Specification Error." *Journal of the American Statistical Association* 67 (Theory and Methods Section): 180–186.

Ramsey, J. B., and P. Schmidt. (1976). "Some Further Results on the Use of OLS and BLUS Residuals in Specification Error Tests." *Journal of the American Statistical Association* 71 (Theory and Methods Section): 389–390.

Ramsey, J. B., and P. Zarembka. (1971). "Specification Error Tests and Alternative Functional Forms of the Aggregate Production Function." *Journal of the American Statistical Association* 57 (Applications Section): 471–477.

Reinfurt, D. W., B. J. Campbell, J. R. Stewart, and J. C. Stutts. (1988, October). *North Carolina's Occupant Restraint Law: A Three Year Evaluation*. Chapel Hill, NC: University of North Carolina Highway Safety Research Center.

Rodriguez, R. J. (1990). "Speed, Speed Dispersion, and the Highway Fatality Rate." *Southern Economic Journal* 57: 349–356.

Saffer, H., and M. Grossman. (1987). "Drinking Age Laws and Highway Mortality Rates: Cause and Effect." *Economic Inquiry* 25: 403–417.

Skinner, D., and P. Hoxie. (1988, April). *Effects of Seatbelt Laws on Highway Fatalities: Update — April 1988*. Cambridge, MA: U.S. Department of Transportation, Research and Special Programs Administration, Transportation Systems Center.

Snyder, D. (1989). "Speeding, Coordination, and the 55-MPH Limit." *American Economic Review* 79: 922–925.

Sommers, P. M. (1985). "Drinking Age and the 55 MPH Speed Limit." *Atlantic Economic Journal* 13: 43–48.

State of Alaska (Rommel Consultants). (1974). *Periodic Motor Vehicle Inspection Survey*. Cited in National Highway Traffic Safety Administration. (1975). *Costs and Benefits of Motor Vehicle Inspection*. Washington, DC: U.S. Department of Transportation.

State of Nebraska Department of Motor Vehicles. (1974). *Status Report on Nebraska's Periodic Motor Vehicle Inspection Program*. Cited in National Highway Traffic Safety Administration. (1975). *Costs and Benefits of Motor Vehicle Inspection*. Washington, DC: U.S. Department of Transportation.

Streff, F. M., R. H. Schultz, and A. C. Wagenaar. (1989, March). *Changes in Police Reported Injuries Associated with Michigan's Safety Belt Law: 1988 Update*. Ann Arbor, MI: The University of Michigan, Transportation Research Institute.

Transportation Research Board. (1984). *55: A Decade of Experience*. Transportation Research Board Special Report 204. Washington, DC: National Research Council.

Treat, J. R., and R. L. Stansifer. (1977, March). *Vehicular Problems as Accident Causes — An Overview of Available Information*. SAE Paper 770117. Warrendale, PA: Society of Automotive Engineers.

Womble, K. B. (1989, January). *The Estimated Effect of Safety Belt Use Laws on Injury Reduction*. Washington, DC: U.S. Department of Transportation, NHTSA.

Zlatoper, T. J. (1991). "Determinants of Motor Vehicle Deaths in the United States: A Cross-Sectional Analysis." *Accident Analysis and Prevention* 23: 431–436.

_____. (1988, March 10–12). "Analyzing U.S. Motor Vehicle Death Rates for 1947–1980: The Issue of Functional Form." Paper presented at the Eastern Economic Association Meetings, Boston, MA.

_____. (1984). "Regression Analysis of Time Series Data on Motor Vehicle Deaths in the United States." *Journal of Transport Economics and Policy* 18: 263–274.

4

Truck Accidents

INTRODUCTION

In December 1989, the U.S. Department of Transportation initiated a drug-testing program for truck drivers. As of February 1990, 10 states had laws that limited the lanes and routes used by trucks; 15 states restricted truck usage of urban highways to certain times of the day (*The Wall Street Journal*, February 5, 1990, p. A7E). The implementation of these measures reflects the increasing concern about truck safety in the United States.

Truck safety is our focus in this chapter. Our treatment of this subject includes the following. We note selected accident and fatality statistics about trucks, comparing some to analogous information for other motor vehicles. To better understand the trucking industry, we then describe types of trucking service, types of trucks, and truck safety regulation. A survey of research findings on purported determinants of truck accidents is then provided. We also discuss research dealing with the relationship between trucking deregulation and safety. In this chapter, we concentrate on medium and heavy trucks, since much of the data and research on truck safety pertains to these vehicles.[1]

ACCIDENT AND FATALITY
STATISTICS FOR TRUCKS

One way of assessing the relative safety of medium and heavy trucks is to compare their rate of accident involvement with that for other types of motor vehicles. Table 2.4 in Chapter 2 reveals that the medium/heavy truck crash-involvement rate (285 crash-involved vehicles per 100 million vehicle miles) was the lowest among all vehicle types in the United States in 1990. This rate was about half as large as that for passenger cars, the predominant vehicle type on the basis of registrations and travel. The medium/heavy truck fatal crash-involvement rate (3.2 vehicles in fatal crashes per 100 million vehicle miles) was second lowest among all vehicle types; but it was 45 percent higher than the passenger-car rate. Thus, while medium/heavy trucks have the lowest overall accident risk among vehicle types, their fatal crash risk exceeds that of passenger cars.

During 1990, approximately 12 percent of all U.S. traffic fatalities occurred in crashes involving medium/heavy trucks; of the 5,254 people killed in these accidents, 13.4 percent were truck occupants, 77.2 percent were occupants of another vehicle, and 9.4 percent were nonoccupants (National Highway Traffic Safety Administration [hereafter NHTSA], 1991a, p. 20). Figure 4.1 plots total fatalities and a distance-based fatality rate (total fatalities per 100 million vehicle miles) for crashes involving medium/heavy trucks for the years 1977–90. Over this period, total fatalities reached a maximum of 6,702 in 1979 and then declined to a minimum of 5,229 in 1982. Subsequently, they rose to 5,734 in 1985 and then trended downward through the remainder of the 1980s. After achieving a maximum of 6.1 in 1979, the fatality rate fell during the 1980s to a low of 3.5 in 1990. Between 1977 and 1990, both the death count and fatality rate for medium/heavy trucks followed patterns similar to those for all motor vehicles combined (see Figures 2.1 and 2.2 in Chapter 2).

TYPES OF TRUCKING SERVICE

There are two types of trucking service:[2] for-hire and private. For-hire trucking firms transport freight owned by another party. Those that haul certain commodities, such as unprocessed agricultural products, between states are exempt from federal economic regulations.[3] Similarly, those providing for-hire service between locations within a state are free from federal economic regulation, although the majority of

FIGURE 4.1
U.S. Medium/Heavy Truck Deaths and Death Rate, 1977–90

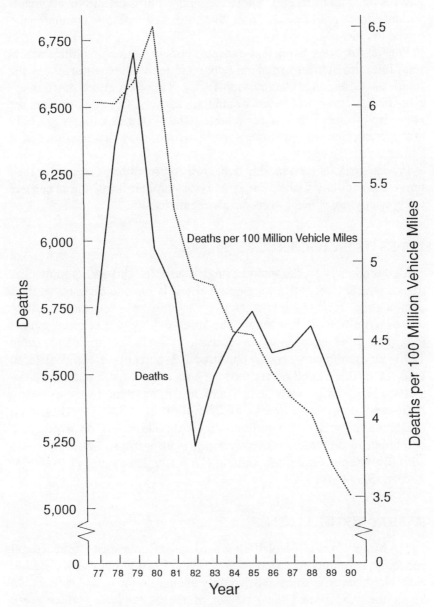

Source: National Highway Traffic Safety Administration. (1991a). *Fatal Accident Reporting System 1990*. DOT HS 807 794. Washington, DC: U.S. Department of Transportation.

states do enforce economic regulations on these carriers. Typically, neither federal nor state economic regulations are placed on local for-hire movements of freight. These exemptions also pertain to shipments within commercial zones, areas that surround and are commercially linked to cities.

For-hire trucking firms that transport nonexempt commodities across state lines are subject to federal economic regulations enforced by the Interstate Commerce Commission (ICC). These regulated carriers are classified as common carriers or contract carriers. Common carriers are authorized to serve the public at large, while contract carriers can only provide service to customers with whom they have contractual agreements.

Private trucking carriers ship their own commodities. The service they provide is ancillary to the primary activities of their firms. These carriers are typically not subject to economic regulations.

TYPES OF LARGE TRUCKS

Medium/heavy trucks include single-unit (straight) and combination trucks. The entirety of a single-unit truck is on one chassis, while a combination truck is either a tractor without a trailer, a tractor pulling one or more trailers, or a single-unit truck pulling one or more trailers (NHTSA, 1993, pp. 55–56). According to Table 2.4 in Chapter 2, in 1990, medium/heavy trucks comprised 3 percent of the registered vehicles in the United States, but they accounted for 7 percent of the total vehicle miles travelled. There are more than twice as many registered single-unit trucks (4.2 million in 1990) as registered combination trucks (1.6 million in 1990). However, on average, a combination vehicle is driven significantly more (60,000 miles annually) than a single-unit vehicle (12,700 miles annually) (NHTSA, 1993, p. 5).

SAFETY REGULATION

The Motor Carrier Act of 1935 provided the framework for the federal economic regulation referred to previously. In addition, this legislation authorized the ICC to establish safety standards for motor carriers. In 1940, the ICC issued the first set of these standards, which were applicable to all common, contract, and private carriers involved in interstate commerce.[4] The regulations pertained to carrier operations, equipment, driver qualifications, and driver hours of service.

Subsequently, Congress enacted several additional laws containing provisions aimed at enhancing motor carrier safety. Among other things, these provisions have pertained to drivers, vehicles, highways, motor carriers, transportation of hazardous materials, accident reporting and investigation, inspection issues, and regulatory responsibilities.[5]

Presently, three U.S. Department of Transportation agencies share regulatory responsibility for motor carrier safety at the federal level: the Federal Highway Administration, the National Highway Traffic Safety Administration (NHTSA), and the Research and Special Programs Administration. The Office of Motor Carriers (previously the Bureau of Motor Carrier Safety) in the Federal Highway Administration establishes and enforces the Federal Motor Carrier Safety Regulations — guidelines for the operations of truck drivers and motor carriers.[6] NHTSA determines and implements safety regulations pertaining to the manufacture of motor vehicles and related equipment. The Research and Special Programs Administration sets and enforces regulations pertaining to the shipment of hazardous materials.

Like the federal government, individual states have established motor carrier safety standards. Matters pertaining to these standards (for example, inspection procedures and enforcement measures) often vary across states.[7] There have been recent initiatives to standardize state motor carrier safety restrictions. For example, the Surface Transportation Assistance Act of 1982, a federal law, set a lower bound (80,000 pounds) on the weight limit states could establish for vehicles travelling on interstate highways. The Surface Transportation Assistance Act also established the Motor Carrier Safety Assistance Program, which provides federal funding for inspection and enforcement programs at the state level.

DETERMINANTS OF TRUCK ACCIDENTS

Assigning causation in truck accidents is a complex task. The complexity is because the event identified as the immediate determinant of an accident (for example, driver error) may have been influenced by a prior occurrence (for example, insufficient driver training) that may have been affected by an earlier policy action (for example, regulation on driver qualifications). Furthermore, societal values or economic considerations may have prompted adoption of the particular policy.

Figure 4.2 demonstrates a portrayal by the Office of Technology Assessment (OTA) (1988) of the linkages among various factors that lead to truck accidents. According to this scheme, at the initial stages of

FIGURE 4.2
Truck Accidents: Causal and Prevention Factors

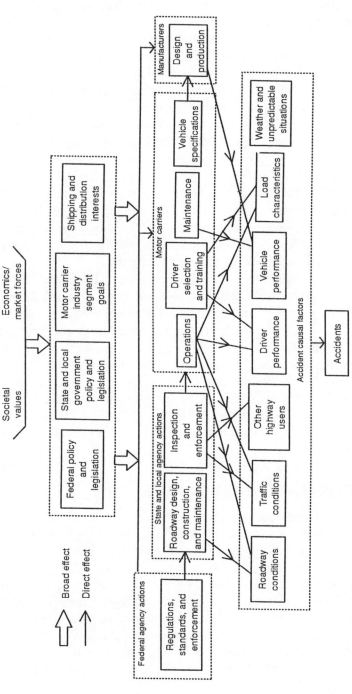

Source: U.S. Congress, Office of Technology Assessment. (1988). *Gearing Up for Safety: Motor Carrier Safety in a Competitive Environment.* OTA-SET-382. Washington, DC: U.S. Government Printing Office. p. 87, Figure 4-4.

the line of accident causation are societal values and economic conditions, both of which shape safety legislation, motor carrier goals, and shipper interests. These initial factors have a broad influence on federal safety restrictions and enforcement activities, which in turn directly affect the actions of three groups: state and local agencies, motor carriers, and vehicle manufacturers. The activities of these three groups have a direct impact on the immediate determinants of truck accidents, the elements in the box labelled "Accident causal factors." Included among the immediate determinants are driver-related (driver performance), vehicle-related (vehicle performance and load characteristics), highway-related (roadway conditions), and environment-related (traffic conditions, other highway users, and weather and unpredictable situations) factors.

In the following five sections, we report statistical findings on the relationship between truck accidents and various potential causes of these accidents.[8] Most of the findings pertain to the immediate accident determinants referred to above. The determinants we discuss are from the following general factor categories: driver, vehicle, highway, environmental, and other. We report two types of statistical information: descriptive and inferential. The descriptive information identifies truck accident patterns and thereby suggests reasons why crashes occur.[9] The inferential results provide statistical evidence on the importance of various determinants in accident causation. The determinants we report on are not an exhaustive collection of the factors causing truck accidents. Rather, they represent factors on which research findings are available.[10]

Driver Factors

Age

Of drivers of medium/heavy trucks involved in fatal or injury crashes in the United States in 1990, 7.9 percent were under 25 years of age, 58.9 percent were 25–44, 31.5 percent were 45–64, and 1.7 percent were over 64.[11] Thus, 90 percent of the drivers were between 25 and 64. This is partly attributable to the fact that most truck drivers are of these ages (NHTSA, 1991c, p. 19).

Gender

Truck driving is predominantly a male occupation. About 96 percent of the drivers of heavy and light trucks in the United States are male

(U.S. Department of Commerce, 1991, p. 397). There is a similarly large male presence in truck crashes. For example, in 1990, almost 97 percent of the drivers of medium/heavy trucks involved in fatal or injury accidents were male.[12]

Alcohol and Other Drugs

Among truck drivers there is a perception that on-the-job usage of drugs and alcohol in their industry is widespread. Beilock and Capelle (1987) asked a sample of nonproduce truckers exiting the Florida Peninsula during 1986 to estimate the percentage of their fellow workers that sometimes drive after using drugs or alcohol. On average, the respondents felt that 37 percent use drugs on the job and 17 percent drive under the influence of alcohol.

Some evidence suggests that relatively few of the truck drivers involved in accidents were under the influence of alcohol. For example, based on police reports, the alcohol-involvement rate for drivers of medium/heavy trucks that crashed in the United States in 1990 was only 1 percent (NHTSA, 1991b, p. 98).[13] Among fatal U.S. crashes in 1990 involving medium/heavy trucks, 5.3 percent of the truck drivers had a blood alcohol concentration of 0.01 percent or more; 2.4 percent of the drivers were intoxicated, having a blood alcohol concentration of 0.10 percent or more (NHTSA, 1991a, p. 30).

Findings from investigations conducted by the National Transportation Safety Board (NTSB) indicate that the use of alcohol and other drugs is a matter of concern in truck safety. Beginning in 1985, NTSB (1988a) analyzed a nonrandom sample of 189 medium/heavy truck crashes in the United States in which the trucks sustained tow away damage. NTSB (1988a, p. 5) found "toxicological evidence of impairment, a police investigator's opinion of impairment, or other evidence of drug or alcohol abuse" in 26 (13.8 percent) of the accidents.[14]

From October 1, 1987, to September 30, 1988, NTSB (1990) investigated a nonrandom sample of 182 driver-fatal medium/heavy truck accidents in eight states (California, Colorado, Georgia, Maryland, New Jersey, North Carolina, Tennessee, and Wisconsin). One-third of the fatally injured drivers had positive results in toxicological tests for alcohol and other drugs of abuse. The drugs found to have been used most frequently were: marijuana (12.8 percent of the fatally injured drivers tested positive), alcohol (12.5 percent), cocaine (8.5 percent), methamphetamine/amphetamines (7.3 percent), other stimulants (7.9 percent), codeine (0.6 percent), and phencyclidine (PCP) (0.6 percent).[15]

Fatigue

Driving too long can decrease alertness and increase the likelihood of driver error. These fatigue-related problems become worse with driver age and during irregular work schedules (Insurance Institute for Highway Safety, 1985, p. 4). According to police reports, in 1990, only 1 percent of the drivers of medium/heavy trucks involved in fatal accidents, and 2 percent of those involved in injury accidents, were fatigued; however, these figures are suspect since it is difficult for police to determine whether accident-involved drivers were fatigued (NHTSA, 1993, p. 20).

Evidence gleaned from detailed investigations by NTSB probably provides a better indication than police reports of the relative extent of weariness among accident-involved drivers. Such evidence suggests that fatigue is widespread among truckers who crash. For example, NTSB (1988a) concluded that fatigue or excessive hours of service was an issue of interest in one-third of the medium/heavy truck accidents that it examined.[16] Similarly, NTSB (1990) found that fatigue was a causal or contributing factor in 31 percent of the driver-fatal truck crashes that it investigated.

Jones and Stein (1987) found evidence that the likelihood of a truck accident increases with driving time. They investigated the role of driver hours of service in crashes on interstates in Washington state. By using regression analysis, they accounted for driver factors and truck operating characteristics. The crash risk associated with driving more than eight hours was found to be twice that associated with driving less than eight hours.

Experience/Training

There is evidence that truck safety improves with driver experience. NTSB (1988a) identified driver experience/training as an issue of interest in nearly one-fourth of the medium/heavy truck accidents that it investigated. Among the driver-fatal crashes it studied, NTSB (1990) found driver inexperience to be a causal or contributing factor in 4.9 percent of the cases.

Regression findings indicate that accident propensity declines with driver experience. For example, Corsi and Fanara (1988b) reported a significant positive relationship between the driver turnover rate and the motor carrier accident rate (accidents per vehicle mile). Bruning (1989) found that this accident rate has a significant negative association with the length of service of accident-involved drivers.

Driver Error

Inappropriate driving decisions can result in accidents. For example, NTSB (1990) identified the following as factors in driver-fatal truck accidents: misjudgement of safe speed (13.5 percent of the accidents); failure to yield, perceive, observe (7 percent); unsafe movement (5.9 percent); and disregard of warnings or signs (2.7 percent). Certain circumstances (for example, alcohol use, fatigue) increase the likelihood of driver error.

Health

There is evidence that driver health problems can lead to truck accidents. In 10 percent of the fatal crashes analyzed by NTSB (1990), the driver's medical condition was deemed serious enough to be a contributing factor, or the likely cause, of the accident. Typically, the health problems associated with crashes were heart-related and were experienced by older drivers. In 90 percent of the cases involving a serious medical condition, there was a cardiac incident when the crash occurred. The average age of drivers in crashes involving medical incidents (55 years) was substantially higher than that of drivers in all other fatal accidents (41 years).

Speed

Evidence suggests that vehicle speed is a factor in trucking accidents. For example, "speeding/too fast for conditions" accounted for 11.4 percent of the truck-attributed factors — which include driver-related and vehicle-related factors — contributing to large truck accidents in Pennsylvania during 1986 (Patten, Carroll, & Thomchick, 1989, p. 273). Also, data indicate that the more severe an accident is, the greater the likelihood it happened at a high velocity. In the United States during 1990, 46 percent of the property-damage-only, 53 percent of the injury, and 73 percent of the fatal crashes involving medium/heavy trucks occurred on highways with speed limits of 50 mph or more (NHTSA, 1993, p. 7).

Along with several other independent factors, Alexander (1992) accounted for the level of speed in regression estimates of models explaining mileage-based accident rates in interstate trucking. He found that his measure of average speed had a statistically significant direct relationship with the accident measures. This result implied that accident risk for trucks increases with velocity.

Speed Variance

Beilock and Capelle (1988) found that many truckers perceive that speed variance has an impact on highway safety. Their study investigated the early impacts on motor carriers of the 1987 federal legislation that allowed states to raise speed limits to 65 mph on rural interstates. The data used in the investigation were drawn from interviews of truck drivers conducted at inspection stations in northern Florida in September 1987. Forty-six percent of those interviewed felt that highways were safer as a result of the higher speed limits, while only 11 percent felt they were unsafe. Nearly two-thirds of those who felt that safety had improved attributed the improvement to better traffic flow. These respondents indicated that there was greater consistency in speeds across vehicles.

In his multiple regression analysis of accident rates in interstate trucking, Alexander (1992) included speed variance as an independent variable. He approximated this factor with the following measure: the eighty-fifth percentile speed minus the average speed. The measure had a statistically significant positive association with accident rates; its effect on these rates was greater than that of average speed.

Vehicle Factors

Mechanical Defects

According to NHTSA (1993, p. 25), police reports suggest that defects are uncommon in accident-involved trucks. In 1990, 93 percent of the medium/heavy trucks in fatal crashes and 91 percent of those in injury crashes had no reported defects. The specific defects reported most often were related to brakes and tires. In the fatal crashes, 3 percent of the trucks had brake deficiencies and 1 percent had tire problems. Brake deficiencies and tire problems were perceived in 2 percent and 1 percent, respectively, of the injury crashes.[17]

Other findings indicate that brake problems may be more prevalent among accident-involved trucks than police reports suggest. For example, NTSB (1988b) determined that at least 32 of the trucks in the 189 medium/heavy truck accidents it investigated had significant brake problems. The most common brake problem was maladjustment. Clarke and others (1987, p. x) estimate "that brake system performance could be involved as a contributing factor in as many as one-third of all truck accidents." They believe that the role of vehicle-related factors in truck accidents is unrecognized and underreported.

Vehicle Age

The majority of medium/heavy trucks involved in crashes in the United States are of a more recent vintage. For example, 58 percent of crash-involved trucks in 1990 had a model year of 1985 or later (NHTSA, 1991b, p. 56). This crash-involvement rate is at least partly attributable to newer vehicles' share of the trucking fleet. For instance, more than 46 percent of the trucks in use in the United States in 1990 had been in use five years or less (U.S. Department of Commerce, 1992, p. 605).

Load Characteristics

Because of its influence on a motor vehicle's center of gravity, cargo load can be a factor in truck crashes. About 70 percent of the medium/heavy trucks involved in fatal crashes are carrying cargo, a proportion comparable to the share of truck miles on which cargo is carried (72 percent) (NHTSA, 1993, p. 26). NTSB (1990) found that load, load shift, or the center of gravity was a causal or contributing factor in 2.7 percent of the driver-fatal truck accidents it investigated.

Truck Type

Aggregate statistics indicate that fatal accident risk is greater for combination trucks than for single-unit trucks. In 1990, the fatal crash involvement rate (vehicles in fatal crashes per 100 million vehicle miles) of combination units (3.9) was more than double the rate for single units (1.8) (NHTSA, 1993, p. 30).

There is considerable variation in accident risk among different types of combination trucks. This was demonstrated by Campbell and others (1988), who computed normalized fatal accident involvement rates for straight (single-unit) trucks and for four categories of combination trucks: straight truck pulling one or more trailers, tractor with no trailer (bobtail), tractor pulling one trailer (single), and tractor pulling two trailers (double).[18] Normalized rates less (greater) than 1.0 indicated underinvolvement (overinvolvement) in fatal accidents. The truck types and their normalized rates were: straight (0.81), straight pulling one or more trailers (1.27), bobtail (2.27), single (1.06), and double (0.90). Thus, straight trucks and tractors pulling two trailers were underinvolved in fatal accidents, while the remaining three types were overinvolved. Particularly noteworthy was the extent of overinvolvement for bobtails.

Several studies have investigated the relative safety of two types of combination trucks: singles and doubles.[19] For example, the Transportation Research Board [TRB] (1986) presented evidence that, under identical operating conditions, doubles are involved in slightly more accidents per mile than singles. However, the study noted that the substitution of doubles for singles reduces truck miles enough to approximately offset doubles' higher accident rate. It concluded that on the U.S. highway system as a whole, tractors pulling two trailers are about as safe as tractors pulling one trailer.

Blower, Campbell, and Green (1993) also presented evidence on the relative safety of singles and doubles. They used log-linear methods to estimate models of accident rates for Michigan-registered truck-tractors operating on Michigan highways from May 1987 through April 1988. In their models, accident rates (accidents per vehicle mile) were hypothesized to depend on vehicle configuration (single, double, or bobtail), road type (limited access, major artery, or other), time of day (day or night), and area type (rural or urban). Estimates of casualty-accident models indicated no significant difference in the accident rates of singles and doubles. They also revealed that accident risk was significantly higher for bobtails than for the other two truck types.

Not all studies have concluded that singles and doubles are equally safe. For instance, using a case-control method on data for Washington state, Stein and Jones (1988) reported that the crash rate per vehicle mile for doubles was more than twice the rate for singles. According to OTA (1988, pp. 95-96), the main reasons for dissimilar results across studies on the relative safety of singles and doubles are:

1) differences in exposure survey methods and uncertainties in the resulting estimates of exposure, 2) unreliable and missing accident data, 3) differences in the definition of an accident and/or large truck, 4) differences in vehicle classification survey methods, 5) differences in driving environment, and 6) inherent stochastic variation associated with small samples.

Highway Factors

Location

Table 4.1 indicates that the fatal crash involvement rate for single-unit trucks was about the same in urban and rural settings during 1990, while

TABLE 4.1
Crash Involvement Rate* by Truck Type and Location, 1990

| | Location | |
Truck Type	Urban	Rural
Fatal Crashes:		
Single-Unit	1.9	1.8
Combination	3.5	4.1
Injury Crashes:		
Single-Unit	106.0	32.0
Combination	119.0	24.0
Property-Damage-Only Crashes:		
Single-Unit	253.0	69.0
Combination	327.0	67.0

*Number of vehicles involved in crashes per 100 million miles of vehicle travel.

Source: National Highway Traffic Safety Administration. (1993). *Summary of Medium and Heavy Truck Crashes in 1990*. DOT HS 807 953. Washington, DC: U.S. Department of Transportation. p. 30, Table 16.

combination trucks had a rate that was about 17 percent higher in rural areas than in urban locations. In contrast, the crash involvement rates for injury crashes and property-damage-only crashes were more than three times greater in urban settings than in rural areas, regardless of truck type.

Controlling for other factors (vehicle configuration, road type, and time of day), Blower, Campbell, and Green (1993) estimated the relationship between accident risk and location for truck-tractors in Michigan. They found that for both casualty crashes and property-damage-only crashes, the risk of accident was significantly higher in rural areas than in urban settings. Greater traffic density in urban areas increases the likelihood of accidents; but this is apparently offset by safer driving conditions attributable to the lower speeds in urban locations.

Highway Type

Relatively few fatal medium/heavy truck accidents occur on interstate highways. As Table 4.2 reveals, in 1990, less than 10 percent of single-unit fatal truck accidents and only about one-fourth of combination fatal truck accidents were on these roadways. Fatal large truck crashes occur most frequently on rural non-interstate highways. In 1990, at least half

TABLE 4.2
Fatal Crash Involvements by Highway Type and Truck Type, 1990

	Truck Type	
Highway Type	Single-Unit (Percent of Crashes)	Combination (Percent of Crashes)
Urban Interstate	6	10
Urban Non-Interstate	39	22
Rural Interstate	3	16
Rural Non-Interstate	50	52

Source: Computed from National Highway Traffic Safety Administration. (1993). Summary of Medium and Heavy Truck Crashes in 1990. DOT HS 807 953. Washington, DC: U.S. Department of Transportation. p. 32, Table 18.

of the fatal accidents that involved single-unit or combination trucks were on these roadways.

For combination trucks, fatal accident risk (measured by fatal accident involvements per vehicle mile) is more than twice as large on urban non-interstate roads than on urban interstates; it is nearly three times greater on rural non-interstates than on rural interstates (University of Michigan Transportation Research Institute [hereafter UMTRI], 1987, p. 53). Design features (for example, limited access, divided highways) are probably major reasons for the relative safety of interstate highways.

Blower, Campbell, and Green (1993) reported evidence on the role of road type in large truck safety. Controlling for other considerations, they found that accident rates for truck-tractors in Michigan were significantly lower on limited access highways than on major arteries and other roads.

Trafficway flow is another distinguishing highway characteristic in trucking accidents. Fatal trucking accidents occur most frequently on two-way, undivided highways. In 1990, 56 percent of fatal crashes involving medium/heavy trucks were on these highways, while 41 percent were on divided roadways (NHTSA, 1993, p. 33).

Environmental Factors

Highway Congestion

Alexander (1992) included a density variable — automobile registrations per highway mileage — in his multiple regression analysis of accident rates in interstate trucking. He hypothesized that greater congestion increases the likelihood of an accident. His regression results supported this hypothesis, indicating a statistically significant positive relationship between his congestion measure and various accident rates.

Weather

Truck accidents typically happen under normal weather conditions. If there are unfavorable conditions at the time of an accident, they usually involve some form of precipitation. For example, during 1990 there were no adverse atmospheric conditions at the time of 83 percent of all fatal crashes involving medium/heavy trucks; it was raining during 11 percent of the crashes; there was fog during 3 percent of the accidents; and 2 percent of the crashes occurred in snow (NHTSA, 1993, p. 34).

In his multiple regression analysis of accident rates in interstate trucking, Alexander (1992) included measures for rain — the average number of rain days per state — and snow — average snowfall per state — among his independent variables. He hypothesized that rain would adversely affect trucking safety since it impairs vision and highway conditions. He was uncertain about the anticipated impact of snow, noting that snow creates slippery highway conditions but may reduce travel. The regression results revealed a statistically significant positive relationship between rain and two accident rates: accidents per highway mileage and injuries per highway mileage. Highway mileage-based rates for accidents, fatalities, injuries, and property damage were all found to have statistically significant negative relationships with snow.

Time

Data for 1990 reveal the following time patterns for fatal or injury crashes in the United States that involved medium or heavy trucks: The majority of fatal (78 percent) and injury (85 percent) crashes were during the week, between Monday 6:00 A.M. and Friday 6:00 P.M. (NHTSA, 1993, pp. 14 and 16). During the week most fatal (69 percent) and injury (81 percent) crashes occurred during the day, between 6:00 A.M. and 6:00 P.M.; but over the weekend most fatal (66 percent) and injury (60 percent) crashes were at night, between 6:00 P.M. and 6:00 A.M. (NHTSA, 1993, pp. 15 and 17).

Most truck accidents occur during the day because this is when trucks typically travel. For example, more than three-fourths of the travel by tractor-semitrailers is in the daytime. However, less than two-thirds of the fatal accidents involving tractor-semitrailers is at that time. Thus, for these vehicles, travel at night is about 2.5 times more dangerous than travel during the day (UMTRI, 1987, pp. 124–26).

In their estimates of models of truck-tractor accident rates in Michigan, Blower, Campbell, and Green (1993) accounted for time of day. They found that casualty accident risk was 1.4 times greater at night than during the day. In evaluating this finding, they noted that night itself does not cause accidents. Rather, factors associated with night (for example, driver fatigue, drunk driving, and poor lighting) are the likely determinants.

UMTRI (1987, pp. 56–59) found evidence of a dawn phenomenon. This pertains to the fact that the distribution of trucking accidents at dawn differs from other time periods. UMTRI reported that police coded substantially higher percentages of truck driver drowsiness in accidents at dawn than at all other times on both divided and undivided rural roads, but truck drivers involved in fatal accidents at dawn tend to have been driving for a shorter period than drivers involved in fatal accidents at other time periods. Thus, the fatigue problem at dawn is more related to problems in human factors (for example, diurnal rhythms) than to driving too long.

Table 4.3 indicates the relative importance of various driver, vehicle, highway, and environmental factors in the driver-fatal accidents investigated by NTSB (1990).[20] As can be seen, the largest number of factors are driver-related, led by fatigue (30.8 percent of the cases), drugs (21.1 percent), unsafe speed (13.5 percent), alcohol (11.9 percent), and physical incapacitation (10.3 percent). Highway or environmental considerations are factors in about 12 percent of the cases. Indicated in more than one-third of the cases, occupant protection is the most frequently cited factor. It pertains to considerations, such as seat belts and the crashworthiness of truck cabs, which affect driver safety in the event of a crash. According to NTSB (1990, pp. 70–71), "The degree of occupant protection in a vehicle does not precipitate an accident, but often was a factor in the accident's survivability."

Other Factors

Seat Belt Usage

Findings of NTSB (1990), previously reported, suggest that occupant safety factors, such as seat belt usage, affect the severity of occupant injury in the event of an accident. According to Clarke and Leasure (1986, p. iii), "Rollovers, ejections, entrapment in crushed cabs, contact

TABLE 4.3
Factors Causing or Contributing to Driver-Fatal
Truck Crashes Investigated by NTSB

Factor	Percent of Cases with This Factor*
Driver-Related:	
Physical Incapacitation	10.3
Impairment Due to Fatigue	30.8
Impairment Due to Alcohol	11.9
Impairment Due to Drugs besides Alcohol	21.1
Driver Inexperience	4.9
Unsafe Movement	5.9
Disregard of Warnings or Signs	2.7
Misjudgement of Safe Speed	13.5
Failure to Yield, Perceive, Observe	7.0
Vehicle-Related:	
Occupant Protection	36.8
Conspicuity	4.9
Brake Adjustment/Deficiencies	4.3
Mechanical/Maintenance	5.9
Load/Load Shift/Center of Gravity	2.7
Highway/Environment-Related:	
Signs, Roadway, Environmental	11.9
Failure for Unknown Reasons	2.7

*Based on investigation of 185 case vehicles. Percentages do not sum to one because more than one factor may have been involved in an accident.

Source: Computed from National Transportation Safety Board. (1990). *Safety Study: Fatigue, Alcohol, Other Drugs, and Medical Factors in Fatal-to-the-Driver Heavy Truck Crashes*, Vol. 1. NTSB/SS-90/01. Washington, DC: National Transportation Safety Board. p. 69, Table 33.

with interior surfaces, and fires are the primary mechanisms responsible for the majority of truck occupant fatalities." In their study, they identified greater restraint system usage as the countermeasure that would be most effective in lowering truck occupant deaths and injuries. Seiff (1991, pp. 3–4) claimed that increased seat belt usage was a likely reason for a 57 percent decline in the distance-based fatality rate for occupants of large trucks over the period 1976–89.

Roadside Inspection

The effect of roadside inspections on large truck safety has been analyzed with state-level data. Patten, Carroll, and Thomchick (1989) assessed the effectiveness of these inspections in identifying factors that are major determinants of large truck accidents in Pennsylvania. To accomplish this, they compared the causes of these accidents with the findings of the Motor Carrier Safety Assistance Program and other comparable roadside inspections. They reported that driver-related factors and vehicle defects accounted for 87 percent and 13 percent, respectively, of the total truck-related causal factors in large truck accidents in Pennsylvania in 1986. In comparison, among the reasons for out-of-service violations identified in Pennsylvania roadside inspections from August 1986 to March 1987, 6.2 percent were driver related and 93.8 percent were vehicle related. The researchers concluded that roadside inspections, as currently conducted, do not effectively deal with driver-related factors that contribute to heavy truck accidents.

Using annual data for California for 1976–87, Kraas (1993) estimated variable coefficients models in which the level of road safety (measured by truck-at-fault accidents per vehicle mile) was a function of government expenditures on safety surveillance (measured by roadside inspections per vehicle mile), the economic environment (measured by real wages of truck drivers per vehicle mile), and a time trend representing factors that enhance road safety. He found a significant inverse relationship between the measures of road safety and government expenditures on safety surveillance, although the estimated coefficient for the latter measure was smaller in absolute value after trucking deregulation. These findings suggest that roadside inspections reduce truck accidents.

Police Enforcement

In his multiple regression analysis of interstate trucking accident rates, Alexander (1992) included a measure — the number of highway police officers per highway mileage — to represent efforts to detect speed and weight violations. He hypothesized that greater police enforcement should promote safer driving and fewer accidents. Consistent with this expectation, the regression results indicated that the measure had a statistically significant negative relationship with various accident rates per truck-miles travelled.

Firm Characteristics

The relationship between large truck safety and company practices or characteristics has been studied. For example, NTSB (1988a) found that oversight of the driver and oversight of equipment were issues of interest in 51.3 percent and 30.2 percent, respectively, of the medium/heavy truck accidents it investigated. Also, NTSB (1990) discovered deficiencies in carrier oversight of the driver or of the vehicle in 62 percent of the driver-fatal truck accidents it examined. NTSB (1990, p. 68) stated that "the high number of these cases is a concern to the Safety Board and indicates a need for more safety oriented management."

Table 4.4 summarizes results from five studies that used multiple regression analysis and carrier-level data to estimate the effect of various firm characteristics on accident rates. Each study utilized data collected by the Bureau of Motor Carrier Safety (BMCS), which is now the Office of Motor Carriers. Corsi, Fanara, and Roberts (1984) used 1981 data to estimate one model for Class I and II carriers and another model for Class III, intrastate, and private carriers.[21] Corsi and Fanara (1988b) used data for 1985 and 1986 to estimate a model for interstate carriers. For Class I and II carriers established prior to the passage of the Motor Carrier Act (MCA) of 1980, Corsi, Fanara, and Jarrell (1988) estimated one model on 1977 data and another one on 1984 data. Corsi and Fanara (1989) used data for 1985 and 1986 to estimate separate models for established carriers (certified by the ICC before passage of the MCA) and new entrants (certified after passage of the MCA). Bruning (1989) estimated various models on 1984 data corresponding to Class I and II general freight carriers and specialized carriers.

In the regressions summarized in Table 4.4, categorical independent factors (for example, commodity operations) were represented by dummy variables; continuous independent variables (for example, driver turnover rate) were expressed either in their original form or as logarithmic transformations. The dependent variable in all of the regressions was a logarithmic transformation of the carrier accident rate (the number of accidents divided by vehicle miles). This rate was computed from information filed with BMCS on accidents resulting in injury, death, or property damage in excess of a certain dollar amount.

Among the independent variables listed in Table 4.4, those that correspond to safety management practices are distinguished from other firm characteristics. Corsi, Fanara, and Roberts (1984), Corsi and Fanara (1988b), and Corsi and Fanara (1989) used information gathered in safety audits of trucking firms to gauge carrier safety practices. In these

TABLE 4.4
Regressions of Mileage-Based Accident Rates on Firm Characteristics

Independent Variables††	Study: A		B	C		D		E**
Carriers Studied:	Class I and II	Class III, Intrastate, and Private	Interstate	Class I and II	Class I and II	Established	New Entrants	General Freight and Specialized
Time Period of Data:	1981	1981	1985–86	1977	1984	1985–86	1985–86	1984
SAFETY MANAGEMENT PRACTICES								
Noncompliance with Regulations:								
Driver Qualifications (R391)	+	+*	*				*	
Driving of Motor Vehicles (R392)			–			–	–	
Accident Reporting (R394)	–	+*	–*			+*	+*	
Hours of Service (R395)	–	–*	+*			+*	+	
Vehicle Inspection and Repairs (R396)	+	+	+			+*	+	
R391 and R396	–*	–				–		
Insurance and Safety Exp./Operating Exp.	+*							
Insurance Payments/Total Miles	+*							
Insurance and Safety Exp./Vehicle Miles				+*	+*			
Maintenance Exp./Vehicle Miles				+	+			
OTHER FIRM CHARACTERISTICS								
Scope of Operations (Intrastate Only)	+	–						
Legal Specification (Contract or Private)	+*	+						
Miles in Owned Vehicles/Total Miles	–							
Miles Rented with Driver as % of Total			+*					
% of Rented Power Units with Drivers				+*	+*			
Driver Turnover Rate				+	+			+

Table 4.4, continued

Study:†	A		B	C		D		E**
Carriers Studied:	Class I and II	Class III, Intrastate, and Private	Interstate	Class I and II	Class I and II	Established	New Entrants	General Freight and Specialized
Time Period of Data:	1981	1981	1985–86	1977	1984	1985–86	1985–86	1984
Independent Variables††								
Average Years of Service of Accident-Involved Drivers								* −
LTL Tons as % of Total				+	−			
Average Length of Haul				−	−*			
Total Operating Expenses	−*							
Vehicle Miles			−*	−*	−	−*	−*	+*
Value of Operating Property				+	+			+
Net Operating Income	−	−		+	+			
Operating Ratio								
Return on Investment				+	*			−*‡
Commodity Operations:								
Tank Operations			+			+	−	
Building Materials			+			+	+*	
Produce, Fruit & Seafood			+*			−	+*	
General Freight			+			+	+	
% of Accidents Due to Defective Equipment								*
Average Tractor Age								+
OTHER FACTOR								
% of Accidents in Bad Weather								−

*The estimated coefficient was significant in a two-tail test at a level of 10 percent or less.

†Study A — Corsi, Fanara, and Roberts (1984); Study B — Corsi and Fanara (1988b); Study C — Corsi, Fanara, and Jarrell (1988); Study D — Corsi and Fanara (1989); and Study E — Bruning (1989).

**Table 4.4 summarizes regression estimates for Bruning (1989) based on the full sample of carriers. Bruning (1989) also reported estimates of models for various carrier subsamples: general freight, specialized carrier, large carrier, medium carrier, and small carrier. The findings for the subsamples were generally consistent with those for the full sample.

††A +(−) to the right of an independent variable indicates that the estimated coefficient associated with the variable was positive (negative). Lack of a sign indicates that the independent variable at the left was not included in the regression.

‡Bruning (1989) used return on investment (ROI) for three different years — 1984, 1982, and 1980 — in alternate regressions. Regardless of its year, ROI was statistically significant.

Source: Compiled by the authors.

audits, federal inspectors ask carrier managers several ques-tions; based on the responses and supporting documentation, they rate the carriers as satisfactory, conditional, or unsatisfactory on each of several of the Federal Motor Carrier Safety Regulations.[22] Studies in Table 4.4 utilized the ratings on at least four of five regulations — driver qualifications (R391), driving of motor vehicles (R392), accident reporting (R394), hours of service (R395), and vehicle inspection and repairs (R396). Ratings of conditional or unsatisfactory were considered to be evidence of noncompliance and were coded as values of one for dummy variables representing the regulations. The researchers expected that regression coefficients corresponding to these variables would be positive, reflecting a direct relationship between accident risk and noncompliance with safety regulations.

Results reported in Table 4.4 imply that accident propensity is linked to nonadherence to federal safety regulations. Noncompliance with any of four regulations — R391, R394, R395, and R396 — is significantly and positively related to accident rates in one or more of the studies. However, contrary to expectations, for each of three of these standards — R391, R395, and R396 — noncompliance also has a significant negative relationship with accident rate in at least one of the regressions summarized in Table 4.4. Among the statistically significant linkages between regulatory noncompliance and accident rate, positive associations outnumber negative ones and are generally more statistically significant.

Regarding other safety management practices, Table 4.4 indicates that measures of spending on insurance and safety have positive, statistically significant associations with accident rates in the regressions for Class I and II carriers in two of the studies. Corsi, Fanara, and Jarrell (1988, p. 35) were not surprised by this positive relationship, explaining that "the higher accident rate experience of the carrier necessitates the additional spending, and the beneficial impact of higher spending in these categories takes time to materialize." These researchers also found that maintenance expenditures per vehicle mile are significantly and positively related to accident rate, which Corsi, Fanara, and Jarrell (1988, p. 35) attribute to "the known association between older equipment and higher accident propensity."

On the subject of other firm characteristics, Table 4.4 reveals that the proportion of total miles in owned vehicles has a negative and statistically significant coefficient in the regression for Class I and II carriers in Corsi, Fanara, and Roberts (1984); and the percentage of miles rented with a driver has a positive, statistically significant coefficient in both regressions in Corsi, Fanara, and Jarrell (1988). These findings suggest that accident risk increases with greater use of owner-operators.[23] Corsi, Fanara, and Jarrell (1988, p. 34) attribute this relationship to "the owner-operator's perceived need to violate hours of service regulations to meet minimum financial needs as well as inability to either replace equipment in a timely fashion or repair it on a regular basis."

There is evidence in Table 4.4 that carrier accident propensity declines with driver experience. For example, in Corsi and Fanara (1988b), the driver turnover rate has a significant positive relationship with accident rate; in Bruning (1989), the accident rate has a significant negative association with the length of service of accident-involved drivers.

Average length of haul has an inverse relationship with accident rate in both regressions in Corsi, Fanara, and Jarrell (1988); the relationship is statistically significant in the 1984 regression. The lower level of accident risk associated with operations of greater length may be attributable to the fact that the major portion of long trips is outside of congested urban areas.

Table 4.4 reveals conflicting findings on the relationship between carrier size and accident risk. In four of the studies, proxies for carrier size — total operating expenses in Corsi, Fanara, and Roberts (1984) and vehicle miles in Corsi and Fanara (1988b, 1989) and Corsi, Fanara, and Jarrell (1988) — are negatively and significantly associated with accident rates. In contrast, the measure of carrier size in Bruning (1989), value of operating property, has a significant direct relationship with accident rate. Although there is not unanimity on the matter, the weight of the evidence from the surveyed studies suggests that trucking firms exhibit economies of scale in terms of supplying safe service.

The operating ratio (operating expenses divided by operating revenue) is significantly and positively linked to accident rate in the 1984 regression in Corsi, Fanara, and Jarrell (1988); return on investment has a significant inverse relationship with accident rate in Bruning (1989). These results suggest that accident risk is lower among firms that are stronger financially.

Table 4.4 indicates that carriers of certain commodities have higher accident rates than other carriers. Corsi and Fanara (1988b, 1989) reported significantly higher rates for general freight carriers. Corsi and Fanara (1989) also found that, among new entrants, haulers of produce, fruit, and seafood have significantly greater accident risk.

Bruning (1989) reported evidence that equipment condition is related to accident risk. He found a significant direct association between the percent of accidents resulting from defective equipment and accident rate.

Like some of the studies in Table 4.4, Moses and Savage (1992b) utilized safety audit information to conduct a regression analysis of the safety performance of trucking firms. However, their study differed from the previous analyses in certain respects. For example, while each of the previous studies had samples consisting of less than 1,000 observations from 1986 or earlier, Moses and Savage used a data set on more than 13,000 firms audited between October 1986 and July 1989. Also, they utilized more of the safety audit information than did the earlier studies; for their estimation procedure, Moses and Savage employed Poisson regression rather than ordinary least squares regression.[24]

Among their independent variables, the earlier studies included carrier ratings on selected federal safety regulations. Instead of doing this, Moses and Savage incorporated the answers to 57 questions posed to the carriers during the safety audits. Along with these answers, they included several firm characteristics as independent variables. Since Poisson regressions were estimated, they used count information — on total accidents and on the number of fatalities and injuries — as dependent variables.

In their regression results pertaining to the audit information, Moses and Savage found that safety practices leading to significantly fewer accidents include: appointment of a safety director, background checks on new drivers, and compliance with regulations on accident reporting and drivers' hours of service. However, contrary to expectations, they also found many instances in which poorer safety procedures were significantly associated with better safety performance. They offered the following rationale for these counter-intuitive results: Many small firms that have safe operations are unfamiliar with federal regulations, while many large carriers with unsafe practices may be savvy enough to receive favorable ratings on safety audits.

Moses and Savage's findings on the relationship between firm characteristics and accident performance were generally consistent with results reported in earlier studies. For example, they found that accident rates have significant inverse linkages with firm size (measured by total fleet miles) and trip distance (measured by the percentage of drivers employed on trips over 100 miles). Their results also revealed that accidents increase less than proportionally with vehicle miles. In addition, findings indicated that, relative to other carriers, agricultural carriers have significantly lower accident rates, and general freight haulers have significantly higher rates. Through closer analysis, Moses and Savage found that the safety problem is particularly acute for the smallest and largest general freight firms. Using an age variable based on the number of years since incorporation, Moses and Savage unexpectedly found that older firms have significantly higher accident rates than newer firms.

Moses and Savage noted that carriers with the worst safety ratings demonstrate improved safety performance after they are reinspected. However, there is a paucity of such firms, and the chance of their being audited is low. As a result, Moses and Savage concluded that the program since 1986 of increased federal safety audits has not led to a lower accident rate in the trucking industry.

In another study, Moses and Savage (1992a) again analyzed the effects of safety practices and other firm characteristics on safety performance. The data used in the analysis pertained to more than 75,000 firms audited by federal safety inspectors between October 1986 and November 1991. As in their previous study, Moses and Savage estimated a model by Poisson regression. The dependent variable in the model was reportable accidents, which are crashes that result in death, injury, or property damage exceeding $5,000. The independent variables were selected firm characteristics as well as the answers to 57 questions asked in the safety audits.

As in their previous study, Moses and Savage found counter-intuitive evidence that a poor performance on much of the safety audit was linked to a better safety record. However, consistent with expectations, findings indicated that carriers have significantly lower accident rates when they file accident reports, monitor drivers' hours of service, and discipline drivers involved in preventable accidents. They also revealed that carriers who appoint a safety director have better safety records.

Moses and Savage reported that accident rates are significantly lower for larger firms, private carriers, and agricultural carriers; and the rates are significantly higher for carriers of hazardous materials and long-distance haulers. The finding for long-distance operators was contrary to that reported in the previous study; but the study considered here dealt with the most serious accidents that are more likely to occur at the higher speeds characteristic of long hauls. In contrast to results in their previous study, Moses and Savage found that, relative to other firms, general freight carriers and older haulers do not have significantly higher rates of reportable accidents.

In another study, Moses and Savage (1991) focused on the safety performance of hazardous materials carriers. Here, they used Poisson regression analysis and information from more than 13,000 federal safety audits conducted between October 1986 and July 1989. Regression estimates, which were based on the entire sample and which controlled for several factors (firm size; long distance operations; general freight, rural, and hazardous materials operations; and performance on safety audits), indicated that, compared to other carriers, hazardous materials haulers have significantly higher accident, fatality, and injury rates.

In this study, Moses and Savage also estimated regressions on a subsample pertaining to 1,905 carriers of hazardous materials. The estimates revealed that accident rates are significantly higher for older firms and for general freight carriers, but the rates have a significant negative relationship with firm size. They also indicated that long-distance carriers have significantly lower accident rates but significantly higher fatality and injury rates. Moses and Savage attributed the latter results to the fact that accidents on high-speed rural roadways tend to be relatively few in number but severe in nature.

Among hazardous materials carriers, Moses and Savage found that those transporting combustible materials have the highest accident, fatality, and injury rates, while tank carriers of flammables have low rates. As in their other studies, they reported that accident rates have significant counter-intuitive relationships with performance on many parts of the safety audit. Surprisingly, they found that hazardous materials carriers rated as satisfactory have accident, fatality, and injury rates that are nearly four times greater than those of firms with poorer safety ratings.

DEREGULATION AND TRUCKING SAFETY

Federal regulatory reform in U.S. transportation commenced in the late 1970s. Among other things, it led to the passage of the Motor Carrier Act of 1980, which deregulated the motor carrier industry at the federal level. According to Talley (1983, p. 40), "The act sought to eliminate unnecessary operating burdens from regulated motor carriers, to liberalize motor carrier entry standards, and to establish a zone of rate freedom."[25]

There has been considerable debate on the linkage between trucking deregulation and highway safety. Some claims and evidence suggest that deregulation has had an adverse impact. For example, Adams (1989) claimed that it has led to a decline in transportation safety. Based on a trend analysis of truck deaths, injuries, or accidents per vehicle mile, Daicoff (1988) concluded that deregulation has been associated with a deterioration in the rate of improvement in motor carrier safety. Regression results of Kraas (1993, p. 186) for California support "the hypothesis that structural changes in the trucking industry induced by economic deregulation have reduced road safety."

There is evidence that refutes the claim that deregulation has led to a decline in highway safety. For example, Moore (1989) noted that the decrease in truck fatalities per billion truck-miles from 1977 to 1985 does not support the claim. Regression estimates of Viscusi (1989) do not indicate that deregulation caused a decline in the safety of transportation workers. Regression results of Alexander (1992, p. 32) pertaining to interstate-trucking "suggest that drivers experience the same accident rate that they did before deregulation, but that the accidents involved fewer fatalities and injuries."

If deregulation has caused trucking safety to deteriorate, it would be informative to determine the manner in which this occurred. Moses and Savage (1989, p. 6) identified four ways in which deregulation may have had an adverse impact on safety. First, declining profits — a result of increased competition after deregulation — may have prompted trucking firms to make decisions on personnel (for example, reduce wages and driver training), equipment (for example, reduce maintenance), and procedures (for example, design schedules that force drivers to violate hours of service regulations) that make travel more dangerous. Second, new entrants into the trucking industry since deregulation may be more inclined than established firms to hire less-experienced and less-qualified personnel and to utilize old, improperly maintained equipment. Third, deregulation has caused freight to be shifted from a safer mode — railroads — to a less-safe one — trucks. Fourth, the increased truck traffic resulting from deregulation may have led to greater congestion and a consequently higher likelihood of accident. In the following three sections, we summarize research pertaining to the first three linkages between deregulation and safety identified by Moses and Savage. To our knowledge, no research has been conducted on the congestion-safety relationship.[26]

Profitability-Safety Relationship

Evidence from several aforementioned regression analyses indicates that accident propensity may decrease with improvements in the financial strength of carriers. For example, Corsi, Fanara, and Roberts (1984) reported that a profitability measure (net operating income) had a negative, though statistically insignificant, linkage with the accident rate of Class I and II carriers during 1981. Corsi, Fanara, and Jarrell (1988) found that their financial performance measure (operating ratio) was positively related to the accident rate of Class I and II carriers in both 1977 and 1984, although the relationship was significant in only the latter year. Bruning's (1989) profitability gauge, return on investment, had a significant inverse relationship with the accident rate of Class I and II carriers in 1984. Moses and Savage (1992a, 1992b) reported that carriers identified in safety audits since 1986 as being unprofitable had significantly more accident occurrences than profitable haulers.

Lacking data on carrier profitability, Kraas (1993) used real wage rates of truck drivers to represent the economic environment in regression models that explained annual truck-at-fault accident rates in California from 1976 to 1987. Controlling for government safety surveillance and a time trend, he found a negative relationship between the wage rates and accident rates both before and after deregulation. However, the association was statistically significant only after deregulation.

Chow (1989) also investigated the hypothesis that financial condition and safety are linked. Lacking the appropriate data, he was unable to estimate the relationship between financial health and safety performance. Instead, he quantified the association between financial condition and four safety-related operating strategies: spending on insurance and safety, spending on maintenance, age of the vehicle fleet, and use of owner-operators. As his primary measure of financial performance, Chow used the C score.[27] He studied the relationship between financial strength and the various safety strategies at both the aggregate and carrier levels.

In his aggregate analysis, Chow used annual data for 1975–85 on four groups of Class I and II general freight carriers. He regressed each safety conduct measure on the C score and dummy variables representing carrier size and class. The coefficients for the C score were statistically significant in every case. Their signs indicated that an improvement in financial strength is associated with increases in insurance, safety, and maintenance spending, and with a decrease in fleet age. Unexpectedly, they also revealed a positive relationship between financial strength and usage of owner-operators.

Chow analyzed carrier-level information on general freight firms reporting to the ICC between 1982 and 1986. Statistically significant results indicated that carriers approaching bankruptcy have older vehicle fleets and make greater use of owner-operators. For carriers not in financial distress, no discernible pattern between safety strategies and financial condition was found.

Blevins and Chow (1988) assessed the profitability-safety linkage by comparing the post-deregulation safety performance of bankrupt and nonbankrupt general freight carriers. Specifically, they conducted univariate analyses on data pertaining to three areas of safety performance: safety expenditures, compliance with federal safety regulations, and accident rates. The data were for the years 1982–86 and came from the BMCS and the ICC.

Blevins and Chow found that, on average, bankrupt carriers spend less than nonbankrupt firms on insurance and safety, maintenance, and equipment replacement. However, none of the differences in averages were statistically significant. The researchers also found that the proportion of carriers rated unsatisfactory in their compliance to various federal safety regulations was greater for bankrupt than for nonbankrupt firms, although the difference in the group proportions was statistically insignificant. Blevins and Chow compared financially distressed and financially sound carriers on the basis of several accident rates. In the majority of cases, the average rate for bankrupt carriers was larger than that for nonbankrupt firms, and in one instance, the difference was highly significant.

Based on interviews of truckers exiting the Florida Peninsula from 1984 through 1986, Beilock and Capelle (1987) found evidence of a linkage between economic pressure and safety. For example, their results indicated that haulers of time-sensitive produce are more likely than nonproduce truckers to have delivery schedules requiring violation of hours-of-service regulations. Beilock and Capelle postulated that the greater competition resulting from deregulation may have increased economic stress and thereby decreased safety. They cited circumstantial evidence of a safety decline under deregulation: 57 percent of the drivers surveyed felt that conditions affecting a hauler's ability to drive safely had deteriorated since 1980; only 10 percent believed that these circumstances had improved. The reasons cited most often for the poorer safety conditions were: increased traffic, deregulation and competition, poor driver skills, and traffic laws and enforcement.

New Entrants-Safety Relationship

Corsi and Fanara (1989) compared accident rates (accidents per 100,000 vehicle miles) of new entrants in the trucking industry with rates of carriers that existed prior to passage of the Motor Carrier Act of 1980. They used BMCS data for 1985 and 1986 to conduct univariate and multivariate analyses. The results of the univariate analysis indicated that new entrants' accident rate and their noncompliance with four federal safety regulations — driver qualifications, accident reporting requirements, hours-of-service regulation, and vehicle inspection and repair — were, on average, significantly higher than those of established carriers. They also indicated that the average vehicle miles for new carriers was significantly less than that for established carriers.

In their multivariate analysis, Corsi and Fanara estimated separate accident-rate regressions for established carriers and new entrants. The estimation results are summarized in Table 4.4. They indicate that the accident rate for both categories of carriers is significantly and positively linked to noncompliance with accident-reporting requirements and is significantly and negatively related to vehicle miles. In addition, the established carrier accident rate has a significant positive association with noncompliance with hours-of-service rules and a significant negative association with violations of vehicle-inspection standards. Also, the accident rate for new entrants has a significant inverse linkage with noncompliance with driver-qualification standards and is significantly and directly related to the carriage of produce, fruit, seafood, and general freight.

Controlling for the effects of the explanatory factors in the regression models, Corsi and Fanara estimated that new entrants have an accident rate that is one-third larger than the rate for established carriers. The researchers did not have data on entrants from other time periods. As a result, they noted that they could not conclude that the safety performance of new entrants born after the Motor Carrier Act of 1980 is worse, or better, than that of new entrants who emerged at other times.

In another study, Corsi and Fanara (1988a) examined the accident rates of established carriers and new entrants, using safety audit data on nearly 7,000 carriers compiled by the Office of Motor Carriers between September 1, 1986, and April 30, 1988. Carriers certified by the ICC prior to July 1, 1980 (the passage date for the MCA) were considered to be established carriers in the analysis. Firms certified after the MCA were considered new entrants, with those certified since January 1985 deemed to be the newest of the new entrants.

Corsi and Fanara compared the average accident rates (accidents per million vehicle miles) for the three categories of carriers. The mean rate for the oldest of the new (0.62) was not significantly different from the average rate for established carriers (0.55). However, the mean rate for the newest of the new firms (0.81) was higher and significantly different from the average rates for the other two categories of carriers. These results demonstrated that the youngest carriers have, on average, the poorest safety record, but the safety performance of the older of the new entrants approaches that of established carriers. Additional findings reported by Corsi and Fanara indicated that the newest of the new entrants have deficient policies and procedures in the areas of driver hours of service, vehicle maintenance, and general safety training; and the policies and procedures in these areas of the oldest of the new carriers are comparable to those of established carriers.

Corsi and Fanara's findings that the safety performance of the newest carriers is worse than that of established carriers conflict with results of Moses and Savage reported above. The latter researchers found that older firms have significantly higher accident rates than younger firms (Moses and Savage, 1991, 1992b).[28]

Modal Shift-Safety Relationship

The deregulation of motor carriers (by the MCA) and railroads (by the Staggers Act of 1980) led to intermodal traffic shifts. Boyer (1989) assessed the impact of these shifts on freight transportation safety. Using *Census of Transportation* data, he estimated that deregulation caused between 1 percent and 7 percent of rail-truck manufactures traffic to be shifted from railroads to motor carriers. Since rail is the less dangerous of the two modes, this traffic shift led to a deterioration in safety. Boyer estimated that between 29 and 236 extra freight transportation deaths per year could be attributed to deregulation. He felt that the lower figure of 29 was the more reasonable estimate. These results suggest that deregulation's effect on safety through modal shifting was relatively small.

Issues in Assessing Deregulation's Effect on Safety

Evaluating the impact of deregulation on trucking safety is a complex task. Various factors must be accounted for in such an undertaking. Researchers have discussed pertinent issues in the deregulation-safety relationship and have either directly stated or implied what should be accounted for in an assessment of this relationship. In this section, we summarize some of this discussion.

Panzar and Savage (1989) have provided a framework for assessing the impact of deregulation on transportation safety. According to them, transportation safety depends on the economic environment and government spending on surveillance (for example, vehicle inspections) and infrastructure (for example, highways). Both types of government spending are presumed to be influenced by the economic environment. Panzar and Savage maintain that this latter influence must be accounted for in assessing the effect of a change in the economic environment (for example, deregulation) on safety. Some of the changes in safety subsequent to deregulation may be attributable to nonoptimal policy responses to deregulation. The authors suggest that the level of preregulation safety should be compared to the level of safety associated with optimal postderegulation policy decisions.

Jovanis (1989) has described the various ways that deregulation is related to transportation safety. He notes that deregulation directly affects the following factors that can influence safety: amount of truck travel, carrier decisions in providing service, and influence of shippers in negotiating terms for service. He also points out that deregulation indirectly affects the following safety-influencing factors: government oversight and enforcement activities and motor carrier safety legislation.[29] Jovanis indicates that there were the following potentially confounding events during the deregulation period: major recession, major economic recovery, and changes in safety oversight.

Winston, Corsi, Grimm, and Evans (1991, pp. 61–62) note that a proper assessment of trucking deregulation's impact on safety requires a counterfactual analysis. This type of analysis would compare the levels of safety under regulated and deregulated regimes. To be properly done, it requires that accidents attributable to regulatory policy be identified. Such identifications are not easily made.

SUMMARY

The safety of medium/heavy trucks in the United States was the focus of this chapter. Recent data revealed that, per vehicle mile travelled, these trucks are involved in fewer crashes than are all other types of motor vehicles; however, they are involved in more fatal accidents per vehicle mile than are passenger cars. In 1990, about 12 percent of all traffic deaths occurred in crashes involving these trucks. More than three-fourths of those killed in these crashes were occupants of other vehicles. The death rate (fatalities per vehicle mile) associated with accidents involving medium/heavy trucks fell during the 1980s.

Like truckers in general, most drivers of medium/heavy trucks involved in crashes are males between the ages of 25 and 64. Evidence from the surveyed studies suggests that driver-related factors that cause or contribute to trucking accidents include: alcohol or drug use, fatigue, medical condition, speed, speed variance, driver inexperience, and driver error.

Data based on police reports indicate that vehicle defects — primarily brake and tire problems — are uncommon in accident-involved trucks. However, some researchers (for example, Clarke and others [1987]) believe that the role of vehicle-related factors in truck accidents is unrecognized and underreported. Cargo-related matters, such as overloading or load shifts, are contributing factors in a small number of accidents. Per vehicle mile travelled, combination trucks have more fatal crashes than single-unit (straight) trucks. Conflicting findings have been reported on the relative safety of two types of combination trucks: truck-tractors pulling one trailer (singles) and tractors pulling two trailers (doubles). Some researchers have concluded that singles and doubles are equally safe, while others have reported findings that singles are safer. There is evidence that accident risk is significantly higher for tractors pulling no trailers (bobtails) than for singles and doubles.

Certain highway-related factors are associated with large truck accidents. For example, controlling for other factors, Blower, Campbell, and Green (1993) found that the risk of truck-tractors being involved in both casualty and property-damage-only accidents is significantly higher on rural highways than on urban highways. They also found that accident risk is significantly lower on limited access roadways, such as interstate highways, than on other types of roads.

Regarding environmental considerations, most truck accidents occur under normal weather conditions. According to recent evidence, such conditions exist in more than 80 percent of the fatal crashes involving medium/heavy trucks. Rain, the most frequent unfavorable weather condition when there is an accident, was found in one study (Alexander [1992]) to have a significant positive relationship with mileage-based injury and accident rates. Most medium/heavy truck accidents occur during the week between 6:00 A.M. and 6:00 P.M. There is evidence that greater highway congestion increases the likelihood of an accident in interstate trucking and that the risk of casualty accidents for truck-tractors is greater at night than during the day.

Investigations conducted by the NTSB (1990) indicate the relative importance of various immediate determinants in a sample of driver-fatal truck accidents. The largest number of contributing factors in these accidents were driver related, led by fatigue (a factor in 30.8 percent of the crashes), drugs (21.1 percent), unsafe speed (13.5 percent), and physical incapacitation (10.3 percent). Although not a cause of accidents, occupant protection (for example, seat belts and crashworthiness of truck cabs) was an important consideration in 36.8 percent of the cases; no other vehicle-related factor played a significant role in more than 6 percent of the crashes. Signs, roadways, or environmental considerations were factors in about 12 percent of the accidents.

Researchers have assessed the effectiveness of certain deterrent strategies in either reducing the severity of injuries sustained in trucking accidents or preventing these accidents. For example, the increase in seat belt usage by drivers has been cited as a probable reason for the decline in the large truck occupant death rate. Kraas (1993) found a statistically significant negative relationship between the number of roadside inspections per vehicle mile and truck-at-fault accidents per vehicle mile. However, Patten, Carroll, and Thomchick (1989) have suggested that the role of these inspections in crash prevention is limited because they deal ineffectively with driver-related accident causes. Moses and Savage (1992b) concluded that an increase in federal safety audits has not led to a lower accident rate in the trucking industry. There is statistically significant evidence that accident rates fall when there is greater police enforcement.

The role of management in trucking safety has been examined. For instance, based on its accident investigations, NTSB has found carrier oversight of drivers and equipment to be a matter of concern. Also, several regression studies have used carrier-level data to estimate the effect of various firm characteristics on accident rates. They reported mixed results on the relationship between safety management practices, as gauged by safety audit information, and accident risk. Safer and more dangerous practices were both significantly linked to better safety performance (that is, lower accident rates). Other statistically significant results from these studies suggest that carrier accident rates are directly related to the extent of owner-operator usage, spending on insurance and safety, and maintenance expenditures. They also indicate that accident risk is higher for carriers of certain commodities (for example, general freight, perishable food items, and hazardous materials). In addition, findings suggest that accident rates are inversely and significantly related to driver experience, carrier size, and average length of haul.

There has been much debate on the relationship between trucking safety and the economic deregulation formalized by passage of the MCA of 1980. Regarding the profitability-safety linkage considered in the debate, evidence from regression analyses suggests that accident propensity may decrease as carrier financial strength increases. There are conflicting findings on the new entrants-safety relationship. Results reported by Corsi and Fanara (1989) indicate that new entrants have a significantly higher accident rate than established carriers. In contrast, Moses and Savage (1991, 1992b) found that older firms have a significantly higher accident rate than younger firms. Boyer (1989) concludes that deregulation's effect on safety through modal freight shifting is relatively small.

The complexity of assessing deregulation's impact on truck safety has been noted. Among the factors to be accounted for in such an assessment are: the economic environment, government enforcement activities, infrastructure spending, carrier decisions, and safety laws. Also, the data available for calculating the impact are less than ideal.

NOTES

1. According to the NHTSA (1991b, p. 127), medium and heavy trucks have gross vehicle weight ratings of more than 10,000 pounds. For research on the safety of light trucks, see the U.S. General Accounting Office (1990).

2. The source for the material in this section is OTA (1988, pp. 34–37).

3. Economic regulation of transportation firms has been concerned with rates, entry, service, and financial aspects. A description of these aspects of economic regulation is found in Talley (1983, pp. 41–52).

4. The source for the information in this section is OTA (1988, pp. 81–82).

5. OTA (1988, pp. 80–82) provides a chronology and historical framework of federal laws pertaining to the motor carrier industry from 1935 through 1987. Phillips and McCutchen (1991, pp. 334–337) summarize federal truck safety legislation enacted between 1982 and 1990.

6. American Trucking Associations (ATA) (1993) catalogues federal motor carrier safety regulations.

7. The allowable length for truck trailers provides an example of how states differ on safety-related matters. In 1988, the legal maximum length for one trailing unit ranged from 48 to 59.5 feet (OTA, 1988, p. 56, Figure 3-1).

8. For descriptions of several data bases used in statistical studies of truck safety, see TRB (1990, Chapter 2). The existing data are inadequate in certain respects. For example, estimates of the number of nonfatal truck crashes vary across data sources; a consistent series of annual truck travel information broken down by truck type, highway class, and geographic region does not exist (TRB, 1990, pp. 1–2).

9. It should be kept in mind that correlation between the presence of a particular factor and the occurrence of an accident need to imply that a causal relationship exists.

10. Several studies have described the factors that cause truck accidents and have reviewed the statistical literature on accident causation. Examples of such studies include: OTA (1988), Jovanis (1987), Clarke and others (1987), and TRB (1986).

11. These percentages were computed using information reported by NHTSA (1993, p. 19, Table 6).

12. This percentage was computed using information provided in NHTSA (1993, p. 19, Table 6).

13. Alcohol involvement was indicated when police found evidence of the presence of alcohol. It does not necessarily mean that individuals involved in the accident were tested for alcohol (NHTSA, 1991b, p. 125).

14. The NTSB (1988a, p. 5) suspected alcohol or drug use in additional cases, but the information needed to determine impairment was insufficient or unavailable.

15. The percentages add up to more than 33 percent, the portion of fatally injured drivers who tested positive for alcohol and other drugs, because some of the drivers used more than one drug.

16. Issues of interest are probable causes, contributing factors, or other factors uncovered during the investigations that may have not caused or contributed to the accident but are important considerations in trucking safety (NTSB, 1988a, p. 2).

17. Police typically report defects only when a mechanical part is obviously faulty (NHTSA, 1991c, p. 25). Thus, NHTSA probably underestimates the extent of mechanical deficiencies in accident-involved vehicles.

18. The normalized rate equalled the raw rate (the number of fatal crash involvements per vehicle mile) divided by the overall raw rate.

19. For surveys of studies on the relative safety of singles and doubles, see Chirachavala and O'Day (1981, pp. 13–29), TRB (1986, pp. 304–329), OTA (1988, pp. 95–97), and Blower, Campbell, and Green (1993, pp. 308–309).

20. We, not NTSB, arbitrarily assigned factors to the driver, vehicle, and highway/environmental categories.

21. Class I motor carriers have annual gross operating revenues from motor carrier operations of $5 million or more; Class II carriers have revenues of $1 million to $4,999,999; and Class III carriers have revenues of less than $1 million (ATA, 1992, p. 31).

22. See Moses and Savage (1992b, pp. 480–481) for a detailed description of the safety audit process.

23. Owner-operators are independent contractors who can transport exempt commodities, lease their services to certificated carriers, or haul regulated commodities under ICC operating authority (OTA, 1988, p. 38).

24. See Greene (1993, pp. 676–679) for a formal description of the Poisson regression model.

25. See Talley (1983, pp. 198–201) for a discussion of the arguments for and against federal trucking deregulation and for a discussion of economic regulation under the MCA.

26. Moses and Savage (1989, p. 217) note that the congestion issue is less relevant to motor carrier deregulation than it is to airline deregulation. While greater truck traffic may contribute to increased congestion, only a small proportion of motor vehicles on highways are trucks.

27. The C score employed by Chow (1989, p. 225) was a weighted combination of retained earnings/total tangible assets, total liabilities/total tangible assets, shareholder equity/total tangible assets, current liabilities/total tangible assets, and working capital/total tangible assets.

28.   Carrier age was determined differently by the two sets of researchers. Corsi and Fanara based it on time since certification, while Moses and Savage based it on time since incorporation.

29.   Several pieces of federal truck safety legislation have been enacted since the trucking industry was deregulated. These include: the Surface Transportation Assistance Act of 1982, the Motor Carrier Safety Act of 1984, the Commercial Motor Vehicle Safety Act of 1986, the Truck and Bus Safety and Regulatory Reform Act of 1988, and the Motor Carrier Safety Act of 1990. See Phillips and McCutchen (1991, pp. 334–337) for summaries of these laws.

REFERENCES

Adams, B. (1989). "Deregulation's Negative Effect on Safety." In Moses, L. N., and I. Savage (Eds.), *Transportation Safety in an Age of Deregulation* (pp. 21–27). New York: Oxford University Press.

Alexander, D. L. (1992). "Motor Carrier Deregulation and Highway Safety: An Empirical Analysis." *Southern Economic Journal* 59: 28–38.

American Trucking Associations. (1993). *Federal Motor Carrier Safety Regulations: Management Edition*. Alexandria, VA: American Trucking Associations.

____. (1992). *American Trucking Trends 1991-92 Edition*. Alexandria, VA: American Trucking Associations.

Beilock, R., and R. B. Capelle, Jr. (1988). "The Effect of the 65 Mile Per Hour Speed Limit on Motor Carrier Schedule Tightness and Driver Perceptions of Safety Conditions." *Journal of the Transportation Research Forum* 29: 9–17.

____. (1987). "Economic Pressure, Long Distance Trucking, and Safety." *Journal of the Transportation Research Forum* 28: 177–185.

Blevins, M. W., and G. Chow. (1988). "Truck Safety and Financial Distress: A Preliminary Analysis." *Journal of the Transportation Research Forum* 29: 18–23.

Blower, D., K. L. Campbell, and P. E. Green. (1993). "Accident Rates for Heavy Truck-Tractors in Michigan." *Accident Analysis and Prevention* 25: 307–321.

Boyer, K. D. (1989). "The Safety Effects of Mode Shifting Following Deregulation." In Moses, L. N., and I. Savage (Eds.), *Transportation Safety in an Age of Deregulation* (pp. 258–276). New York: Oxford University Press.

Bruning, E. R. (1989). "The Relationship between Profitability and Safety Performance in Trucking Firms." *Transportation Journal* 28: 40–49.

Campbell, K. L., D. F. Blower, R. G. Gattis, and A. C. Wolfe. (1988). *Analysis of Accident Rates of Heavy-Duty Vehicles*. Ann Arbor: University of Michigan Transportation Research Institute.

Chirachavala, T., and J. O'Day. (1981). "A Comparison of Accident Characteristics and Rates for Combination Vehicles with One or Two Trailers." UM-HSRI-81-41. Ann Arbor: University of Michigan Highway Safety Research Institute.

Chow, G. (1989). "Deregulation, Financial Distress, and Safety in the General Freight Trucking Industry." In Moses, L. N., and I. Savage (Eds.), *Transportation Safety in an Age of Deregulation* (pp. 219–240). New York: Oxford University Press.

Clarke, R. M., and W. A. Leasure, Jr. (1986). *Truck Occupant Protection*, DOT HS 807 081. Washington, DC: National Highway Traffic Safety Administration.

Clarke, R. M., W. A. Leasure, Jr., R. W. Radlinski, and M. Smith. (1987). *Heavy Truck Safety Study*. DOT HS 807 109. Washington, DC: National Highway Traffic Safety Administration.

Corsi, T. M., and P. Fanara, Jr. (1989). "Effects of New Entrants on Motor Carrier Safety." In Moses, L. N., and I. Savage (Eds.), *Transportation Safety in an Age of Deregulation* (pp. 241–257). New York: Oxford University Press.

____. (1988a). "Deregulation, New Entrants, and the Safety Learning Curve." *Journal of the Transportation Research Forum* 29: 3–8.

____. (1988b). "Driver Management Policies and Motor Carrier Safety." *Logistics and Transportation Review* 24: 153–163.

Corsi, T. M., P. Fanara, Jr., and J. L. Jarrell. (1988). "Safety Performance of Pre-MCA Motor Carriers, 1977 Versus 1984." *Transportation Journal* 27: 30–36.

Corsi, T. M., P. Fanara, Jr., and M. J. Roberts. (1984). "Linkages Between Motor Carrier Accidents and Safety Regulation." *Logistics and Transportation Review* 20: 149–164.

Daicoff, D. W. (1988). "Deregulation and Motor Carrier Safety." *Logistics and Transportation Review* 24: 175–183.

Greene, W. H. (1993). *Econometric Analysis*. 2nd ed. New York: Macmillan Publishing Company.

Insurance Institute for Highway Safety. (1985). *Big Trucks*. Washington, DC: Insurance Institute for Highway Safety.

Jones, I. S., and H. S. Stein. (1987). "Effect of Driver Hours of Service on Tractor-Trailer Crash Involvement." Arlington, VA: Insurance Institute for Highway Safety.

Jovanis, P. P. (1989). "A System Perspective on the Effects of Economic Deregulation on Motor Carrier Safety." In Moses, L. N., and I. Savage (Eds.), *Transportation Safety in an Age of Deregulation* (pp. 277–286). New York: Oxford University Press.

____. (1987). "A Perspective on Motor Carrier Safety Issues in the 1980s." Proceedings, Transportation Deregulation and Safety Conference (pp. 530–550). Evanston, IL: Northwestern University Transportation Center.

Kraas, A. (1993). "The Impact of the US Motor Carrier Act 1980 on Road Safety in California: An Econometric Policy Evaluation." *Logistics and Transportation Review* 29: 179–192.

Moore, T. G. (1989). "The Myth of Deregulation's Negative Effect on Safety." In Moses, L. N., and I. Savage (Eds.), *Transportation Safety in an Age of Deregulation* (pp. 8–20). New York: Oxford University Press.

Moses, L. N., and I. Savage. (1992a). "The Effect of Firm Characteristics on Motor Carrier Accidents." Paper presented at the 6th World Conference on Transportation Research, Lyon, France, June 29–July 3, 1992.

____. (1992b). "The Effectiveness of Motor Carrier Safety Audits." *Accident Analysis and Prevention* 24: 479–496.

____. (1991). "Motor Carriers of Hazardous Materials: Who Are They? How Safe Are They?" Paper presented at Hazmat Transport '91: A National Conference on the Transportation of Hazardous Materials and Waste, Northwestern University, July 17–19, 1991.

____. (1989). "Introduction." In Moses, L. N., and I. Savage (Eds.), *Transportation Safety in an Age of Deregulation* (pp. 3–7). New York: Oxford University Press.

National Highway Traffic Safety Administration. (1993). *Summary of Medium and Heavy Truck Crashes in 1990.* DOT HS 807 953. Washington, DC: U.S. Department of Transportation.

____. (1991a). *Fatal Accident Reporting System 1990.* DOT HS 807 794. Washington, DC: U.S. Department of Transportation.

____. (1991b). *General Estimates System 1990.* DOT HS 807 781. Washington, DC: U.S. Department of Transportation.

____. (1991c). *Summary of Medium and Heavy Truck Crashes in 1989.* DOT HS 807 739. Washington, DC: U.S. Department of Transportation.

National Transportation Safety Board. (1990). *Safety Study: Fatigue, Alcohol, Other Drugs, and Medical Factors in Fatal-to-the-Driver Heavy Truck Crashes* (Vol. 1). NTSB/SS-90/01. Washington, DC: National Transportation Safety Board.

____. (1988a, October). *Safety Study: Case Summaries of 189 Heavy Truck Accident Investigations.* NTSB/SS-88/05. Washington, DC: National Transportation Safety Board.

____. (1988b, November). *Safety Study: Braking Deficiencies on Heavy Trucks in 32 Selected Accidents.* NTSB/SS-88/06. Washington, DC: National Transportation Safety Board.

Panzar, J. C., and I. Savage. (1989). "Regulation, Deregulation, and Safety: An Economic Analysis." In Moses, L. N., and I. Savage (Eds.), *Transportation Safety in an Age of Deregulation* (pp. 31–49). New York: Oxford University Press.

Patten, M. L., J. L. Carroll, and E. A. Thomchick. (1989). "The Efficacy of Roadside Inspections in Reducing Heavy Truck Accidents." *Journal of the Transportation Research Forum* 29: 269–276.

Phillips, K. B., and J. A. McCutchen. (1991). "Economic Regulation vs. Safety Regulation of the Trucking Industry — Which More Effectively Promotes Safety?" *Transportation Quarterly* 45: 323–340.

Seiff, H. E. (1991). "Large Truck Safety in the United States." Paper presented at the 13th Experimental Safety Vehicle Conference. Paris, France. November 4–7.

Stein, H. S., and I. S. Jones. (1988). "Crash Involvement of Large Trucks by Configuration: A Case-Control Study." *American Journal of Public Health* 78: 491–498.

Talley, W. K. (1983). *Introduction to Transportation.* Cincinnati, OH: South-Western Publishing Co.

Transportation Research Board. (1990). *Data Requirements for Monitoring Truck Safety.* Special Report 228. Washington, DC: National Research Council.

____. (1986). *Twin Trailer Trucks.* Special Report 211. Washington, DC: National Research Council."Truckers Face Accelerating Safety Drive," *The Wall Street Journal*, February 5, 1990, p. A7E.

U.S. Congress, Office of Technology Assessment. (1988). *Gearing Up for Safety: Motor Carrier Safety in a Competitive Environment.* OTA-SET-382.

Washington, DC: U.S. Government Printing Office.
U.S. Department of Commerce. (1992). *Statistical Abstract of the United States 1992*. Washington, DC: U.S. Government Printing Office.
____. (1991). *Statistical Abstract of the United States 1991*. Washington, DC: U.S. Government Printing Office.
U.S. General Accounting Office. (1990). *Highway Safety: Fatalities in Light Trucks and Vans*. GAO/PEMD-91-8. Washington, DC: General Accounting Office.
University of Michigan Transportation Research Institute. (1987). Large Truck Survey Program. Proceedings, National Truck Safety Symposium, June 1987. Washington, DC: Motor Vehicle Manufacturers Association.
Viscusi, W. K. (1989). "The Effect of Transportation Deregulation on Worker Safety." In Moses, L. N., and I. Savage (Eds.), *Transportation Safety in an Age of Deregulation* (pp. 70–89). New York: Oxford University Press.
Winston, C., T. M. Corsi, C. M. Grimm, and C. A. Evans. (1991). *The Economic Effects of Surface Freight Deregulation*. Washington, DC: The Brookings Institution.

5

Air Accidents

INTRODUCTION

In this chapter, we turn our attention to U.S. air accidents. We begin by discussing measures of unsafe air travel. Then the impact of U.S. airline deregulation on air safety is analyzed — impacts of market forces, new entrants, and congestion under deregulation are addressed. A discussion of the costs of air accidents follows. Finally, we present determinants of aircraft accidents, commuter versus certificated airlines having unsafe air occurrences, and the severity of unsafe air occurrences.

MEASURES OF UNSAFE AIR TRAVEL

Because the safety of air travel (heretofore referred to as air safety) cannot be observed directly, and a reduction in unsafe air travel is also an improvement in air safety, measures of unsafe air travel have been used as proxies for air safety. Both input and outcome proxies have been used. Input proxies represent actions by airlines, airports, and government that decrease the probability of unsafe air service; outcome proxies represent unsafe outcomes of air travel. Aircraft maintenance and pilot training expenditures are examples of input proxies; aircraft accidents and incidents are examples of outcome proxies. Since little is known of the extent to which safety inputs translate into air safety, outcome proxies may be more reliable proxies of air safety than input proxies — thus the rationale for the extensive use of outcome rather than input proxies for air safety.

Various outcome proxies for air safety have been used by government, the airline industry, and academia. The particular proxy that is chosen will depend upon the purpose in investigating air safety, for example, comparing air safety over time and across airlines, investigating the probability of passenger fatalities and injuries, and investigating determinants of unsafe air travel. Henceforth, we will refer to outcome proxies for air safety as unsafe air occurrences.

The National Transportation Safety Board (NTSB) classifies unsafe air occurrences as either aircraft accidents or incidents. The NTSB defines an aircraft accident as "an occurrence associated with the operation of an aircraft which takes place between the time any person boards the aircraft with the intention of flight and all such persons have disembarked, and in which any person suffers death or serious injury, or in which the aircraft receives substantial damage" (*Code of Federal Regulation*, 1987, p. 741). The NTSB defines an aircraft incident as "an occurrence other than an accident, associated with the operation of an aircraft, which affects or could affect the safety of operations" (*Code of Federal Regulation*, 1987, p. 741). Examples of aircraft incidents include flight control system malfunction or failure; inability of any required flight crewmember to perform normal flight duties as a result of injury or illness; failure of structural components of a turbine engine excluding compressor and turbine blades and vanes; inflight fire; inflight collision of aircraft; damage to property, other than the aircraft, estimated to exceed $25,000; and electrical and hydraulic system failures, loss of power of two or more engines, and evacuation of aircraft (where the emergency egress system is utilized) for a large multi-engine aircraft.

The NTSB compiles detailed data on individual aircraft accidents and incidents that it investigates. Accident detection is quite accurate; incident detection is less accurate — the non-reporting of incidents is more difficult to detect. A safety-conscious airline may appear to be more unsafe than a non-safety-conscious airline if the former encourages more complete reporting of incidents than the latter. If so, accident comparisons will be more appropriate than incident comparisons for making safety performance comparisons (over time and across airlines).

In addition to aircraft accident and incident data collected by the NTSB, the Federal Aviation Administration (FAA) keeps a record of reported near midair collisions. A near midair collision is defined by the FAA (1987, p. xi) as "an incident associated with the operation of an aircraft in which the possibility of a collision occurs as a result of proximity of less than 500 feet to another aircraft, or a report is received from a pilot or flight crew member stating that a collision hazard existed between two or more aircraft." As for aircraft incidents, there is concern about the accuracy of the reporting of near midair collisions, since reporting is voluntary. The FAA also keeps a record of operational errors — "an occurrence attributed to an element of the air traffic control system which results in less than the applicable separation minimums between two or more aircraft or between an aircraft and terrain or obstacles and obstructions" (FAA, 1987, p. xi).

An unsafe air occurrence is an unintended happening. A robust measure of unsafe air occurrences would encompass all unintended happenings, regardless of their severity. While fatal and serious-injury occurrences are dramatic and newsworthy, a non-injury occurrence may be an indication of more serious occurrences in the future. The difference between an occurrence where there are passenger fatalities and one in which the passengers escape injury is often very small.

In comparing unsafe air occurrences (for example, aircraft accidents) among airlines and over time, it has become customary to adjust these occurrences for exposure to risk (for example, by number of aircraft or passenger departures) in order to make meaningful safety comparisons. Most accidents occur during aircraft takeoffs and landings; thus the risk of passenger fatalities and injuries increase during these phases of flight. Since every landing is associated with a prior takeoff, aircraft accidents are often adjusted for exposure to risk by expressing them as accidents rates, that is, aircraft accidents per aircraft departure or per passenger departure.

Consider two types of airlines — a long-haul airline flying long flight stages (and thus having a relatively small number of aircraft takeoffs and landings) with relatively large passenger loads and a short-haul airline flying short flight stages (and thus having a relatively large number of aircraft takeoffs and landings) with relatively small passenger loads. Being exposed to less risk, we would expect the former airline to incur less aircraft accidents than the latter airline. Safety performance comparisons based upon aircraft accidents will favor the long-haul airline; aircraft accidents per aircraft departure will favor the short-haul airline, other factors remaining the same. The systematic bias in favor of or against a specific type of airline in using one of these safety measures can be reduced by using instead the aircraft accident rate, the number of aircraft accidents per passenger departure (Oster and Zorn, 1989b). Having discussed measures of unsafe air travel, we now turn our attention to the relationship between economic deregulation of airline service and air safety.

DEREGULATION

Airline economic deregulation provides airlines with greater freedom for entry and pricing, thereby increasing the influence of market forces on air service. U.S. air service was deregulated with the passage of the Airline Deregulation Act in 1978 (Morrison and Winston, 1986; Levine, 1987; Kahn, 1988; Hawk, 1989). Australian domestic air service was deregulated in 1990 and domestic air service of the United Kingdom is scheduled for deregulation. Deregulated U.S. airlines operate more efficiently and move more passengers a greater distance, with more full planes and fewer staff (Moore, 1986). Between 1977 and 1986, the average revenue per passenger mile for U.S. air service increased by only 30 percent, passenger miles increased from 226 to 366 billion (62 percent), and passenger enplanements increased by 52 percent (Moses and Savage, 1989). The downside associated with these benefits was increases in travel time (from hub-and-spoke operations), travel uncertainty, and lost or damaged baggage. In addition, there is public uneasiness or fear that deregulation may bring (or has brought) significant increases in travel hazards to airline passengers.

Air Safety Statistics

Will airlines retain their commitment to safety or will they be tempted to reduce this commitment in a competitive environment? Evidence suggests that U.S. air safety has not deteriorated under deregulation (Kanafani and Keeler, 1990; Transportation Research Board, 1991; Rose, 1992). Table 5.1 presents total aircraft accidents and the accident rate (total aircraft accidents per 100,000 aircraft departures) for U.S. certificated air carriers in the provision of scheduled service from 1966 through 1990. Certificated ("Part 121") air carriers are jet air carriers that account for the bulk of U.S. commercial air travel.[1] The accident rate data in Table 5.1 indicate that the declining trend in these data under regulation has continued under deregulation. However, a caveat is in order. The accident rate data for each of the last four years (1987–90) is greater than that for each of the previous three years (1984–86). The former data, though not sufficient to indicate a rising trend, may nonetheless be the beginning of such a trend. Based upon an estimated declining trend line for accident rates for the same air service over the period 1955–90, Rose (1992) found that the accident rates (measured in million departures) for 1987–90 lie slightly above the trend line. Although four years of data are not enough to make inferences, Rose (1992) suggests continued scrutiny of aggregate air safety performance in the future.

In addition to certificated air carriers, the accident rates of U.S. commuter air carriers providing scheduled service, air taxi carriers providing nonscheduled service, and general aviation also exhibit declining trends in the current deregulated environment.[2] Accident rates

TABLE 5.1
Aircraft Accidents and Accident Rates for Scheduled
Air Service: U.S. Certificated Air Carriers

Year	Total Aircraft Accidents	Accident Rate*
1966	56	1.28
1967	54	1.09
1968	56	1.06
1969	51	0.95
1970	43	0.84
1971	43	0.86
1972	46	0.93
1973	36	0.70
1974	43	0.91
1975	29	0.62
1976	21	0.43
1977	19	0.38
1978	20	0.40
1979	23	0.43
1980	15	0.27
1981	25	0.46
1982	16	0.29
1983	22	0.42
1984	13	0.23
1985	17	0.28
1986	21	0.29
1987	32	0.43
1988	31	0.41
1989	24	0.33
1990	24	0.33

*Total aircraft accidents per 100,000 aircraft departures.
Source: From data provided by the Federal Aviation Administration.

(total aircraft accidents per 100,000 aircraft hours flown) for the period 1979–90 are presented in Table 5.2. For a basis of comparison, accident rates of certificated air carriers are also included in Table 5.2. The data suggest that air travel by commuter, air taxi, and general aviation in the deregulated environment is less safe than by certificated air carriers.

The decline in U.S. air accident rates is in part attributable to improvements in aircraft and aviation technology — improvement in radar technology, advances (such as power, range, and operating altitude) in jet aircraft, metallurgical and material advances in aircraft, introduction and improvement in navigational and landing aids, and improvement in pilot training practices (Rose, 1989). Oster and Zorn (1989b), in a study of the decline in U.S. aircraft accidents per 1 million aircraft departures from 1979 to 1985, found that there had been significant decreases in most causes of air accidents — equipment failure, weather, pilot error, air traffic control, and the failure of passengers to fasten seat belts.

Although accident rate data suggest that U.S. air safety has not deteriorated under deregulation, John Nance (1989) argues that the

TABLE 5.2
Accident Rates for U.S. Certificated Air Carriers, Commuter Air Carriers, Air Taxi Carriers, and General Aviation
(per 100,000 aircraft hours flown)

Year	Certificated[a]	Commuter[a]	Air Taxi[b]	General Aviation
1979	0.34	4.45	4.34	9.88
1980	0.21	3.23	4.73	9.86
1981	0.37	2.50	5.42	9.51
1982	0.22	2.00	4.05	10.06
1983	0.32	1.13	5.48	9.90
1984	0.17	1.26	4.74	9.55
1985	0.21	1.21	5.46	8.95
1986	0.21	0.87	3.98	8.80
1987	0.31	1.64	3.41	8.45
1988	0.29	0.93	3.45	7.97
1989	0.23	0.88	3.83	7.25
1990	0.22	0.63	3.28	7.01

[a]Scheduled service.
[b]Nonscheduled service.
Source: From data provided by the Federal Aviation Administration.

safety margin for air service — in terms of input proxies for air safety — has deteriorated. Nance (1989) states that, in the regulated environment, U.S. air carriers maintained maintenance, pilot training, and operational levels far above the federally mandated minimum levels. Air carriers could afford such levels in the regulated environment but not in the deregulated environment. In the competitive deregulated environment, "all airlines have engaged in cost cutting in maintenance, training, operations, and wages to some extent to stay viable" (Nance, 1989, p. 192). The cuts in safety-related expenditures have reduced the safety margin for air travel. The safety margin has also been reduced by the substitution of service vacated by certificated air carriers on nonprofit-able routes by service provided by less-safe commuter air carriers and by the fact that resources committed to the FAA, the federal agency that oversees air safety, have not kept pace with the growth in deregulated air travel. In 1978, there were 16,750 FAA air traffic controllers; by 1987, the number had declined to 12,847 (Morrison and Winston, 1989, p. 106).

Market Forces and Safety

The notion that airline deregulation (that is, a market environment) will have an adverse impact on air safety has been popularized by the media. This notion, also referred to as the profit-safety argument (Talley, 1993), states that there is a positive relationship between profitability and safety in the airline industry; therefore, adverse financial conditions expected under airline deregulation would have an adverse effect on airline safety. This argument opposes market forces for promoting air safety and, thus, favors regulation and more stringent public-sector enforcement for such promotion. Market forces, however, may in fact promote air safety. The market-response argument (Chalk, 1987b; Talley, 1993) states that airlines anticipating a deterioration in their financial condition following an accident will take safety precautions in a market environment. This argument thus favors deregulation and less stringent public-sector enforcement for promoting air safety.

Results from empirical investigations of the profit-safety argument are mixed. Golbe (1986) found no significant statistical relationship between air safety (measured by the square root of aircraft accidents) and profits in the airline industry. If there is a relationship, it is likely to be negative — more profitable airlines have more accidents and, hence, are less safe. Two sets of U.S. domestic data were utilized in the investigation — a pooled time-series, cross-sectional data set consisting of 11 U.S. certificated airlines for the years 1963–70 and a time-series data set for the U.S. certificated airline industry as a whole for the years 1952–72. Two measures of airline profitability were considered: net income after taxes but before special items, deflated by the GNP price deflator, and the rate of return on regulatory investment.

In a time-series investigation of the profit-safety argument for the certificated airline industry, Rose (1989) also found no significant statistical relationship between accidents and profits. The data consist of annual accidents by the industry in the provision of scheduled service for the period 1956–84. This result holds for total aircraft accidents, accident rates (total aircraft accidents per 100,000 aircraft departures), and for total fatal aircraft accidents. Airline profitability was measured by the average operating margin, defined as one minus the ratio of operating expenses to operating revenues, lagged one time period.

In the same study, Rose (1989) also investigated the profit-safety argument utilizing pooled time-series, cross-sectional data, that is, annual data of 26 scheduled certificated airlines for the period 1957–86. A statistically significant and negative relationship was found between aircraft accidents per 100,000 departures and the operating margins (lagged one time period) of the airlines — the negative relationship implies that lower profit margins correspond to higher accident rates. To test for the robustness of the relationship, the data set was divided into three time periods: 1957–65, 1966–75, and 1976–86. For these three time periods, the relationship remains negative, but is only statistically significant for the 1966–75 time period — thus providing mixed evidence on the robustness of the results.

In a more recent study, Rose (1990) investigated the profit-safety argument, utilizing a slightly larger data set — 35 large scheduled airlines for the years 1957–86. Rose concludes that higher operating margins (or operating profits) are associated not only with reduced accident rates but also with reduced incident rates. Operating margins were lagged one time period in the investigation. Rose (1990) further concludes that the effect seems strongest for the smaller airlines (among the large scheduled airlines) and is particularly noticeable for airline incident data. Rose (1992) suggests that the strength of this profitability-safety link may be due to greater flexibility in safety investment choices by smaller airlines (for example, FAA regulators may scrutinize these airlines less closely than larger airlines). Further, the results may help to explain why earlier studies, which tended to focus on very large airlines, failed to detect a profitability-safety link. A summary of the profit-related results for the above studies is presented in Table 5.3.

TABLE 5.3
Estimates of the Effects of Profits on Air Safety

Study	Profit Variable	Effect of Profit on Dependent Variable[a]	Dependent Variable	Type of Data[b]
Golbe (1986)	Rate of return on regulatory investment; net income after taxes deflated by GNP price deflator	+/insig	Square root of accidents	TS/CS (1963–70); TS (1952–70)
Rose (1989)	Operating margin = 1 – (operating expense/operating revenue)	+/insig	Accidents, accidents per 100,000 departures and fatal accidents	TS (1956–84)
	Operating margin = 1 – (operating expense/operating revenue)	–/sig	Accidents per 100,000 departures	TS/CS (1957–86)
Rose (1990)	Operating margin = 1 – (operating expense/operating revenue)	–/sig	Accidents	TS/CS (1957–86)
	Operating margin = 1 – (operating expense/operating revenue)	–/sig	Incidents	TS/CS (1981–86)

[a]Significant coefficients at the 5–10 percent significance level or better are denoted as "sig," while insignificant coefficients are denoted as "insig."

[b]"TS/CS" indicates pooled time-series, cross-sectional data, and "TS" indicates time-series data.

Source: Compiled by the authors.

An underlying argument to the airline profit-safety argument is that a positive relationship exists between airline profits and safety expenditures (for example, aircraft maintenance), and these expenditures, in turn, have a positive influence on airline safety — a decrease in profits will lead to a decrease in safety expenditures, which, in turn, will lead to an increase in accidents. An investigation of this linkage is found in Talley (1993) utilizing time-series accident data of U.S. certificated airlines (providing scheduled service) for the years 1959–84. A highly statistically significant positive relationship was found between airline operating margins, that is, one minus (operating costs/operating revenue), and relative maintenance expenditures (that is, the ratio of maintenance expenditures to total operating costs) — thus implying that a decrease in profits will result in a decrease in maintenance expenditures. However, a statistically insignificant relationship was found between relative maintenance expenditures and aircraft accidents. Thus, the hypothesized scenario is only supported in part. A liberal interpretation of these results is that lower profits lower the safety margin (for example, maintenance expenditures) of airlines, but the lower safety margin may not lead to more aircraft accidents. The results also suggest that the validity of the profit-safety argument will depend upon which safety investments affect aircraft accidents and whether these investments are affected by the financial condition of airlines. Phillips and Talley (1992) found that certain safety investments are expected to affect airline safety, but others may not.

A test of the market-response argument is found in a study by Mitchell and Maloney (1989). Specifically, Mitchell and Maloney (1989, p. 329) address the following question: "Are consumers reluctant to fly with airlines that have poor safety records or do they treat crashes merely as random events that bear no reflection on the quality of the airline?" If the former is true, the goodwill (or the value of the brand name) of the airline will decline, having an adverse effect on the performance of the airline's stock; if the latter is true, a crash will not affect the performance of the stock. The authors investigated the abnormal stock market performance of airlines immediately following a crash. Two groups of crashes were considered: those caused by pilot error and those in which the airline was judged by the press or by the FAA not to be at fault. Between 1964 and 1987, 56 such crashes were examined. For crashes caused by pilot error, the airline experienced significantly negative stock returns; for crashes for which the airline was not at fault, there was no stock market reaction. Mitchell and Maloney (1989, p. 355) conclude: "Since our results suggest the market is quite efficient at punishing airlines for at-fault crashes, the need for increased airline safety regulation is not apparent."

Mitchell and Maloney's (1989) results suggest that whether deregulation will have an impact on air safety via the market response argument will depend upon who is at fault in air accidents. However, even if the market response argument is operative, it may be negated by economic forces not related to safety (Scheraga & Ornstein, 1991; Karels, 1989).

Airlines that are near bankruptcy might choose to reduce safety expenditures and risk an increase in accidents in an effort to avoid bankruptcy. If airline accident rates increase as a consequence, the goodwill of these airlines will erode and their value to potential acquirers is likely to be lower. The tendency for failing airlines leaving the industry is to leave by merger or acquisition rather than by liquidation of assets. Apparently, the cost of leaving the industry by liquidation of assets (or by bankruptcy) is perceived by failing airlines to be higher than the cost to be incurred in leaving by merger or acquisition. Hence, even failing airlines may have a market incentive to encourage safety, and thereby avoid raising the risk of bankruptcy (Rose, 1989).

New Entrants, Congestion, and Safety

In addition to the general concern that a deregulated (or market) environment would have an adverse impact on airline safety, there is also concern for the safety performance of new entrants into the deregulated airline industry. The relative inexperience of new entrants would make them less safe. Further, new airlines are expected to be financially weaker than established airlines, thus spending less on safety than established airlines. The empirical evidence addressing this concern is mixed, however.

In their investigation, Kanafani and Keeler (1989) conclude that there is no difference in the safety performance of established U.S. airlines and new entrants who joined the industry following deregulation. Their conclusion follows from investigations of the maintenance expenditures, FAA safety inspection results, near midair collisions, and accidents following deregulation for both established airlines and new entrants. However, with respect to passenger fatalities, Barnett and Higgins (1989) reach a different conclusion — new entrants were substantially more risky than established airlines. Also, Oster and Zorn (1989b) report that new entrant jet carriers had a substantially higher aggregate rate of fatal accidents per million departures than established jet carriers over the period 1979–85.

Airport congestion attributable to airline deregulation may also have an adverse impact on airline safety. U.S. air service (measured in aircraft departures) has increased significantly in the deregulation environment (see Table 5.4), placing stress on airport and air traffic control capacities. One manifestation of this stress is airport congestion — flight delays due to demand conditions. Although the empirical evidence relating airport congestion to airline safety is very poor, it is reasonable to assume, all other things being equal, that an increase in the level of airport congestion increases the probability of an air accident (Arnott and Stiglitz, 1989). The available, poor empirical evidence may be attributable to the difficulty of distinguishing among flight delays caused by demand (that is, congestion) and flight delays attributable to weather, airline, and government practices. Contrary to popular belief, weather, and not congestion or airline practices, is the primary cause of flight delays (Bailey and Kirstein, 1989).

Actions by both airlines and government have compounded flight delays in the deregulated airline environment. Airlines, for example, have adopted hub-and-spoke operations. Whereas air service has increased to many city-pair markets where traffic would otherwise not be sufficient to support it, flight delays at airports designated as hubs

TABLE 5.4
U.S. Scheduled Aircraft Departures
(in millions)

Year	Certificated Airlines	Commuter Airlines
1979	5.4	1.9
1980	5.6	1.8
1981	5.4	1.8
1982	5.1	2.0
1983	5.2	2.3
1984	5.7	2.7
1985	6.1	2.6
1986	7.0	2.7
1987	7.2	2.8
1988	7.3	2.9
1989	7.3	2.9

Source: From data provided by the Federal Aviation Administration

have increased. Planes are stacked up at hub airports during peak hours, contributing to flight delays and concern for too high a utilization of airspace and the airport's air traffic control system.

Government has also contributed to flight delays. In 1981, the Reagan Administration dismissed 11,500 striking FAA air traffic controllers. In response to the Professional Air Traffic Controllers Organization strike and dismissals, the FAA changed many of its procedures to reflect the less experienced and reduced air traffic controller staff (Cunningham and Davis, 1987). For example, if bad weather or congestion exists at a destination airport, air traffic controllers are instructed to keep the plane on the ground at the origin airport — thus contributing to flight delays at the destination airport.

AIR ACCIDENT COSTS

An underlying assumption to the argument that market forces promote air safety is that costs of air accidents are of sufficient magnitude to provide an incentive to both airlines and aircraft manufacturers to promote air safety. Because airlines typically carry quite complete aircraft and passenger liability, the primary airline accident-related costs are expected to be increased insurance premiums and reduced demand (that is, prospective losses) rather than actual cash outlays. The primary accident-related costs incurred by aircraft manufacturers are expected to be the costs of lost sales (that is, reduced demand) rather than actual cash outlays. The typical approach adopted in the literature for investigating accident-related costs borne by both airlines and aircraft manufacturers is to investigate the reaction of the stock market — that is, accident-related costs are reflected in the decline in the stock market value of airlines and manufacturers. In the following discussion, estimates of these costs utilizing this approach are presented. However, whether these costs are of sufficient magnitude to provide an incentive for airlines and aircraft manufacturers to promote (that is, for market forces to promote) air safety is debatable.

Airline Costs

In investigating the reaction of airline stocks to air accidents, Chance and Ferris (1987) and Mitchell and Maloney (1989) restrict their investigations to air crashes. Chance and Ferris's (1987, p. 160) findings suggest that the stock market responds immediately to the news of an air crash — "the abnormally low rate of return does not continue beyond the date of the crash." That is, the value of the stock is only affected momentarily by a crash. Further, the stock market value of airlines not involved in crashes was not affected, suggesting that investors did not perceive airline crashes to be an industry-wide phenomenon. These findings are based upon domestic airline crashes from 1962 through 1985.

Mitchell and Maloney (1989) dichotomize air crashes into an airline being at fault versus not at fault. Their data set consisted of fatal airline crashes involving U.S. airlines between 1964 and 1987. In instances where the airline was not at fault, there was no stock market reaction; where the airline was at fault (that is, caused by pilot error), there was a significant negative stock market response. The latter represents a one-day decline of roughly 1.6 percent and a two-day decline of roughly 2.3 percent, representing an average loss in equity value of $22–$31 million in 1990 dollars (Rose, 1992, p. 91). At most, 42 percent of the stock market losses are explained by insurance cost increases and the remainder are attributable to expected loss of consumer demand (or goodwill) — not only do insurance firms revise their expectations about the probability of accidents for the at-fault airlines but passengers do so as well.[3]

Borenstein and Zimmerman (1988) investigate the reaction of airline stocks to accidents utilizing fatal aircraft accidents of U.S. certificated airlines for the period 1962–85. Air accidents were restricted to at least one on-board fatality and some damage to aircraft. They find an average decline in stock market value of roughly 1.3 percent on the first trading day following the accident, and 1.5 percent over the first two days following the accident. These declines represent an average loss of $12 million in 1990 dollars (Rose, 1992, p. 91).

Borenstein and Zimmerman (1988) also estimate airline passenger demand loss. Airline demand (measured in monthly revenue passenger miles) is modeled as a function of price, income, a time trend, and seasonal variables. Estimates for individual airlines for both regulated (1960–77) and deregulated (1978–85) periods were found. The estimated functions, in turn, were used to estimate passenger demand responses to accidents. Borenstein and Zimmerman (1988) found that before deregulation passengers did not respond to air accidents to an extent that is statistically discernible; for post-deregulation, the response appears to have increased but is only weakly significant. Most of the latter effect appears to occur in the first two months following a fatal accident. However, the demand losses imply an average airline revenue loss of over $100 million in 1990 dollars (Rose, 1992, p. 92). The validity of this estimate, however, has been questioned: the estimate is based upon a relatively small sample and it greatly exceeds the estimated declines in equity value (Rose, 1992).[4]

Aircraft Manufacturer Costs

One investigation of the reaction of the stock market value of aircraft manufacturers to aircraft accidents is found in a study by Chalk (1987a). The response was performed utilizing a sample of 76 air crashes involving at least one fatality for the period 1966–81. Since the primary interest of the investigation was the effect on manufacturer stock value of accidents, in which it appears the aircraft design may be the cause, the sample of airline crashes was separated into crashes for which the aircraft design is suspect and those for which the design is not suspect. The former were further classified into crashes where the aircraft types were still in production and where the aircraft types were not in production at the time of the crash.

For those crashes for which the manufacturer is implicated and the aircraft is still in production, Chalk's (1987a) investigation finds a decline of 4.0 percent (or $21 million) on average in manufacturer equity value over the five business days following an accident. Since this loss is far greater than the expected FAA fines, cleanup, and investigation costs of crashes to the manufacturer, Chalk (1987a) concludes that most of the decrease in stock value would appear to be related to future increases in liability insurance premiums and market forces that lead to reduced demand for aircraft. In contrast to crashes implicating the manufacturer, crashes that did not implicate the manufacturer did not result in any stock price effect. Further, crashes involving one type of aircraft had no statistically negative impact on the stock market value of manufacturers producing other types of aircraft.

On May 25, 1979, an American Airlines DC-10 aircraft crashed at Chicago's O'Hare Airport resulting in 273 fatalities and the "first legally-mandated grounding of a passenger jet aircraft" (Chalk, 1986, p. 43). The early speculation that McDonnell Douglas, the manufacturer of the aircraft, was liable was found to be incorrect; American Airlines maintenance procedures were quickly identified as the likely cause of the crash. A study by Karels (1989) indicates that the cumulative abnormal stock market returns to McDonnell Douglas were not statistically significant. Further, American Airlines experienced no significant abnormal returns nor did other airlines flying the DC-10. Having discussed the costs of air accidents, we now turn our attention to determinants of air accidents.

DETERMINANTS

An aircraft accident seldom has a single unambiguous cause. Causes are often a sequence of causes (or events). For example, the initial cause of an accident may be engine failure just after takeoff. If the pilot subsequently fails to land the aircraft safely, both equipment failure and pilot error will be listed as causes by the NTSB. Two possible approaches have been suggested for selecting a single accident cause: select the initial cause or the last cause (beyond the initial cause) in the sequence of causes at which the accident could have been prevented (Oster and Zorn, 1989a).

Accident Causes: An Inspection Perspective

In their inspection of aircraft accidents, NTSB staff are required to list contributing factors to accidents. Categorizations of these contributing factors are found in studies by Morrison and Winston (1988) and Oster and Zorn (1989a).

The Morrison and Winston (1988) study categorized the major NTSB contributing factors of fatal aircraft accidents of U.S. certificated airlines into six categories: pilot error, weather, air traffic control, equipment failure (aircraft/engine), maintenance, and airport facilities (for example, a service truck colliding with a parked aircraft). The frequency of these contributing factors for the regulated period (1965–75) and the deregulated period (1976–86) are found in Table 5.5. The year 1976 was selected as the starting date for deregulation because administrative fare

TABLE 5.5
Frequency of Major Contributing Factors to Fatal
Accidents of U.S. Certificated Airlines

Contributing Factor	1965–75 Frequency	1976–86 Frequency
Pilot error	32	12
Weather	18	8
Traffic control	9	5
Equipment failure	7	4
Maintenance	2	1
Airport facilities	0	2

Source: S. A. Morrison, and C. Winston. (1988). "Air Safety, Deregulation, and Public Policy." *The Brookings Review* 6: 12.

deregulation began in that year. Since the number of major contributing factors exceeds the number of fatal certificated airline accidents for each period (that is, 42 for 1965–75 and 15 for 1976–86), there is generally more than one major contributing factor for each accident.

Table 5.5 reveals that pilot error was the most frequent major contributing factor to fatal accidents for both the regulated and the deregulated period, followed by weather. It is worth noting that the frequency of occurrence for all factors (except for airport facilities) declined under deregulation and that deficient maintenance contributed to only two fatal accidents under regulation and one under deregulation.

The Oster and Zorn (1989a) study investigated initial causes of fatal aircraft accidents. Accidents of certificated and commuter airlines as well as accidents of air taxis and general aviation were considered. The former accidents were for the period 1979–86 and the latter for the period 1983–86. The initial causes were classified into one of eight possible categories: equipment failure, environment (weather), pilot error, air traffic control, ground crew, other aircraft, company operations, and other. The other category includes collisions between two aircraft either in the air or on the ground; company operations includes accidents that result from the policies or procedures of the company operating the aircraft.

The percent of accidents for each of the four types of air transport attributable to a given initial cause are found in Table 5.6. These percentages are based upon 8, 24, 23, and 1,681 fatal aircraft accidents for certificated airlines, commuter airlines, air taxis, and general aviation, respectively. Excluding the other category, pilot error, equipment failure, and the environment (weather) represent the largest percentage of initial causes of accidents. Pilot error has the largest percentage for all four air transport segments except for commuters; equipment failure is generally ranked second followed by the environment. Pilot error represents 64 percent of the initial causes of general aviation accidents and a progressively smaller percentage for air taxis, certificated, and commuter airlines. Differences among these percentages across air transport segments are likely attributable to differences in pilot experience among these segments. Most general aviation pilots have either private or student licenses; by comparison, certificated, commuter, and air taxi pilots have commercial license ratings. Hence, the level of experience and training is typically lower for general aviation pilots. Further, all certificated service and almost all commuter service have co-pilots as opposed to general aviation and air taxis service, where this is generally not the case.

TABLE 5.6
Percent of Fatal Aircraft Accidents for Air
Transport Segments by Initial Cause

Initial Cause	Certificated*	Commuter*	Air Taxis	General Aviation
Equipment Failure	12.5	37.5	13.0	11.6
Environment	25.0	25.0	13.0	4.2
Pilot Error	25.0	20.8	39.1	64.0
Air Traffic Control	12.5	0.0	4.4	0.3
Ground Crew	12.5	4.2	0.0	0.4
Other Aircraft	0.0	8.3	8.7	3.2
Company Operations	0.0	4.2	0.0	0.0
Other	12.5	0.0	21.7	16.5

*Domestic scheduled service.

Source: C. V. Oster, Jr. and C. K. Zorn. (1989). "Aviation Safety: The Experience of General Aviation." Journal of the Transportation Research Forum 30: 190.

Accident Determinants: An Analytical Perspective

An alternative to the inspection of air accidents for investigating their causes is to rely upon analytical (or statistical) models for finding factors that are statistically significant in explaining the variation in these accidents. Those hypothesized determinants (or factors) that are significant may be interpreted as determinants of air accidents, that is, causes or deterrents to air accidents. One such study by Talley and Bossert (1990) investigated the relationship between U.S. certificated airline accidents and a number of hypothesized determinants: number of aircraft miles flown (level of air service), relative maintenance expenditure (the ratio of maintenance expenditure to total operating expenditures), pilot expertise (ratio of air transport pilot ratings to the total number of U.S. commercial air pilot ratings), and number (in 10,000s) of FAA air traffic controllers. A binary deregulation variable (assigned a one for a deregulation time period and zero otherwise) was also included, as well as a time trend variable (whose values are consecutive positive integers corresponding to consecutive time periods). Annual time-series data for the period 1959–84 were used in the estimation.

For the hypothesized accident function, three variables were found to significantly explain the variation in aircraft accidents. Both pilot expertise and the number of air traffic controllers were found to be highly significant and to have a negative impact on accidents (that is, an increase in their values leads to a decrease in aircraft accidents); the deregulation binary variable was significant at the 5 percent level and negative. The former suggests that pilot expertise and the number of air traffic controllers are deterrent determinants of air accidents and are consistent with the results of Morrison and Winston (1988). The latter study found that pilot error and air traffic control are frequent major contributing factors (or causes) of fatal accidents of certificated airlines. The negative coefficient of the deregulation binary variable provides support for the argument that aircraft accidents of certificated airlines have declined during the post-deregulation period.

Safety of Commuter versus Certificated Airlines

A major development of U.S. post-deregulation airline service has been the transfer of much low-density, small community service from certificated to commuter airlines. The accelerated growth in commuter service gave rise to the concern that small-community passengers faced greater safety risk because of the relatively poor safety record of commuter airlines. Although the data suggest that the safety performance of commuter and certificated airlines has improved during the post-deregulation period (see Table 5.2), they also suggest that commuter air travel remains more risky than travel by certificated airlines.

Why does travel on commuter airlines remain relatively risky? One approach to addressing this question is to investigate determinants of the difference in the safety risks of travel on commuter and certificated airlines. A study by Phillips and Talley (1993) adopted this approach by investigating determinants of the probability that an accident or incident will be that of a commuter rather than a certificated airline. If the probability increases, the safety risk of the commuter increases relative to that of the certificated airline; conversely, if the probability decreases. NTSB accident and incident data for commuter and certificated airlines for the post-deregulation period 1983–86 and the probit statistical model were utilized in the study.[5]

Four factors, two pilot and two aircraft engine characteristics, were found to be highly significant in explaining the variation in the probability of a commuter versus a certificated airline having an accident or an incident. Pilot experience (in hours of flight time) decreases and pilot utilization (number of pilot landings during the last 90 days) increases the probability. Pilot utilization has increased during the post-deregulation period because of the expansion of service under deregulation and a shortage of pilots by some airlines, thereby raising concerns about air safety. The policy implications of these results for improving the safety performance of commuter airlines (as well as reducing the variation in the safety performance among commuter and certificated airlines) are to increase the required flight time experience of commuter pilots and limit the number of aircraft landings allowed by commuter pilots during a specified time period.

The number of engines per aircraft and the type of engine (piston versus turbine or jet) also affect the probability. Specifically, commuter aircraft with one or two engines rather than four, and with piston rather than turbine engines, increase the probability of commuters relative to certificated airlines having accidents and incidents. Commuter airlines are restricted to using propeller-driven aircraft — piston and turbine engines — seating 60 passengers or less. Piston engines have far more moving parts and, thus, have a higher rate of equipment failure than turbine and jet engines.

The policy implications of the aircraft engine results for improving commuter air safety are to require these airlines to utilize a greater number of multi-engine and non-piston engine aircraft. However, a conflict between airline cost efficiency and safety is likely to arise from such policies. If the aircraft presently used by commuter airlines are cost efficient for commuter markets, then four-engine and non-piston engine aircraft are expected to be cost inefficient for these markets.

Severity of Unsafe Air Occurrences

Investigating determinants of aircraft accidents and incidents is made difficult by the heterogeneous nature of these occurrences (Moses and Savage, 1990). An aircraft accident, for example, may involve fatal injuries without damage to the aircraft or aircraft damage without fatal injuries. The more heterogeneous accidents and incidents are, the greater the difficulty in discerning their determinants. Addressing this problem, Phillips and Talley (1992) investigated determinants of the severity of the aircraft damage of accidents and incidents.

For each accident or incident that it investigates, the NTSB classifies aircraft damage into one of four possible categories: no damage, minor damage, substantial damage, and aircraft destroyed. Phillips and Talley (1992) utilized these ordinal observations to proxy an index of the severity of aircraft damage. Determinants of the latter were investigated using NTSB accident and incident data of U.S. certificated and commuter airlines for the years 1983-86 and the multichotomous probit statistical model. Phillips and Talley (1992) hypothesized that the severity of aircraft damage for a given accident or incident is a function of the following factors: pilot age, pilot experience (flight time in hours), pilot utilization (landings by pilot during the last 90 days), aircraft size (in pounds), number of aircraft engines, aircraft age (cumulative flight time in hours on airframe), phase of aircraft flight (that is, airstrip versus off airstrip), visual flying conditions exist versus do not exist, time of day (that is, night versus day), stall warning system installed in aircraft versus not installed, cumulative flight time (in hours) of aircraft since last periodic mechanical and safety inspection, and type of airline (that is, commuter versus a certificated airline).

Seven factors were found to have a significant relationship with the severity of aircraft damage: pilot experience (a negative relationship), pilot age (a positive relationship), pilot utilization (a positive relationship), visual flying conditions (a negative relationship), occurrence at night (a positive relationship), stall warning system installed (a negative relationship), and a commuter airline (a positive relationship). These results suggest that the severity of aircraft damage may be reduced by airlines by utilizing more experienced and younger pilots, reducing the number of aircraft landings by pilots during a specified time period, reducing the safety risk of flights flown during poor visibility conditions, and reducing the safety risk of commuter flights. Phillips and Talley (1991) also investigated determinants of the severity of aircraft accidents with respect to passenger and crew injuries. The proportion of injuries (fatal and non-fatal) in air accidents was expressed as a function of the same hypothesized factors (discussed above) affecting aircraft damage severity. Utilizing the NTSB data set (excluding incidents) in estimation of this function, three factors were found to have a significant relationship with this proportion: pilot experience (a negative relationship), visual flying conditions (a negative relationship), and a commuter airline (a positive relationship). These results suggest that less injuries are expected to occur flying with more experienced pilots and when visual flying conditions exist. Further, an aircraft accident involving a commuter airline is expected to be more severe from a passenger and crew perspective than one involving a certificated airline (other factors remaining the same).

SUMMARY

Since safety of air travel cannot be observed directly, measures of unsafe air travel have been used as proxies. Input proxies represent actions by airlines, airports, and government that decrease the probability of unsafe air travel; outcome proxies represent unsafe outcomes of air travel. Since little is known of the extent to which safety inputs translate into air safety, outcome proxies may be more reliable proxies for air safety. Input proxies include aircraft maintenance and pilot training expenditures; output proxies include aircraft accidents and incidents. For comparative purposes, the latter are often adjusted for exposure to risk (for example, by number of aircraft departures).

Does economic deregulation compromise air safety? In the United States, evidence suggests that air safety has not deteriorated under deregulation. It has been argued that there is a positive relationship between airline profitability and air safety, therefore, adverse financial conditions existing in a market environment is expected to have an adverse effect on airline safety. Empirical results are mixed, however, in their support of the profit-safety argument. It also has been argued that market forces may promote air safety. Airlines anticipating a deterioration in their financial condition following an accident will take safety precautions in a market environment (that is, the market-response argument). Although there is some empirical support for this argument, the evidence is not conclusive.

The literature has investigated accident-related costs borne by both airlines and aircraft manufacturers by investigating the reaction of the stock market. Since airlines typically carry quite complete aircraft and passenger liability, the primary airline accident-related costs are expected to be increased insurance premiums and reduced passenger demand rather than actual cash outlays. The primary costs incurred by aircraft manufacturers are also not expected to be actual cash outlays but rather lost sales (that is, reduced demand for aircraft). Accident-related costs for both airlines and aircraft manufacturers are argued to be reflected in the decline in their stock market values. Estimates of average equity losses incurred by airlines involved in accidents range from $12 million to $31 million. The average equity loss for aircraft manufacturers has been estimated to be $21 million. Whether these losses are of sufficient magnitude to provide an incentive for airlines and aircraft manufacturers to promote (that is, for market forces to promote) air safety is debatable.

Determining causes of unsafe air travel is complicated by the fact that a given unsafe air occurrence seldom has a single unambiguous cause. In their inspection of aircraft accidents, NTSB staff are required to list contributing factors to accidents. Surveys of these inspection reports for U.S. fatal accidents (during regulated and deregulated time periods) reveal that pilot error and weather were the most frequently listed contributing factors. For the deregulated time period, empirical evidence suggests that airlines may reduce the severity (measured in aircraft damage severity or proportion of passenger injuries) of unsafe air occurrences by utilizing more experienced pilots, reducing the safety risk of flights flown during poor visibility conditions, and reducing the safety risk of commuter flights.

NOTES

1.   A certificated air carrier is defined by the FAA as "an air carrier operator who conducts operations in accordance with FAR Part 121, who provides scheduled services on specified routes in aircraft with more than 30 passenger seats and a payload capacity of more than 7,500 pounds. These air carriers may also provide non-scheduled or charter service as a secondary operation" FAA (1987, p. ix).

2.   A commuter air carrier is defined by the FAA as "an aircraft operator who operates under FAR Part 135 who carries passengers on at least five round trips per week or at least one route between two or more points according to published flight schedules that specify the times, day of the week, and places between which these flights are performed. A commuter operates aircraft with 30 or less passenger seats and a payload capability of 7,500 pounds or less" FAA (1987, p. x). An air taxi carrier is defined by the FAA as "an aircraft operator who conducts operations in accordance with FAR Part 135, that is for hire or compensation in aircraft with 30 or less passenger seats and a payload capacity of 7,500 pounds or less. They operate on an on-demand basis and do not meet the flight schedule qualifications of a commuter air carrier" FAA (1987, p. ix). General aviation is defined by the FAA as "all civil aviation activity except that of air carriers certificated in accordance with FAR Parts 121, 123, 127 and 135. The types of aircraft used in general aviation activities cover a wide range; e.g., from corporate multi-engine jet aircraft to amateur-built single engine piston aircraft" FAA (1987, p. xi).

3.   A study by Morrison and Winston (1988, p. 14) concludes that "deregulation lowered airline insurance expenses by roughly 22 percent over what they would have been had regulation continued. Apparently the strength of market forces (from potential and actual competition) leading to increases in safety has outweighed the alleged tendency for air carriers to sacrifice safety in the face of increased competition."

4.   Other studies investigating airline equity losses following air accidents include Bruning and Kuzma (1989) and Mansur, Cochran, and Froio (1989).

5.   The probit statistical model assumes a cumulative normal distribution function and utilizes an interactive maximum likelihood procedure to maximize the value of the likelihood function.

REFERENCES

Arnott, R. J., and J. E. Stiglitz. (1989). "Congestion Pricing to Improve Air Travel Safety." In Moses, L. N., and I. Savage (Eds.), *Transportation Safety in an Age of Deregulation* (pp. 167–185). New York: Oxford University Press.

Bailey, E. E., and D. M. Kirstein. (1989). "Can Truth in Airline Scheduling Alleviate the Congestion and Delay Problems?" In Moses, L. N., and I. Savage (Eds.), *Transportation Safety in an Age of Deregulation* (pp. 153–166). New York: Oxford University Press.

Barnett, A., and M. Higgins. (1989). "Airline Safety: The Last Decade." *Management Science* 35: 1–21.

Borenstein, S., and M. B. Zimmerman. (1988). "Market Incentives for Safe Commercial Airline Operation." *American Economic Review* 78: 913–935.

Bruning, E. R., and A. T. Kuzma. (1989). "Airline Accidents and Stock Return Performance." *Logistics and Transportation Review* 25: 157–168.

Chalk, A. (1987a). "Market Forces and Commercial Aircraft Safety." *Journal of Industrial Economics* 36: 61–81.

———. (1987b). Market Outperforms FAA as Air-Safety Enforcer." *Wall Street Journal* (September 1): 30.

———. (1986). "Market Forces and Aircraft Safety: The Case of the DC-10." *Economic Inquiry* 24: 43–60.

Chance, D. M., and S. P. Ferris. (1987). "The Effect of Aviation Disasters on the Air Transport Industry." *Journal of Transport Economics and Policy* 21: 151–165.

Code of Federal Regulation. (1987). Washington, DC: U.S. Government Printing Office.

Cunningham, W. A., and G. M. Davis. (1987). "A Preliminary Analysis of the Impact of the PATCO Strike on Airline Safety." *Annual Proceedings of the Transportation Research Forum* 28: 21–24.

Federal Aviation Administration. (1987). *Selected Statistics Concerning Pilot Reported Near Midair Collisions (1983–1986).* Washington, DC: U.S. Government Printing Office.

Golbe, D. L. (1986). "Safety and Profits in the Airline Industry." *Journal of Industrial Economics* 34: 305–318.

Hawk, B. E. (1989). "Airline Deregulation After Ten Years: The Need for Vigorous Antitrust Enforcement and Intergovernmental Agreements." *The Antitrust Bulletin* 34: 267–305.

Kahn, A. E. (1988). "Surprises of Airline Deregulation." *American Economic Review* 78: 316–322.

Kanafani, A., and T. E. Keeler. (1990). "Air Deregulation and Safety: Some Econometric Evidence from Time Series." *Logistics and Transportation Review* 26: 203–209.

———. (1989). "New Entrants and Safety." In Moses, L. N., and I. Savage (Eds.), *Transportation Safety in an Age of Deregulation* (pp. 115–128). New York: Oxford University Press.

Karels, G. V. (1989). "Market Forces and Aircraft Safety: An Extension." *Economic Inquiry* 27: 345–354.

Levine, M. E. (1987). "Airline Competition in Deregulated Markets: Theory, Firm Strategy, and Public Policy." *Yale Journal of Regulation* 4: 393–494.

Mansur, I., S. J. Cochran, and G. L. Froio. (1989). "The Relationship Between the Equity Return Levels of Airline Companies and Unanticipated Events: The

Case of the 1979 DC-10 Grounding." *Logistics and Transportation Review* 25: 355–365.

Mitchell, M. L., and M. T. Maloney. (1989). "Crisis in the Cockpit? The Role of Market Forces in Promoting Air Travel Safety." *Journal of Law and Economics* 32: 329–355.

Moore, T. G. (1986). "U.S. Airline Deregulation: Its Effects on Passengers, Capital and Labor." *Journal of Law and Economics* 29: 1–28.

Morrison, S. A., and C. Winston. (1989). "Enhancing the Performance of the Deregulated Air Transportation System." In Bailey, M., and C. Winston (Eds.), *Brookings Papers on Economic Activity* (pp. 61–123). Washington, DC: The Brookings Institution.

____. (1988). "Air Safety, Deregulation, and Public Policy." *The Brookings Review* 6: 10–15.

____. (1986). *The Economic Effects of Airline Deregulation.* Washington, DC: The Brookings Institution.

Moses, L. N., and I. Savage. (1990). "Aviation Deregulation and Safety: Theory and Evidence." *Journal of Transport Economics and Policy* 24: 171–188.

____. (1989). "Introduction." In Moses, L. N., and I. Savage (Eds.), *Transportation Safety in an Age of Deregulation* (pp. 3–7). New York: Oxford University Press.

Nance, J. J. (1989). "Economic Deregulation's Unintended but Inevitable Impact on Airline Safety." In Moses, L. N., and I. Savage (Eds.), *Transportation Safety in an Age of Deregulation* (pp. 186–205). New York: Oxford University Press.

Oster, C. V., Jr., and C. K. Zorn. (1989a). "Aviation Safety: The Experience of General Aviation." *Journal of the Transportation Research Forum* 30: 187–194.

____. (1989b). "Is It Still Safe to Fly?" In Moses, L. N., and I. Savage (Eds.), *Transportation Safety in an Age of Deregulation* (pp. 129–152). New York: Oxford University Press.

Phillips, R. A., and W. K. Talley. (1993). "Improving Commuter Air Carrier Safety Performance." *Transportation Quarterly* 47: 247–256.

____. (1992). "Airline Safety Investments and Operating Conditions: Determinants of Aircraft Damage Severity." *Southern Economic Journal* 59: 157–164.

____. (1991). "Determinants of the Severity of Airline Accidents: A Passenger Perspective." *Proceedings of the Transportation Research Forum* 115–122.

Rose, N. L. (1992). "Fear of Flying? Economic Analysis of Airline Safety." *Journal of Economic Perspectives* 6: 75–94.

____. (1990). "Profitability and Product Quality: Economic Determinants of Airline Safety Performance." *Journal of Political Economy* 98: 944–964.

____. (1989). "Financial Influences on Airline Safety." In Moses, L. N., and I. Savage (Eds.), *Transportation Safety in an Age of Deregulation* (pp. 93–114). New York: Oxford University Press.

Scheraga, C. A., and S. Ornstein. (1991). "Market Forces and Airline Safety: An Empirical Reevaluation." *Journal of the Transportation Research Forum* 31: 278–285.

Talley, W. K. (1993). "The Impact of Deregulation on Airline Safety: Profit-Safety and Market-Response Arguments." In Beesley, M., D. Hensher, and A. Talvitie

(Eds.), *Privatization and Deregulation in Passenger Transportation* (pp. 205–211). Forssa, Finland: Auranen, Ltd..

Talley, W. K., and P. A. Bossert, Jr. (1990). "Determinants of Aircraft Accidents and Policy Implications for Air Safety." *International Journal of Transport Economics* 17: 115–130.

Transportation Research Board. (1991). *Winds of Change: Domestic Air Transport Since Deregulation.* Washington, DC: National Research Council.

6

Recreational Boating Accidents

INTRODUCTION

In this chapter, we turn our attention to water transportation accidents. The discussion is restricted to recreational boating accidents. Commercial vessel accidents are discussed in Chapter 7. We begin with an overview of recreational boating accidents in the United States. Various boating accident statistics are presented (for example, fatalities, fatality rates, and fatalities and injuries by type of boating accident). A discussion of alcohol involvement in boating accidents follows; evidence and effects on operator performance and drownings are discussed. Finally, we present determinants of the operator at fault and the severity of boating accidents.

ACCIDENT STATISTICS

Among U.S. transportation modes, recreational boating accidents currently rank second behind motor vehicle accidents (see Table 1.1). Prior to 1982, railroad accidents ranked second behind motor vehicle accidents. Since 1981, there has been a general decline in railroad accidents, but a general increase in recreational boating accidents. Among U.S. transportation fatalities (see Table 1.2), recreational boating fatalities rank second behind motor vehicle fatalities except for the years 1981 and 1982, when general aviation fatalities were slightly higher.

The trend in U.S. boating fatalities during the 1980s (see Table 1.2) was one of general decline. By comparison, the number of recreational boats increased (see Table 6.1). Consequently, boating fatality rates (fatalities per 100,000 boats) declined during the 1980s. During the 1960s, we observe double digit fatality rates. Since 1975, we observe single digit fatality rates. In the 1980s, boating fatality rates were in single digits, even though the number of boats was more than twice the number in the 1960s.

TABLE 6.1
Recreational Boats and Fatality Rates

Year	Boats (millions)	Fatality Rate (Per 100,000 boats)	Year	Boats (millions)	Fatality Rate (per 100,000 boats)
1961	5.85	20.8	1976	12.75	9.9
1962	5.95	18.7	1977	13.30	9.9
1963	6.05	19.3	1978	13.60	9.7
1964	6.20	19.2	1979	14.10	9.9
1965	6.35	21.4	1980	14.60	9.3
1966	6.50	20.3	1981	15.10	8.0
1967	6.65	19.7	1982	15.50	7.6
1968	6.85	19.6	1983	15.80	7.9
1969	7.10	19.0	1984	16.30	6.5
1970	7.40	19.2	1985	16.70	6.7
1971	7.85	20.2	1986	17.30	6.2
1972	8.50	16.9	1987	17.70	5.9
1973	9.60	18.3	1988	18.40	5.1
1974	10.75	13.5	1989	19.00	4.7
1975	11.80	12.4	1990	19.50	4.4

Source: U.S. Coast Guard, U.S. Department of Transportation. (1991). Boating Statistics 1990. Washington, DC: U.S. Government Printing Office.

Recreational boating accidents are classified by the U.S. Coast Guard according to type of accident. In a grounding accident, a vessel runs aground, striking or pounding on rocks, reefs, or shoals. In a capsizing accident, a vessel overturns — the vessel's bottom becomes uppermost, except in the case of a sailboat that lies on its side. A swamping accident is one in which the vessel fills with water, particularly over the side, but retains sufficient buoyancy to remain on the waterway's surface; for a flooding accident, the ingress of water filling may be from any method. In a sinking, the vessel settles below the surface of the waterway.

A fire/fuel-explosion boating accident involves the accidental burning or explosion of a vessel's fuels or their vapors. A fire/other-explosion accident involves the accidental burning or explosion of any material on board a vessel except vessel fuels or their vapors. A collision/another-vessel accident is one in which there is the striking together of two or more vessels, regardless of operation at time of the accident. A collision/fixed-object accident is one where a vessel strikes any fixed object, above or below the surface of the waterway. In a collision/floating-object accident, the vessel strikes any waterborne object except another vessel (above or below the surface of the waterway) that is free to move with the tide, current, or wind.

In a falls-overboard-victim boating accident, a person on board a vessel falls overboard. A person on board a vessel falls within the boat in a falls-within-boat-victim accident. In a non-boat-victim accident, a person who is not on board a vessel is struck by a boat or its propeller.

From inspection of Table 6.2, we see that for both 1985 and 1990 the accident type with the greatest number of accidents is collision with

TABLE 6.2
Boating Accidents, Fatalities, and Injuries: By Type of Accident

Type of Accident	Accidents		Fatalities		Injuries	
	1985	1990	1985	1990	1985	1990
Grounding	358	390	9	14	122	240
Capsizing	623	545	378	289	225	259
Swamping/ Flooding	247	252	73	60	31	55
Sinking	297	210	31	11	47	38
Fire/Explosion (Fuel)	339	274	16	14	193	141
Fire/Explosion (Other)	80	97	1	2	16	22
Collision/Another Vessel	2,123	2,242	79	81	993	1,376
Collision/Fixed Object	754	864	107	76	381	545
Collision/Floating Object	306	269	13	13	74	100
Falls-Overboard Victim	436	451	287	239	178	260
Falls-Within-Boat Victim	46	139	3	1	49	164
Non-boat Victim	111	183	16	7	98	180
Other	517	495	103	58	350	442
Total	6,237	6,411	1,116	865	2,757	3,822

Sources: U.S. Coast Guard, U.S. Department of Transportation. (1988). *Boating Statistics 1987*. Washington, DC: U.S. Government Printing Office; U.S. Coast Guard, U.S. Department of Transportation. (1991). *Boating Statistics 1990*. Washington, DC: U.S. Government Printing Office.

another vessel, followed by collision with fixed object, capsizing, and falls overboard, respectively (excluding the "other" category). The accident type with the greatest number of fatalities for 1985 is capsizing, followed by falls overboard, collision with fixed object, and collision with another vessel, respectively (excluding the "other" category). For 1990 fatalities, the order is the same except the accident types — collision with fixed object and collision with another vessel — are reversed.

From inspection of Table 6.2, we also notice that although collision with another vessel ranks first in number of accidents, it is fourth in 1985 and third in 1990 in number of fatalities; whereas, falls overboard ranks fourth in number of accidents, but second in number of fatalities for both years. Further, although capsizing ranks third in number of accidents, it ranks first in number of fatalities for both years.

In terms of the fatality accident rate (fatalities per accident), falls-overboard-accidents had the highest rate in 1985 and tied with capsizing in 1990 for the highest rate (see Table 6.3). The magnitude of the differences among the fatality accident rates is noteworthy. For 1985, the fatality accident rates for falls-overboard and capsizing were more than four times greater than those rates for collision accidents. For 1990, the former rates were more than five times greater than the latter rates.

TABLE 6.3
Fatality and Injury Accident Rates: By Type of Accident

Type of Accident	Fatality Accident Rate		Injury Accident Rate	
	1985	1990	1985	1990
Collision/Another Vessel	0.037	0.036	0.468	0.614
Collision/Fixed Object	0.142	0.088	0.505	0.631
Capsizing	0.607	0.530	0.361	0.475
Falls Overboard Victim	0.658	0.530	0.408	0.576

Source: Compiled by the authors. Data used in computations were taken from Table 6.2.

For 1985, the accident type with the greatest number of injuries (see Table 6.2) is collision with another vessel, followed by collision with fixed object, capsizing, and fire/fuel-explosion, respectively (excluding the "other" category). In 1990, collision with another vessel and collision with fixed object also ranked first and second, respectively, in number of boating injuries. However, falls-overboard ranks third and capsizing ranks fourth for 1990 boating injuries (excluding the "other" category). Remember that collision with another vessel and collision with fixed object also rank first and second, respectively, in number of boating accidents (see Table 6.2). Table 6.3 reveals that the differences among the injury accident rates (injuries per accident) are substantially less than that for the fatality accident rates.

Before concluding this section, let us relate boating fatalities to the type of boat involved. A noteworthy statistic is that in 1990 over 53 percent of all boating fatalities involved an open motorboat (see Table 6.4). The next largest percentage is 10 percent for canoe or kayak. An open motorboat is defined by the U.S. Coast Guard as a craft of open construction specifically built for operating with a motor. A cabin motorboat is a motorboat with a cabin that can be completely closed by means of doors or hatches. A motorboat is any vessel equipped with propulsion machinery, not more than 65 feet in length. The distinction among the remaining types of boats in Table 6.4 is obvious except for personal watercraft. The latter is defined by the U.S. Coast Guard as craft less than 13 feet in length designed to be operated by a person or persons sitting, standing, or kneeling on the craft, rather than within the confines of a hull.

TABLE 6.4
1990 Boating Fatalities: By Type of Boat

Type of Boat	Fatalities	Percentage
Open Motorboat	462	53.4
Cabin Motorboat	69	8.0
Sailboat	38	4.3
Rowboat	69	8.0
Canoe or Kayak	90	10.4
Inflatable Boat	24	2.8
Personal Watercraft	29	3.4
Other/Unknown	84	9.7
Total	865	100.0

Source: U.S. Coast Guard, U.S. Department of Transportation. (1991). Boating Statistics 1990. Washington, DC: U.S. Government Printing Office.

ALCOHOL INVOLVEMENT
IN BOATING ACCIDENTS

The philosophy of the U.S. National Transportation Safety Board (NTSB) toward alcohol involvement in recreational boating is revealed in a statement appearing in an NTSB (1983, p. 14) report — the NTSB "believes that the reduction of alcohol involved accidents, fatalities, and injuries in recreational boating activities should be a major national safety initiative." The same report also states that the use of alcohol by recreational boating operators has been a concern of the NTSB, the U.S. Coast Guard, State Boating Law Administrators, and others since the early 1970s. In the discussion that follows, we present evidence of the extent of alcohol involvement in recreational boating. Whether this evidence supports the above concerns, however, is open to debate.

Evidence

A boating accident where alcohol is involved may be one where the operator of the boat, a passenger on board the boat, or a person not on board the boat used alcohol. "Passenger intoxication can have a very significant influence on the fatal accident risk in boating because passengers can cause boating accidents, unlike automobiles or general aviation where only operators are likely to cause accidents" (U.S. Department of Transportation, 1988, pp. 4–5).

In investigating alcohol involvement in boating accidents, a distinction should be made between alcohol involvement in fatal versus non-fatal boating accidents. Since nearly all fatal boating accidents are reported to the U.S. Coast Guard but only approximately 10 percent of all non-fatal boating accidents are reported, a measurement of alcohol involvement in fatal accidents is expected to be more reliable than that for non-fatal accidents. For fatal boating accidents in 1987 and 1988 (reported to the U.S. Coast Guard), 19.7 percent involved alcohol; for non-fatal boating accidents, 6.8 percent involved alcohol (Anderson and Talley, 1993). In 1988, 7.6 percent of all boating accidents (fatal and non-fatal) reported to the U.S. Coast Guard involved alcohol; by 1990, the percentage was 8.9 percent (U.S. Coast Guard, 1991, pp. 11 and 17). In 1988, 15.4 percent of boating fatalities were involved in alcohol-involved boating accidents; by 1990, the percentage was approximately the same at 15.5 percent (U.S. Coast Guard, 1991, pp. 11 and 17).

Alcohol involvement in boating accidents has also been measured by the proportion of boating fatalities where their blood alcohol concentration (BAC) levels equals or exceeds certain levels. At the national level, BAC information on boating fatalities is limited. In addition, only four states — California, Maryland, New Jersey, and North Carolina — collect BAC information for over 50 percent of its boating accident fatalities. In the majority of states that have a boating BAC standard, boat operators are considered intoxicated if their BAC is 0.10 or higher. A BAC of 0.10 is also the BAC standard for operator intoxication for automobile drivers in all states except for three — Idaho, Maryland, and Utah — where the BAC standard is 0.08.

Utilizing BAC information on boating fatalities (in the early to mid-1980s) for California, Maryland, New Jersey, and North Carolina, a U.S. Department of Transportation (1988) study found that 30 percent of the fatalities with known BACs had a BAC at or above 0.10; another 21 percent with known BACs had a BAC above 0.04 and below 0.10; the remaining 49 percent with known BACs had either no alcohol in their blood (40 percent) or very low levels of alcohol (9 percent). The fatalities with known BACs represented 75 percent of all fatalities.

The analysis of the above sample also revealed that almost 40 percent of the fatalities in the high BAC category (that is, a BAC at or above 0.10) were falls-overboard fatalities. Further, the falls-overboard fatalities (with high BACs) were likely to be on board boats where other persons were also consuming alcohol — thus, perhaps because of alcohol impairment were unable to rescue the victim. Given the known effects of alcohol on a person's coordination, the implication is that alcohol is a cause of falls-overboard fatalities.

Effects on Performance and Drownings

It is well known that alcohol affects human performance. Specifically, alcohol affects balance, increases risk-taking behavior, increases choice reaction time (the time a person needs to decide which of two responses is correct), has a detrimental effect on hand-eye coordination, and reduces one's ability to make precise positioning movements of limbs (U.S. Department of Transportation, 1988).

In boating, water may interact with alcohol and compound alcohol's effects on human performance. Specifically, alcohol can magnify the effects of caloric labyrinthitis — becoming disoriented, nauseous, or both, when water different from normal body temperature enters one's ears. An intoxicated person whose head is immersed may become so disoriented as to swim down to death instead of up to safety. Cold water can affect muscle control (peripheral hypothermia) and, thus, compound alcohol's effects on physical coordination, further impairing a swimmer's abilities. Also, cold water may further impair an intoxicated swimmer's air supply. The combination of inhalation (or gasp) response when suddenly placed in cold water and alcohol induced hyperventilation can result in aspiration of water and rapid drowning.

Because alcohol affects balance, intoxicated boaters are more likely to fall overboard than sober boaters. Given that water compounds the effects of alcohol on human performance, intoxicated boaters are thus less likely to recover from falling overboard than sober boaters.

DETERMINANTS

Concern about alcohol involvement in recreational boating accidents prompted the U.S. Congress to pass an anti-alcohol rider to the Coast Guard Appropriations Act, effective as of December 1987. This rider was modeled after highway per se laws and established a federal safety-regulation policy regarding alcohol consumption and recreational boating. Highway per se laws make operating a vehicle at or above a certain BAC level conclusive evidence of operator intoxication (that is, per se). Under the anti-alcohol rider, boat operators are considered intoxicated if their BAC is 0.10 or higher; if so, Coast Guard personnel may terminate the use of the vessel, and convicted operators may receive a maximum penalty of one year imprisonment and a $10,000 fine. Unlike highway per se laws, there is no potential license forfeiture, since operator licenses are not required for recreational boating.

The federal boating BAC (or per se) standard of 0.10 applies to states that have not set their own impairment levels; for those states that have done so, the state BAC (or per se) standard is the one that is enforced. Similar to highway laws, boat operators (and not passengers) are subject to anti-alcohol boating laws. The intent of anti-alcohol boating laws is to reduce boating accidents by reducing alcohol consumption by operators. The implicit assumption is that alcohol consumption by operators is a determinant of operators at fault in boating accidents. Hence, an alternative approach for investigating the effectiveness of the laws for reducing boating accidents is to investigate the validity of this hypothesis.

Operator at Fault

Determinants of the likelihood that an operator will be at fault because a boating accident has occurred have been investigated by Anderson and

Talley (1993). Thus, determinants of a cause of boating accidents — the operator at fault — were investigated. Accident case data (obtained from the U.S. Coast Guard for all 50 states) for 1987 and 1988 for both fatal and non-fatal recreational boating accidents were utilized in the investigation. For fatal accidents, the sample consisted of 254 accidents — 133 for 1987 and 121 for 1988; for non-fatal accidents, the sample consisted of 3,610 accidents — 1,833 for 1987 and 1,777 for 1988. The accidents were restricted to motorboat accidents only.

Fault of operator, as defined by the U.S. Coast Guard (1991, p. 32), may include:

speeding; overloading; improper loading, not properly seating occupants of boat; no proper lookout; carelessness; failure to heed weather warnings; operating in a congested area; not observing the Rules of the Road; unsafe fueling practices; lack of experience; ignorance of aids to navigation; lack of caution in an unfamiliar area of operation; improper installation or maintenance of hull, machinery or equipment; poor judgment; recklessness; overpowering the boat; panic; proceeding in an unseaworthy craft; operating a motorboat near persons in the water; starting engine with clutch engaged or throttle advanced; irresponsible boat handling such as quick, sharp turns.

Hypothesized determinants of the likelihood (or probability) that a boat operator will be at fault in a given boating accident include boat, boat operation, operator, waterway, type of accident, weather/visibility, and alcohol involvement characteristics of the accident. Boat character- istics are represented by type of motorboat (open versus cabin), length of boat, horsepower of boat, and the year the boat was built. Boat operation characteristics include whether the boat was at anchor, drifting, or cruising at the time of the accident and the number of people on board the boat. Operator characteristics include age of operator and operator boating experience.

Waterway characteristics are represented by type of waterway and condition of waterway. Types of waterways include: river, lake, and restricted waterways such as bays, sounds, harbors, or intracoastal waterways. Waterway conditions include: calm (waves less than six inches), choppy (waves between six inches and two feet), rough (waves over two feet but less than or equal to six feet), very rough (waves greater than six feet), and strong current conditions. Type of accident characteristics include: capsizing; swamping; collision with another boat, or fixed or floating object; and a victim falling overboard. Weather/visibility characteristics are presented by type of weather and time of day. Types of weather include: foggy, rainy, and clear. Time was classified as day or night.

Although the data do not include specific information on the extent of alcohol consumption by an operator, whether alcohol was involved or not in a given boating accident was reported. A binary variable representing alcohol involvement versus non-involvement was used as a proxy for consumption by the operator. This assumption is reasonable, since "when one person on a boat has been drinking, others on the boat are more likely to have been drinking" (U.S. Department of Transportation, 1988, p. 41). The probit statistical technique (see Pindyck and Rubinfeld, 1981, pp. 280–287) was used to estimate a linear probability model, where the probability of operator at fault is expressed as a linear function of the above hypothesized determinants. Probit estimations were performed separately for fatal and non-fatal accidents. In Table 6.5, hypothesized determinants that were significant at the 10 percent level or better and whether their effect on the probability of operator at fault is positive or negative (denoted by plus (+) and minus (–) signs, respectively) for both fatal and non-fatal accidents are presented.

The fatal-accident results suggest that operating a boat that is anchored or drifting versus cruising reduces the probability that an operator will be at fault in a fatal accident. The inexperience level of the operator being less than or equal to 100 boating hours versus greater than 500 hours increases this probability. Further, operating a boat in a river or lake versus a restricted waterway increases the probability, whereas if the condition of the waterway is choppy, rough, or very rough versus calm decreases this probability. The latter results may be because authorities excuse operator mistakes when made under adverse waterway conditions; perhaps operators being aware that they lack sufficient skill avoid adverse waterway conditions disproportionately.

Although the variable — alcohol involved in accident — had the predicted positive sign, surprisingly it was not statistically significant. Anderson and Talley (1993) support this result by demonstrating that when the variable — alcohol involved in accident — is introduced (after the other hypothesized determinants have been introduced) into the probability equation, the probability of operator at fault in a fatal accident is affected only marginally. Finding no evidence of statistical modeling errors, Anderson and Talley (1993, p. 1240) conclude that "there is no persuasive evidence of alcohol contributing substantially to operator fault in fatal accidents."

Non-fatal-accident results (see Table 6.5) suggest (in contrast to the fatal-accident results) that alcohol involvement increases the probability

TABLE 6.5
Operator at Fault Probability Model: Probit Estimation Results

Hypothesized Determinant	Effect (+ or –)/Significance Level	
	Fatal Accidents	Non-Fatal Accidents
Anchored (versus cruising)	–/5 percent	–/1 percent
Drifting (versus cruising)	–/1 percent	–/1 percent
Cabin Motorboat (versus open motorboat)		–/10 percent
Number of People on Board		+/1 percent
Age of Operator		–/1 percent
Operator Inexperience (≤100 hours versus >500 hours)	+/5 percent	+/1 percent
River (versus restricted waterway)	+/5 percent	–/5 percent
Lake (versus restricted waterway)	+/10 percent	–/5 percent
Choppy Waters (versus calm waters)	–/5 percent	–/10 percent
Rough Waters (versus calm waters)	–/1 percent	–/10 percent
Very Rough Waters (versus calm waters)	–/1 percent	–/5 percent
Capsizing Accident (versus victim-falls-overboard)		–/5 percent
Swamping Accident (versus victim-falls-overboard)		–/1 percent
Collision Accident (versus victim-falls-overboard)		–/1 percent
Foggy (versus clear weather)		+/5 percent
Daytime (versus nighttime)		–/1 percent
Alcohol Involved in Accident		+/1 percent

Source: E. E.Anderson, and W. K. Talley. (1993). "Alcohol Involvement in Recreational Boating: Implications for Safety Regulation." *Applied Economics* 25: 1238.

of operator at fault in non-fatal accidents — alcohol involvement has the predicted positive sign and is highly significant. The same variables that were found to be significant in the fatal-accident results were also found to have a significant impact on the probability of operator at fault in non-fatal accidents. Operating a boat that is anchored or drifting versus cruising reduces the probability; the inexperience level of the operator being less than or equal to 100 boating hours versus greater than 500 boating hours increases the probability; the condition of the waterway being choppy, rough, or very rough versus calm reduces the probability. However, unlike the fatal accident results, the non-fatal accident results suggest that operating a boat in a river or lake versus a restricted waterway reduces (rather than increases) the probability of operator at fault.

A number of other hypothesized determinants were found to be significant beyond those found in the fatal-accident results (see Table 6.5). Operating a cabin motorboat versus an open motorboat reduces the probability that an operator will be at fault in a non-fatal accident. An increase in the number of people on board increases the probability; older operators reduce the probability; a capsizing, swamping, or collision accident versus a victim-falls-overboard accident reduces the probability; foggy versus clear weather increases the probability; and daytime versus nighttime reduces the probability.

Severity

"Alcohol use has long been suspected by the Coast Guard (as well as by state marine boating law authorities) of being a major factor in the number of recreational boating fatalities" (NTSB, 1983, p. 3). Does Anderson and Talley's (1993) operator-at-fault result related to alcohol involvement contradict this view? The answer is no if alcohol involvement increases the probability that an accident will be fatal without increasing the probability that an operator will be at fault in a fatal accident. Anderson and Talley (1993) investigated this hypothesis by using the same data as used in their operator-at-fault investigation to investigate determinants of the probability of a boating accident being fatal versus non-fatal. The hypothesized determinants were also the same as considered in their operator-at-fault investigation. The probit statistical technique and combined fatal and non-fatal accident data were used to estimate a linear probability model. In Table 6.6, hypothesized determinants that were significant at the 10 percent level or better and whether their effect on the probability of a fatal accident is positive or negative (denoted by plus (+) and minus (−) signs, respectively) are presented.

The result of primary interest found in Table 6.6 is that the hypothesized determinant — alcohol involved in accident — is positive and highly significant (that is, significant at the 1 percent level). This evidence thus suggests that alcohol involvement increases the probability that a boating accident will be fatal, thus supporting the view held by boating safety regulators that alcohol involvement is a cause of fatal boating accidents.

Rationale for Alcohol Involvement Results

Anderson and Talley's (1993, p. 1243) conclusions suggest that "alcohol involvement causes fatal boating accidents, but does not cause

TABLE 6.6
Accident-Severity (Fatal Versus Non-Fatal) Probability
Model: Probit Estimation Results

Hypothesized Determinant	Effect (+ or –)/ Significance Level
Motor Power (horsepower)	–/1 percent
Drifting (versus cruising)	+/1 percent
Age of Operator	+/1 percent
Operator Inexperience (≤100 hours versus >500 hours)	+/10 percent
Choppy Waters (versus calm waters)	–/10 percent
Strong Current Waters (versus calm waters)	+/5 percent
Capsizing Accident (versus victim-falls-overboard)	–/1 percent
Swamping Accident (versus victim-falls-overboard)	–/1 percent
Collision Accident (versus victim-falls-overboard)	–/1 percent
Alcohol Involved in Accident	+/1 percent

Source: E. E.Anderson, and W. K. Talley. (1993). "Alcohol Involvement in Recreational Boating: Implications for Safety Regulation." *Applied Economics* 25: 1241.

the operator to be at fault in fatal accidents." Rationale for this conclusion is found in the type of accident that increases the probability of a fatal accident without increasing the probability that the operator will be at fault in a fatal accident, that is, the type of accident — victim-falls-overboard.

The operator-at-fault results for fatal accidents (see Table 6.5) indicate that falls-overboard accidents do not increase the probability of the operator at fault in fatal accidents. This is revealed by the insignificance of the binary variables representing types of accidents — capsizing, swamping, and collision versus victim-falls-overboard. Alternatively, in the severity investigation (see Table 6.6), these binary variables were highly significant and negative — suggesting that falls-overboard accidents increase the probability of fatal accidents.

Anderson and Talley (1993) also investigated correlations (utilizing their data) between types of boating accidents (that is, capsizing, swamping, collision, and victim-falls-overboard) and alcohol involvement in these accidents. A positive correlation was found between victim-falls-overboard and alcohol involvement; the correlations between the remaining accident types and alcohol involvement were all negative. They conclude that the evidence suggests that it is alcohol consumption by victims falling overboard that explains how alcohol can cause fatal accidents without leading operators to cause fatal accidents.

SUMMARY

Since 1981, recreational boating accidents rank second behind motor vehicle accidents among U.S. transportation modes. The type of boating accident that incurs the greatest number of accidents is collision with another vessel, followed by collision with fixed object, capsizing, and falls-overboard, respectively. Capsizing accidents incur the greatest number of fatalities, followed by falls-overboard.

Boating safety regulators have long been concerned with alcohol involvement in recreational boating. In 1987 and 1988, 19.7 percent of fatal boating accidents involved alcohol, whereas 6.8 percent of non-fatal boating accidents involved alcohol. It is well known that alcohol affects human performance (for example, balance, risk-taking behavior, and choice reaction time). However, in boating, water interacting with alcohol is expected to compound alcohol's effect on human performance (for example, magnify the effects of caloric labyrinthitis and further impair an intoxicated swimmer's air supply).

The intent of anti-alcohol boating laws is to reduce boating accidents by reducing alcohol consumption by operators — thus, the implicit assumption that alcohol consumption by operators is a determinant of operators at fault in boating accidents. The evidence suggests that alcohol involvement is a determinant of the operator at fault in non-fatal accidents but not in fatal accidents. However, evidence also suggests that alcohol involvement increases the probability that a boating accident will be fatal — thus supporting the view held by boating safety regulators. Rationale for these conclusions are: falls-overboard accidents, which are positively correlated with alcohol involvement in boating accidents (unlike other accident types that are negatively correlated), increase the probability of fatal accidents but do not increase the probability that operators will be at fault in fatal accidents.

REFERENCES

Anderson, E. E., and W. K. Talley. (1993). "Alcohol Involvement in Recreational Boating: Implications for Safety Regulation." *Applied Economics* 25: 1233-1243.

National Transportation Safety Board. (1983). *Recreational Boating Safety and Alcohol.* Washington, DC: U.S. Government Printing Office.

Pindyck, R. S., and D. L. Rubinfeld. (1981). *Econometric Models and Economic Forecasts.* 2nd ed. New York: McGraw-Hill Book Company.

U.S. Coast Guard, U.S. Department of Transportation. (1991). *Boating Statistics 1990.* Washington, DC: U.S. Government Printing Office.

____. (1988). *Boating Statistics 1987*. Washington, DC: U.S. Government Printing Office.

U.S. Department of Transportation. (1988). *Alcohol in Fatal Recreational Boating Accidents*. Washington, DC: U.S. Government Printing Office.

7

Commercial Vessel Accidents

INTRODUCTION

In this chapter, we continue our discussion of water transportation accidents by addressing commercial vessel accidents. Commercial vessels provide for the commercial transport of freight and/or passengers. We begin with a discussion of U.S. commercial vessel accidents. Statistics include vessel accidents, vessel total and non-total losses, and accident fatalities and injuries over time. Accident statistics are classified by type of accident; fatalities and injuries are classified by type of accident and type of vessel. Then, safety standards and enforcement are addressed. Finally, we present determinants of the severity of tankship and oil barge accidents.

ACCIDENT STATISTICS

Among U.S. transportation accidents (see Table 1.1), commercial vessel accidents in 1981 ranked fourth behind motor vehicle, railroad, and recreational boating accidents (ranked first, second, and third, respectively). However, since 1984, the number of accidents for the two water transportation modes — recreational boating and commercial vessel — now rank second and third, respectively, among U.S. modal accidents (with motor vehicle accidents still ranked first).

The statistics in Table 7.1 suggest an upward trend in the number of U.S. commercial vessel accidents for fiscal years 1967–80; for the recent calendar years 1981–89, the number has remained relatively stable. These interpretations are borne out in the estimation of trend equations. In regressing vessel accidents of the fiscal years as a linear function of time (measured in years), a highly significant and positive relationship was found — on average, accidents increased by 223 per fiscal year. For the calendar years, no significant relationship was found between vessel accidents and time. Among the remaining vessel statistics found in Table 7.1, only two significant trends were found. For the fiscal years, a highly significant and positive relationship was found between the number of vessels involved in accidents that were non-total losses and time — on

TABLE 7.1
U.S. Commercial Vessel Accidents, Vessels Involved, Fatalities, and Injuries for U.S. Flagged Vessels in U.S. Waters

Year*	Accidents	Total Losses[a]	Non-Total Losses[a]	Fatalities[b]	Injuries[b]
1967	2,353	294	3,079	178	118
1968	2,570	341	3,670	140	89
1969	2,684	373	3,810	217	173
1970	2,582	348	3,715	178	105
1971	2,577	366	3,786	243	163
1972	2,424	309	3,808	177	110
1973	3,108	321	4,656	131	74
1974	3,388	362	5,051	199	104
1975	3,306	325	5,226	190	74
1976	4,211	446	6,704	269	153
1977	3,574	294	5,846	216	136
1978	4,268	220	6,898	179	119
1979	4,865	330	7,829	NA	118
1980	5,738	462	9,088	147	180
1981	3,858	393	5,035	99	145
1982	3,198	460	5,210	227	161
1983	3,727	391	5,512	262	143
1984	3,151	370	4,742	507	308
1985	3,387	401	5,259	146	169
1986	3,026	282	4,847	162	240
1987	3,128	285	5,171	154	361
1988	3,786	349	5,967	92	298
1989	3,693	462	5,144	82	219

NA (Not Available).
*Fiscal years 1967–80; calendar years 1981–89.
[a]By number of vessels.
[b]For commercial vessel accidents only.

Source: U.S. Coast Guard annual reports of vessel casualties for the years 1967–89.

average these vessel losses increased by 408 per fiscal year. For the calendar years, a significant (at the 10 percent level) and positive relationship was found between number of injuries and time — on average the number of injuries increased by 18 per calendar year.[1]

A commercial vessel accident may be one of several types (as classified by the U.S. Coast Guard). In a foundering, a vessel fills with water or is flooded. In a fire/explosion vessel accident, fire or explosion is the initiating event reported, except where the first event is a hull/machinery failure leading to the fire or explosion. A collision occurs when a vessel strikes or is struck by another vessel on the water surface, or strikes a stationary object. A grounding occurs when the vessel comes in contact with the waterway's bottom or a bottom obstacle. A hull/machinery damage accident is attributable to vessel material and equipment failure. The "other" accident classification includes missing vessels and various miscellaneous accidents.

From inspection of Table 7.2, we see that vessel accident types with the greatest number of accidents are groundings and hull/machinery damage. For 1983, 1984, 1988 and 1989, grounding accidents ranked first, followed by hull/machinery damage accidents. For 1985, 1986 and 1987, hull/machinery damage accidents ranked first, followed by groundings. For all years, collision accidents rank third.

Although accidents incurred by vessel groundings and hull/machinery damage are greater in number than that for other vessel accident types, they do not incur the greatest number of fatalities or injuries. From inspection of Table 7.3, we notice that foundering accidents rank first in number of fatalities for 1983–87; for 1988 and 1989, collisions had the

TABLE 7.2
U.S. Commercial Vessel Accidents: By Type of Accident

Type of Accident	1983	1984	1985	1986	1987	1988	1989
Foundering	315	263	416	356	165	241	273
Fire/Explosion	250	256	202	121	142	151	153
Collision	721	644	589	550	466	703	635
Grounding	1,149	904	902	734	911	1,294	1,117
Hull/Machinery Damage	838	728	1,027	1,066	1,017	817	880
Other	454	356	251	199	427	580	635
Total	3,727	3,151	3,387	3,026	3,128	3,786	3,693

Source: U.S. Coast Guard annual reports of vessel casualties for the years 1983–89.

greatest number of fatalities. Collision fatalities ranked second for 1983, 1985, 1986, and 1987 (excluding the "other" category) with fire/explosion fatalities ranking second in 1984 and foundering fatalities ranking second in both 1988 and 1989. Among injuries, collisions rank first for every year from 1983 through 1989 except for 1984, when fire/explosion injuries ranked first.

TABLE 7.3
Fatalities/Injuries of U.S. Commercial Vessel
Accidents: By Type of Accident

Type of Accident	1983	1984	1985	1986	1987	1988	1989
Foundering	196/11	258/6	72/21	69/19	76/6	24/8	24/19
Fire/Explosion	6/33	63/125	17/43	23/45	24/48	7/39	14/55
Collision	19/41	36/90	24/71	55/119	27/194	39/185	25/55
Grounding	5/9	14/2	8/12	3/9	6/9	5/10	2/24
Hull/Machinery Damage	11/17	6/23	5/12	4/42	3/83	1/47	7/42
Other	25/32	130/62	20/18	8/6	18/21	16/9	10/24
Total	262/143	507/308	146/169	162/240	154/361	92/298	82/219

Source: U.S. Coast Guard annual reports of vessel casualties for the years 1983–89.

Let us now relate commercial vessel fatalities and injuries to type of vessel. A noteworthy statistic (see Table 7.4) is that for every year, 1983–89, commercial fishing vessels incurred the greatest number of fatalities (excluding miscellaneous vessels). For this same time period, fishing vessels also rank first in number of injuries for every year except 1986 and 1987 (excluding miscellaneous vessels). In 1986, injuries on tug/towboat vessels ranked first; in 1987, injuries on passenger vessels ranked first.[2]

SAFETY STANDARDS AND ENFORCEMENT

The United States has long been among those nations with the highest maritime safety standards (Gracey, 1985). The U.S. commercial vessel safety program has evolved from congressional action following marine disasters. The U.S. Coast Guard, in turn, has implemented safety regulations based upon congressional mandate, its safety experience, and the safety experience of the marine community.

TABLE 7.4
Fatalities/Injuries of U.S. Commercial Vessel
Accidents: By Type of Vessel

Type of Vessel	1983	1984	1985	1986	1987	1988	1989
Freightship	34/9	4/5	5/6	10/10	0/10	0/10	0/11
Tankship	1/7	6/10	0/8	7/33	0/16	1/11	5/10
Passenger Vessel	1/15	5/22	4/26	10/37	12/170	0/50	8/44
Tug/Towboat	25/27	42/18	6/18	21/50	3/25	20/48	6/30
Fishing Vessel	94/29	56/33	79/56	64/35	80/32	53/66	51/54
Freight Barge	5/1	10/22	4/3	5/16	0/0	0/0	0/1
Tank Barge	9/14	10/13	5/9	16/27	0/20	0/1	0/3
Miscellaneous Vessels	93/41	374/195	43/43	29/32	59/88	18/112	12/68
Total	262/143	507/308	146/169	162/240	154/361	92/298	82/219

Source: U.S. Coast Guard annual reports of vessel casualties for the years 1983–89.

The worldwide maritime safety program has also evolved from government or regulatory action following marine disasters. A recent example relates to fire protection standards for cruise (or passenger) ships. In 1990, a disastrous fire swept through the cruise ship *Scandinavian Star* during a trip in the North Sea. Nearly 160 adults and children died from fire, smoke, and intense heat. Investigation of the accident found weak fire alarms, defective fire doors, and other equipment problems. As a consequence of this accident, the International Maritime Organization, the maritime safety agency of the United Nations, adopted sweeping new fire protection standards for ships carrying more than 36 passengers. New fire standards require existing ships to be retrofitted, starting in 1994, with a host of new fire safety-related equipment. By 1997, all existing ships must be equipped with smoke detectors, sprinklers, alarms, and other detection and extinguishing equipment (Adams, 1992). It should be noted, however, that these standards are voluntary for each member nation and the International Maritime Organization has no enforcement powers of its own.

Although there is a trend toward worldwide parity in commercial vessel safety standards, there are significant differences among nations in their enforcement of safety standards. "Disparities in enforcement do much more than economic damage — they serve to undermine the safety system" (Gracey, 1985, p. 10C). Worldwide classification societies (about 40) that certify ship safety have been accused of relaxing standards to win business in a depressed shipping market. Allegedly, some vessel operators (that is, shipowners) shop for societies that offer low classification rates and lax inspections. The societies (some dating back more than 200 years) inspect ships to ensure that vessels are seaworthy, that they meet national-flag requirements and conform to international safety standards. No underwriter will insure a ship if it is not classed.

Both the smallest and the largest classification societies have been criticized for lax safety inspections. In November 1986, the oil/ore (169,000 deadweight-ton) ship *Kowloon Bridge* was forced to take refuge in Bantry Bay, Southern Ireland, after structural faults were discovered during a storm.[3] The ship was classed as seaworthy by Lloyd's Register of Shipping despite fundamental design flaws (Journal of Commerce Staff, 1986). In 1984, the cruise ship *Sundancer* sank shortly after running aground off the coast of British Columbia. Just before the accident occurred, the ship had undergone an $85,000 inspection by the American Bureau of Shipping. Evidence suggests that an undetected construction flaw in converting the ship from a ferry to a luxury liner and not the grounding was the cause of the sinking (Abrams, 1992). The Lloyd's Register of Shipping and the American Bureau of Shipping are two of the four largest classification societies in the world; the remaining two are the Bureau Veritas of France and the Det Norske Veritas based in Norway.

In the past, marine insurers have only required a vessel to hold a classification certificate as evidence that it is safe. However, in December 1991, concern for the reliability of these certificates led London marine underwriters to begin their own inspections of ships they considered a high safety risk. Only 6 of the first 28 ships they inspected passed their safety inspection criteria — however, all 28 held classification certificates (Abrams, 1992).

ACCIDENT SEVERITY DETERMINANTS

Determinants of the extent of damage to commercial vessels involved in accidents (that is, vessel damage severity) have been investigated by Anderson and Talley (1993). Specifically, the study investigated vessel damage severity of tankship and oil barge accidents. Data include tankship and oil barge accidents reported by the U.S. Coast Guard for 1981–89. The number of tankship accidents totalled over 700, whereas the number of oil barge accidents in the data totalled over 2,000.

Hypothesized determinants of vessel damage severity include vessel safety investments, operating conditions, safety regulations, and type of accident. Vessel safety investments consist of actions by the operators (or carriers) to improve the safety of vessel service. These investments include hiring more experienced personnel and utilizing newer and larger vessels. Vessel operating conditions describe the environment in which vessel service is provided. These conditions are represented by the phase of vessel service (that is, whether the vessel was underway, docked, moored, or adrift at the time of the accident), type of waterway where the accident occurred (that is, coastal, inland, or ocean waterway), and weather/visibility characteristics. Weather characteristics include precipitation (that is, rain or snow versus no precipitation) and wind speed. Visibility is proxied by time of day — night versus day. Safety regulations are proxied by whether the vessel is U.S. versus foreign flagged (for tankships only, since all barges in the data are U.S. flagged). The type of accident is classified as a collision, fire-explosion, material-equipment failure, or grounding.

Two measures of vessel damage severity were considered: the occurrence of severe vessel damage (or non-seaworthiness) and real vessel damage cost per gross ton (of ship size). The non-seaworthiness variable was assigned a one if the seaworthiness of the vessel was not affected; set equal to two if the seaworthiness of the vessel was affected; and set equal to three if the vessel was a total loss in the accident. The linear probability model, where the probability of the non-seaworthiness of the vessel is expressed as a linear function of the above hypothesized determinants, was estimated by the probit statistical technique (Pindyck and Rubinfeld, 1981, pp. 280–287). With vessel damage severity measured as real vessel damage cost per gross ton, the vessel damage severity function was estimated by the Tobit statistical technique rather than by the linear regression technique. The former technique was used rather than the latter, since some of the observations for real vessel damage cost per gross ton were zero (Pindyck and Rubinfeld, 1981, p. 294).

In Table 7.5, hypothesized determinants of tankship damage severity that were significant at the 10 percent level or better and their effect on the measurement of vessel damage severity (that is, positive or negative as denoted by plus (+) and minus (–) signs, respectively) are presented. The results of both models suggest that collision, fire-explosion, and material-equipment failure tankship accidents are expected to result in greater vessel damage than grounding tankship accidents. Also, larger tankships are expected to incur less damage in accidents than smaller tankships (after adjusting for other factors), whereas adrift tankships are expected to incur greater damage in accidents than when they are docked or moored. The results of the Tobit model also suggest that tankship accidents on coastal and inland waterways are expected to incur less damage than in the ocean; night accidents are expected to incur less damage than day accidents; older tankships are expected to incur greater damage than newer tankships (other factors remaining the same).

TABLE 7.5
Tankship Damage Severity: Probit and Tobit Estimation Results

Hypothesized Determinant	Effect (+ or –)/Significance Level	
	Probit Model	Tobit Model
Coastal (versus ocean waterway)		–/5 percent
Inland (versus ocean waterway)		–/10 percent
Night (versus day)		–/5 percent
Collision Accident (versus grounding)	+/1 percent	+/1 percent
Fire-Explosion Accident (versus grounding)	+/1 percent	+/1 percent
Material-Equipment Failure Accident (versus grounding)	+/1 percent	+/1 percent
Age of Vessel		+/10 percent
Size of Vessel	–/5 percent	–/10 percent
Adrift (versus docked or moored)	+/5 percent	+/1 percent

Source: E. E.Anderson, and W. K. Talley. (1993). "Vessel Oil Spill Risk and Severity: Evidence from Tanker and Barge Accidents." Paper presented at the 1993 Annual Meeting of the Allied Social Science Associations, Anaheim, California, January 5–7.

In Table 7.6, hypothesized determinants of oil barge damage severity that were significant at the 10 percent level or better and their effect on the measurement of vessel damage severity (that is, positive or negative as denoted by plus (+) and minus (–) signs, respectively) are presented. Results of both the probit and Tobit models suggest that collision, fire-explosion, and material-equipment failure oil barge accidents are expected to result in greater vessel damage than grounding oil barge accidents (as for tankship accidents). Also, older oil barges (similar to older tankships) are expected to incur greater damage in accidents than newer barges. Further, barges that are adrift or underway are expected to incur less damage in accidents than when docked or moored (opposite from tankship accidents). In contrast to the tankship damage results, larger oil barges are expected to incur greater damage in accidents than smaller barges as well as greater damage at night than at day.

TABLE 7.6
Oil Barge Damage Severity: Probit and Tobit Estimation Results

	Effect (+ or –)/Significance Level	
Hypothesized Determinant	Probit Model	Tobit Model
Night (versus day)		+/5 percent
Collision Accident (versus grounding)	+/1 percent	+/1 percent
Fire-Explosion Accident (versus grounding)	+/1 percent	+/1 percent
Material-Equipment Failure Accident (versus grounding)	+/1 percent	+/1 percent
Age of Vessel	+/5 percent	+/10 percent
Size of Vessel	+/1 percent	
Adrift (versus docked or moored)	–/1 percent	–/1 percent
Underway (versus docked or moored)	–/1 percent	–/1 percent

Source: E. E.Anderson, and W. K. Talley. (1993). "Vessel Oil Spill Risk and Severity: Evidence from Tanker and Barge Accidents." Paper presented at the 1993 Annual Meeting of the Allied Social Science Associations, Anaheim, California, January 5–7.

SUMMARY

For fiscal years 1967–80, there was an upward trend in the number of U.S. flagged commercial vessel accidents in U.S. waters; for the calendar years 1981–89, the number has remained relatively stable. In recent years, the vessel accident types with the greatest number of accidents are grounding and hull/machinery damage. In contrast, vessel accident types with the greatest number of fatalities are generally foundering and collision; collisions also generally rank first in number of injuries. Among types of commercial vessels, fishing vessels generally rank first in number of fatalities and injuries.

Although there is a trend toward worldwide parity in commercial vessel safety standards, significant differences exist among nations in their enforcement of safety standards. The United States has long been a nation with relatively high maritime safety standards.

An investigation of determinants of the accident damage severity of tankships and oil barges suggests that collision, fire-explosion, and material-equipment failure accidents are expected to result in greater vessel damage than grounding accidents. Also, older vessels are expected to incur greater damage in accidents than newer vessels. Larger tankships are expected to incur less damage in accidents than smaller tankships. Conversely, larger oil barges are expected to incur greater damage in accidents than smaller barges.

NOTES

1. A discussion of the statistical technique, linear regression analysis — ordinary least squares — is found in the appendix to Chapter 2.

2. Freightships are self-propelled vessels that carry non-liquid cargo; alternatively, tankships are self-propelled vessels that carry liquid cargo. Passenger vessels are self-propelled and designed for the transport of passengers. Fishing vessels are self-propelled and designed for catching and the transport of fish and other water species. A towboat is a powerful shallow-draft vessel designed to push tow barges over inland waterways. A tugboat is a heavily powered vessel designed for towing various types of vessels. A barge is a flat bottom vessel with no self-propulsion. A freight barge carries non-liquid cargo, whereas a tank barge carries liquid cargo.

3. A vessel's deadweight tonnage is the number of tons of 2,240 pounds that it can hold.

REFERENCES

Abrams, A. (1992, July 8). "Cruise Ship Case Raises Doubts About Vessel Inspection Process." *Journal of Commerce*, pp. 1A,3A.

Adams, M. (1992, August 12). "Nations Move to Upgrade Safety Standards for Ocean Liners." *Journal of Commerce*, pp. 10B.

Anderson, E. E., and W. K. Talley. (1993). "Vessel Oil Spill Risk and Severity: Evidence from Tanker and Barge Accidents." Paper presented at the 1993 Annual Meeting of the Allied Social Science Associations, Anaheim, California, January 5–7.

Gracey, J. S. (1985, May 20). "Many Question Value of Drive for Vessel Safety Standards." *Journal of Commerce*, p. 10C.

Journal of Commerce Staff. (1986, November 20). "Ship Classing Under Pressure: Inspection Requirements Meet Growing Criticism." *Journal of Commerce*, pp. 1A, 20A.

Pindyck, R. S., and D. L. Rubinfeld. (1981). *Econometric Models and Economic Forecasts*. 2nd ed. New York: McGraw-Hill Book Company.

8

Railroad Accidents: Deterrent Policies and Other Observations

INTRODUCTION

Railroads have been of major importance in not only the transportation of goods, animals, and people but also the development of countries. The development of the United States is a good case in point, where the formation and growth of the West and the cattle industry were greatly dependent upon the railroads. Clearly, big business was centered around, or at least greatly tied to, the railroads in the United States at the end of the nineteenth and turn of the twentieth centuries. Scandals and business improprieties were also well known. The business environment established by such huge business enterprises as Standard Oil during the early days of railroads in the United States helped define a regulatory mood for the country along with a general legal environment that remains to this day.

The accidents and associated fatalities and injuries borne by railroad employees, passengers, and other victims were not insignificant. Unions became important in the latter part of the nineteenth century in American railroads. They were concerned with, among other things, attempting to establish safety in this dangerous, but essential, industry. The importance of railroads for the well-being of the nation assured their prominence in the business world. Nonetheless, as mentioned above, railroad accidents, injuries, and fatalities are not inconsequential. Table 8.1 provides a time-series of railroad fatalities and accidents for 1969–88. As can be seen readily, the bulk of fatalities are associated with grade crossing only. As portrayed in Table 8.1, fatalities on railroad only declined from 752 to 510 or 32.2 percent. Grade crossing only fatalities declined from 1,490 to 689 between 1969 and 1988. This is a 53.8 percent decline. One can readily see a convergence in the number of fatalities between those on railroad only and those at grade crossing only. In 1969, the ratio of fatalities at grade crossing only to on railroad only was 1.98 to 1 while in 1988 the ratio was 1.35 to 1. Overall, fatalities between 1969 and 1988 declined from 2,242 to 1,199 or 46.5 percent.

Railroad accidents, as seen from Table 8.1, have declined between 1969 and 1988 from 8,543 to 2,854 or 66.6 percent. Data on injuries,

TABLE 8.1
Railroad Fatalities and Accidents, 1969–88

Year	Fatalities			Accidents†
	Railroad Only*	Grade Crossing Only	Total	
1969	752	1,490	2,242	8,543
1970	785	1,440	2,225	8,095
1971	654	1,356	2,010	7,304
1972	685	1,260	1,945	7,532
1973	730	1,186	1,916	9,698
1974	689	1,224	1,913	10,694
1975	575	966	1,541	8,041
1976	510	1,174	1,684	10,248
1977	534	996	1,530	10,362
1978	582	1,064	1,646	11,277
1979	546	883	1,429	9,740
1980	584	833	1,417	8,451
1981	556	728	1,284	5,781
1982	512	607	1,119	4,589
1983	498	575	1,073	3,906
1984	598	649	1,247	3,900
1985	454	582	1,036	3,275
1986	475	616	1,091	2,620
1987	541	624	1,165	2,512
1988	510	689	1,199	2,854

*Fatalities resulting from train accidents, train incidents and nontrain incidents.
†Train accidents only — also includes those rail-highway grade crossing accidents that have been classified as train accidents.

Source: Research and Special Programs Administration. *Transportation Safety Information Report*. Various annual reports. Cambridge, MA: U.S. Department of Transportation, Transportation Systems Center, Center for Transportation Information.

provided in Table 8.2, also portray a reduction, declining from 74,126 in 1979 to 34,300 in 1985. This is a 53.7 percent reduction over the period. Unlike in the fatality case, most injuries are attributed to the railroad only situation as compared to grade crossing only injuries. The ratio of railroad only injuries to grade crossing only injuries declined from 15.93 to 1 in 1979 to 11.78 to 1 in 1985. Railroad only injuries declined between 1979 and 1985 from 69,748 to 31,617 or 54.7 percent while grade crossing only injuries declined from 4,378 to 2,683 or 38.7 percent over the same period.[1] One would like to address the determinants of these trends. For example, were deregulation, changes in modes of transporting freight, the use of longer trains, technological changes, and the introduction of new safety features instrumental in these apparent trends?

TABLE 8.2
Railroad Injuries, 1979–85*

Year	Railroad Only†	Grade Crossing Only	Total
1979	69,748	4,378	74,126
1980	58,356	3,890	62,246
1981	49,710	3,293	53,003
1982	37,638	2,637	40,275
1983	32,160	2,631	34,791
1984	35,660	2,910	38,570
1985	31,617	2,683	34,300

*Includes occupational illness.
†Includes train and nontrain data.

Source: Research and Special Programs Administration. *Transportation Safety Information Report*. Various annual reports. Cambridge, MA: U.S. Department of Transportation, Transportation Systems Center, Center for Transportation Information.

As previous chapters have demonstrated, there is a significant body of scholarly and academic literature investigating the determinants of accidents leading to injuries, fatalities, and destruction of property for most modes of transportation. The literature regarding these issues, as well as the impact of policy measures on accidents, is quite extensive when dealing with road transportation in particular. Such is not the case when dealing with railroads. Although there is not as extensive a set of scholarly research published in academic journals, the Federal Railroad

Administration compiles and published a great deal of data regarding rail accidents/incidents. (See, for example, Federal Railroad Administration, 1991a, 1991b.)[2]

Data reported include information on various types of accidents by state and by various possible contributing causes or descriptive categories associated with the accidents. For example, Federal Railroad Administration (1991a) provides, among many other statistics, a time-series of causes of train accidents. These causes are categorized as: human factors, mechanical and electrical failures, track defects, rail-highway crossing impacts, and other. In addition, the Federal Highway Administration conducts studies of highway-railroad safety. Included in these is an analysis of rail-highway crossings. (See Federal Highway Administration, 1989.) Here, descriptive statistics are used to examine various rail-highway accidents and to make policy suggestions. These recommendations relate to the use of at-grade warning devices and the promotion of public education and research to enhance safety. One recommendation is the installation of safety devices, such as flashing lights with gates, to help improve safety at public rail-highway crossings.

In addition to the evaluation of particular safety devices, the U.S. Department of Transportation has been instrumental in developing two procedures that estimate the expected number of accidents and casualties at crossings and then selects crossings for safety improvements, recommending the types of safety devices to be installed. These analytical methods are discussed at length in Federal Railroad Administration (1987). Nevertheless, a great number of federal publications dealing with railroad accidents are concerned with design and engineering issues associated with safety and benefit/cost studies dealing with the risks associated with, for example, transporting toxic material.

THE ACADEMIC LITERATURE REGARDING RAILROAD SAFETY

Very little has been published in academic journals (particularly economics journals) regarding the determinants of railroad accidents in the same manner as for motor vehicle accidents.[3] This does not suggest that academics have not addressed issues concerning the railroads. Winston (1985) provides a rather detailed survey of the literature dealing with the economics of transportation. None of the more than 270 citations appear to deal directly with transportation safety issues in

general, much less safety issues associated with railroads.[4] Rather, for
the most part, they are concerned with such issues as regulatory effects
on railway rates, the determinants of profitability, the effects of mergers,
and the demand for freight transportation.[5] Nevertheless, a few papers
have appeared dealing with safety issues and these are discussed below.

The Safety Literature

The importance of firemen in reducing railroad accidents was a point
of controversy between the railroads and the Brotherhood of Loco-
motive Firemen and Enginemen and the United Transportation Union.
Fisher and Kraft (1971) examine the effect of reducing the number of
firemen on railroad accidents. Employment of firemen (measured in
terms of fireman hours) was reduced by about half between 1963 and
1967 in response to Arbitration Award 282 in November 1963, which
was implemented in the spring of 1964.[6] Following the decline in
firemen employment, there was a substantial increase in accidents
(approximately a 50 percent increase between 1963 and 1967). Fisher
and Kraft examine this association given that other things were also
changing during this time period, making it difficult, just on this
information, to conclude that it was only the reduction of firemen
employed that resulted in the increase in accidents. To circumvent this
problem, Fisher and Kraft used a ratio model relating the ratio of
accidents after and before the implementation of the award to similar
ratios of fireman-to-engineer hours worked, gross ton-miles of traffic,
and a road composite-crew variable. The statistical analysis indicates
that a reduction in firemen results in a significant effect on the number of
collisions. However, Fisher and Kraft (1971, p. 492) also suggest that,
"To the extent that railroads act to offset this by running fewer, but
longer trains with full crews instead of the same number of trains with
smaller crews, they incur a significantly increased risk of derailment."

Golbe (1983), using regression analysis, investigates the need for
price regulation of railroads to reduce accident rates, measured in terms
of accidents per gross ton mile. Using data from 1963 to 1967 on Class I
railroads, Golbe (1983, p. 39) finds an inverse relationship between
accident rates and profitability; a possible positive (if any) relationship
between accidents and profitability when considering only profitable
railroads; and a positive relationship between accident rates and losses
when considering only unprofitable railroads.

Golbe (1983, p. 50) concludes that "so long as firms are not in financial difficulty, regulators need not worry much about safety. Higher prices may, in fact, lead to more accidents, not less." However, regarding unprofitable firms, the author advocates monitoring for the maintenance of safety standards. Golbe (1983, p. 51) concludes that, "If regulation is needed to ensure adequate safety levels, it is preferable to regulate safety directly rather than to rely on price controls."

Boyer (1989) examines fatality, injury, and accident trends for both the railroad and truck industries so as to evaluate the impact of deregulation on safety. More specifically, he examines the impact of the Motor Carrier Act of 1980 and the Staggers Act of 1980 on accidents. The Motor Carrier Act of 1980 deregulated the trucking industry, while the Staggers Act of 1980 did similarly for railroads. Boyer examines the impact of deregulation on safety and intermodal shifting of traffic. This analysis is more similar to other research endeavors reported for other modes of transportation in this volume in that it examines the particular effect of a given policy action on accidents.

Boyer indicates that from 1973 to 1984, the number of truck-involved fatalities (all carriers) had been fairly stable, varying between a low of 2,232 (in 1975) and a high of 3,072 (in 1979), while the number of truck-involved accidents varied between a low of 24,274 (in 1975) and a high of 36,854 (in 1984) (Boyer, 1989, pp. 261–262). Examining statistics for fatal train incidents in 1985, it is clear that most of such incidents result at rail-highway crossings (428 fatalities) and by being struck by locomotives, not at highways (355 fatalities).[7] As such, 95 percent of all fatal train incidents can be described as the aforementioned types (in 1985). Boyer recognizes that rail safety is not likely to be improved by deregulation given the predominance of rail-highway crossing incidents. Rather, Boyer notes, "In view of the importance of grade-crossing accidents, by changing the number of motor vehicles operating on highways, trucking deregulation may have had a more important impact on railroad safety statistics than railroad deregulation had on the same series" (1989, p. 263) Nevertheless, between 1975 and 1985, unlike in the truck case, there were major reductions in deaths (from 1,323 to 982), injuries (12,999 to 8,031), and accidents (19,818 to 10,848) due to train accidents and incidents (p. 266).

Examining various train accident and incident rates, Boyer finds a decline in accidents and incidents per billion ton-miles from 28.48 in 1976 to 12.38 in 1985, while rates measured in terms of million man-hours and million train miles did not decline as significantly. Thus, Boyer (1989, p. 265) speculates that "deregulation appears to have made railroads safer primarily by encouraging a reduction in employment and by causing fewer but heavier freight trains to be run."

Boyer calculates that transporting freight by railroad is much safer than by highway. He states that, "In terms of ton-miles, motor carrier transportation is between 4 and 75 times more likely to produce a fatality compared with the same ton carried on a railroad" (Boyer, 1989, p. 266). If deregulation then resulted in a shift from motor to rail, one would anticipate a reduction in fatalities, all else equal. This is not what was observed. Instead, Boyer finds an increase in the share of manufactured commodities shipped by truck due to a decline in the costs of trucking services. This resulted in an estimated increase of between 29 and 236 fatalities.

THE SAFETY-DEREGULATION RELATIONSHIP: SOME REGRESSION ESTIMATES

To examine the effect of deregulation further, we have estimated a simple model of the form:

$$Y_t = \beta_1 + \beta_2 \, \text{DEREG} + \beta_3 \, \text{TIME} + \varepsilon \tag{8.1}$$

for various measures of deaths, injuries, and accidents for both truck accidents (for the period 1973–84) and train accidents and incidents (for the period 1975 or 1976–85).[8] DEREG is a dummy variable accounting for the period of deregulation, TIME is a time trend, and ε is a random error term. We use the data provided by Boyer (1989). For truck accidents, the dependent variables were measured in terms of levels of deaths, injuries, and accidents (total, all carriers) for the period 1973–84 as well as in terms of per million truck miles and per billion ton-miles (for the same time period).[9] The coefficient associated with DEREG provides an estimate of the effect of deregulation on truck accidents. Only when the dependent variables are measured in terms of levels do we find significant coefficients associated with DEREG that are also negative. When the dependent variable is in terms of rates, the coefficient associated with DEREG is not significant and the sign of the coefficient is usually positive. Table 8.3 provides the regression results associated with levels of fatalities, injuries, and accidents for truck accidents.[10]

Similarly, regressions based on Equation 8.1 were estimated for train accidents and incidents. Data were obtained for the period 1975–85, when the dependent variables were measured in terms of levels, and for

TABLE 8.3
Regression Results on the Effect of Deregulation on
Truck Deaths, Injuries, and Accidents, 1973–84

Independent Variable	Dependent Variable		
	Deaths	Injuries	Accidents
Constant	−231,663.15	−2,004,743.6	−4,114,235.2
	(−2.28)*	(−2.34)	(−3.52)
TIME	118.56	1,029.11	2,095.96
	(2.31)	(2.38)	(3.54)
DEREG	−719.82	−7,468.28	−7,097.98
	(−2.43)	(−2.98)	(−2.38)
Durbin-Watson	1.37	1.47	1.15
Adjusted R^2	0.32	0.42	0.75
Estimation Technique†	CORC	CORC	CORC

*t-statistics are shown in parentheses.
†CORC is the Cochrane-Orcutt estimation procedure. One observation is lost when this procedure is employed.

Source: Estimated by the authors. Data from Boyer (1989).

the period 1976–85, when the dependent variables were measured as rates, that is, deflated by million man-hours, million train miles, and billion ton-miles. Unlike the case of motor carriers, the coefficients

TABLE 8.4
Regression Results on the Effect of Deregulation on Train Accidents and
Incidents, 1976–85

Independent Variable	Dependent Variable (per billion ton-miles)			
	Deaths	Deaths	Injuries	Accidents
Constant	125.63	97.97	2,150.57	3,914.32
	(3.51)*	(3.32)	(4.66)	(5.49)
TIME	-0.06	-0.05	-1.08	-1.96
	(-3.47)	(-3.26)	(-4.62)	(-5.45)
DEREG	-0.1	-0.19	-3.30	-4.43
	(-0.93)	(-2.25)	(-2.77)	(-2.29)
Durbin-Watson	2.90	2.5	1.83	2.23
Adjusted R^2	0.88	0.88	0.96	0.96
Estimation Technique†	OLS	CORC	CORC	CORC

*t-statistics are shown in parentheses.
†OLS is the Ordinary Least Squares Estimation Technique and CORC is the Cochrane-Orcutt estimation procedure. (One observation is lost when the Cochrane-Orcutt procedure is employed.)

Source: Estimated by the authors. Data from Boyer (1989)

associated with DEREG were consistently negative, regardless of whether the dependent variable was measured in terms of levels or rates. Table 8.4 presents the regressions associated with deaths, injuries, and accidents when deflated by billion-ton miles. These are the regressions that tend to have significant coefficients associated with DEREG.[11]

The regression models provide some evidence that deregulation may result in a reduction of fatality, injury, and accident rates when rates are measured in terms of billion-ton miles for the case of train accidents and incidents.

SOME CONCLUDING THOUGHTS

A dearth of scholarly research on railroad safety issues vis-à-vis is found for motor vehicle accidents in the economics (and economics/ transportation) literature.[12] Perhaps that may be attributed to problems associated with measurement, for example, defining accidents versus incidents, or a greater concern regarding the transportation of hazardous material. Alternatively, there may be only modest interest in addressing these issues as railroad specific problems, given that many railroad related fatalities involve, for example, automobiles, and these fatalities might then be addressed when investigating this other mode of transportation. However, there is a good deal of interest directed at reducing accidents by investing in safety devices, such as warning lights and gates. These issues are indeed well documented in federal documents and the engineering literature and are beyond the scope of this study. Nonetheless, these are issues that may prove of great value in reducing accidents and fatalities. In addition, a good deal of literature is available concerning the transportation of hazardous materials, designing containers, track design (geometry), and other engineering concerns. Once again, these issues are not investigated in this volume, but they are indeed important matters deserving attention.

In conclusion, the descriptive statistics show a marked decline in railroad fatalities between 1969 and 1988. Railroad injuries also declined substantially between 1979 and 1985. Railroad accident data also trend down between 1969 and 1988 but with the downward trend more noticeable between 1978 and 1988.

NOTES

1.   Caution should be used when comparing injury data with fatality data because injury data include occupational illness.

2.   The differences between accidents and incidents pertain to the amount of damage done to railroad on-track equipment. In addition, differences may arise regarding whether reportable deaths, injuries, or illness result (see Research and Special Programs Administration, 1989). More specifically, Research and Special Programs Administration (1989, p. 118) defines train accidents and train incidents as follows:

Train Accident — is a collision, derailment, fire, explosion, . . . , or other event involving operation of railroad on-track equipment which, while it does not necessarily result in a reportable death, injury, or illness, results in more than $4,900 in damages to railroad on-track equipment, signals, track, track structures, or roadbed. Prior to 1985, this threshold stood at $4,500; prior to 1983, at $3,700; prior to 1981, at $2,900; prior to 1979, at $2,300; prior to 1977, at $1,750; and prior to 1975, at $750.

Train Incident — is a collision, derailment, fire, explosion, . . . , or other event involving operation of railroad on-track equipment, which results in a reportable death, injury, or illness, but involves less than $4,900 in damages to railroad on-track equipment, signals, track, track structures, or roadbed. Prior to 1985, this threshold stood at $4,500; prior to 1983, at $3,700; prior to 1981, at $2,900; prior to 1979, at $2,300; prior to 1977, at $1,750; and prior to 1975, at $750.

3.   A substantial body of literature is available dealing with problems associated with, for example, the transportation of hazardous materials by railroads. See, for example, Barkan, Glickman, and Harvey (1991) and Mintz, Bertram, Saricks, and Rowland (1991). In addition, see Lerner, Ratte, and Walker (1990) for references pertaining to accidents at railroad-highway crossings.

4.   Based on the titles of the citations. In addition, the references cited by Moses and Savage (1989) further indicate the sparsity of scholarly literature on this issue.

5.   See Braeutigam (1993) for such a discussion on the effects of regulatory reform in the U.S. railroad industry.

6.   Arbitration Award 282 "permitted railroads to eliminate some fireman jobs." See Fisher and Kraft (1971, p. 471).

7.   See Boyer (1989, p. 243). Boyer (1989, p. 263) indicates the difference between train accidents and incidents is dependent upon "whether damage to railroad equipment exceeds a reporting threshold, which varies according to the price level and stood at $4,900 in 1985."

8.   Caution should be used when considering models like these in that specification errors, such as the omission of variables, may bias results.

9.   Chapter 4 provides further discussion of deregulation and trucking safety. Because of the shift of transporting freight from train to truck, we examine regressions for both modes of transportation here.

10.   Alexander (1992) uses cross-sectional state data for 1977, 1982, and 1987 to examine the effect of truck deregulation on rates of accidents, fatalities, injuries, and property damage. The rates are measured in terms of truck-miles travelled, as well as highway mileage. Alexander finds the coefficients associated with his dummy variable accounting for years deregulation is in effect were always negative and tend to be significant except in the case of accident rates. Data differences (pooled cross-sectional

significant except in the case of accident rates. Data differences (pooled cross-sectional versus time-series) along with differences in model specifications may account for discrepancies between the results reported here and those reported by Alexander.

11.   These models also had the highest R^2s and adjusted R^2s. One should note that comparison of models by the R^2 statistics should only be done when the models use identical dependent variables. See Pindyck and Rubinfeld (1991) on this.

12.   A good deal of literature does exist pertaining to other economic issues. See Winston (1985).

REFERENCES

Alexander, D. L. (1992). "Motor Carrier Deregulation and Highway Safety: An Empirical Analysis." *Southern Economic Journal* 59: 28–38.

Barkan, C. P. L., T. S. Glickman, and A. E. Harvey. (1991). "Benefit-Cost Evaluation of Using Different Specification Tank Cars to Reduce the Risk of Transporting Environmentally Sensitive Chemicals." *Transportation Research Record* 1313: 33–43.

Braeutigam, R. R. (1993). "Consequences of Regulatory Reform in the American Railroad Industry." *Southern Economic Journal* 59: 468–480.

Boyer, K. D. (1989). "The Safety Effects of Mode Shifting Following Deregulation." In Moses, L. N., and I. Savage (Eds.), *Transportation Safety in an Age of Deregulation* (pp. 258–276). New York: Oxford University Press.

Federal Highway Administration, Office of Highway Safety. (1989, April). *Rail-Highway Crossings Study — Report of the Secretary of Transportation to the United States Congress*. Washington, DC: U.S. Department of Transportation.

Federal Railroad Administration, Office of Safety Analysis. (1991a, July). *Accident/Incident Bulletin, No. 159, Calendar Year 1990*. Washington, DC: U.S. Department of Transportation.

____. (1991b, July). *Rail-Highway Crossing Accident/Incident and Inventory Bulletin, No. 13, Calendar Year 1990*. Washington, DC: U.S. Department of Transportation.

____. (1987, August). *Rail-Highway Crossing Resource Allocation Procedure, User's Guide*, 3rd ed. Washington, DC: U.S. Department of Transportation.

Fisher, F. M., and G. Kraft. (1971). "The Effect of the Removal of the Firemen on Railroad Accidents, 1962-1967." *The Bell Journal of Economics* 2: 471–494.

Golbe, D. L. (1983). "Product Safety in a Regulated Industry: Evidence from the Railroads." *Economic Inquiry* 21: 39–52.

Lerner, N., D. Ratte, and J. Walker. (1990, June). *Driver Behavior at Rail-Highway Crossings*. FHWA-SA-90-008. Washington, DC: U.S. Department of Transportation, Federal Highway Administration, Office of Highway Safety.

Mintz, M., K. Bertram, C. Saricks, and R. Rowland. (1991). "Hazardous Materials Emergencies in Railyards: Preparedness Guidance for Railroads and Adjacent Communities." *Transportation Research Record* 1313: 44–48.

Moses, L. N., and I. Savage (Eds.). (1989). *Transportation Safety in an Age of Deregulation*. New York: Oxford University Press.

Pindyck, R. S., and D. L. Rubinfeld. (1991). *Econometric Models and Economic Forecasts*. 3rd ed. New York: McGraw-Hill Book Company.

Research and Special Programs Administration. (1989, December). *Transportation Safety Information Report.* Cambridge, MA: U.S. Department of Transportation, Transportation Systems Center, Center for Transportation Information.

Winston, C. (1985). "Conceptual Developments in the Economics of Transportation: An Interpretive Survey." *Journal of Economic Literature* 23: 57–94.

9

Improving Transportation Safety: Lessons Learned

INTRODUCTION

While in previous chapters we examined transportation safety from the perspective of individual modes, in this concluding chapter we take a multimodal approach to the subject. We begin by summarizing and comparing findings on the determinants of safety for the various transportation modes considered in this book. Then we discuss research results on the relationship between safety and deregulation across the modes. We conclude by discussing issues pertaining to cross-modal policies for improving transportation safety.

DETERMINANTS OF TRANSPORTATION SAFETY: A CROSS-MODAL COMPARISON

Because transportation safety cannot be observed directly and a decrease in unsafe travel represents an improvement in safety, measures of unsafe travel have been used as proxies for transportation safety. In this book, we focused on outcome proxies for unsafe travel that were accident related. They included accidents, accident risk, and accident severity. Accidents were measured by counts of accidents, injuries, or fatalities; accident risk was approximated by accident measures standardized for levels of transportation activity; and accident severity was calculated by the extent of human injury or vehicle damage sustained in accidents.

In previous chapters, we reported research findings on the determinants of accident-related outcomes separately for the following modes: motor vehicles, trucks, aircraft, recreational boating, commercial vessels, and railroads. Our intent here is to summarize and compare findings for the various modes drawn from two methodological approaches: accident investigation and statistical inference. To ensure consistency across modes in information from the former methodological approach, we provide investigative findings from one source, the National Transportation Safety Board (NTSB). The results reported from the statistical inference approach were significant at a level of 10 percent or better in statistical studies cited in previous chapters.

Table 9.1 provides a tabular summary of the determinants of accident-related outcomes. The information is categorized by both mode and determinant factor category. The determinant factor categories include: driver, vehicle, way/travel/environmental, firm characteristics, policy, and other. Driver factors include descriptive characteristics of vehicle operators (for example, gender and age) as well as personal circumstances and choices likely to have a bearing on driver performance (for example, driving experience, health, alcohol use, and vehicle speed). Vehicle factors include physical characteristics (for example, size) and operating characteristics (for example, mechanical defects) of vehicles. Way/travel/environmental factors include characteristics of the way (for example, location and type), travel conditions (for example, volume of travel and traffic density), and environmental circumstances (for example, weather and lighting). Firm characteristics account for practices (for example, safety management decisions) and descriptive aspects (for example, size) of for-hire transportation carriers. Policy factors include governmental policies initiated to improve transportation safety. Other factors include considerations not accounted for in the previous categories.

Two types of determinants are accounted for: causes and deterrents. Causes are factors that increase accident-related outcomes, while deterrents decrease these outcomes. In Table 9.1, some determinants are followed by plus (+) and/or minus (–) in parentheses. A plus indicates a causal factor that was found to have a statistically significant positive relationship with one or more of the accident-related measures — accidents, accident risk, and accident severity — in at least one of the studies surveyed in this book.[1] Any factor followed by minus is a deterrent that had a significant negative association with one or more of the accident-related measures in at least one of the surveyed studies. In addition, the figure in square brackets reveals the percentage of accident

TABLE 9.1
Determinants of Transportation Accidents, Accident Risk, and/or Accident Severity by Mode

Determinant Category[a]	Motor Vehicle	Truck[b]	Aviation[c]
Driver factors	Alcohol use (+)	Impairment due to fatigue [30.8%]	Pilot error [77.2%]
	Male drivers (+)	Impairment due to drugs [21.1%]	Pilot age (+)
	Young drivers (+/–)	Misjudgement of safe speed [13.5%]	Pilot experience (–)
	Elderly drivers (+/–)	Impairment due to alcohol [11.9%]	Pilot utilization (+)
	Speed (+)	Physical incapacitation [10.3%]	
	Speed variance (+)	Failure to yield, perceive, observe [7.0%]	
		Unsafe movement [5.9%]	
		Driver inexperience [4.9%]	
		Disregard of warnings or signs [2.7%]	
		Driving time (+)	
		Speed (+)	
		Speed variance (+)	
Vehicle factors	Vehicle size (–)	Occupant protection [36.8%]	Equipment failure [19.3%]
	Vehicle age (+)	Mechanical/maintenance [5.9%]	Maintenance [5.3%]
	Truck activity (+)	Conspicuity [4.9%]	Stall warning system installed (–)
	Mandated safety features (–)	Brake adjustment/deficiencies [4.3%]	
		Load/load shift/center of gravity [2.7%]	
		Bobtail (versus single or double) (+)	
		Defective equipment (+)	

Table 9.1, continued

Determinant Category[a]	Motor Vehicle	Truck[b]	Aviation[c]
Way/travel/ environmental factors	Interstate highways (–) Urban highways (–) Volume of travel (+) Urban density (+) Rural density (–) Overall density (+/–) Snow (–) Precipitation (–) Temperature (+) Altitude x alcohol (+)	Signs, roadways, environmental [11.9%] Traffic density (+) Police enforcement (–) Rain (+) Snow (–) Rural highways (+) Limited access highways (–) Night (+)	Weather[45.6%] Traffic control [24.6%] Airport facilities [3.5%] Number of air traffic controllers (–) Occurrence at night (+) Visual flying conditions exist (–)
Firm characteristics		Safety management practices (+/–) Owner-operator use (+) Driver turnover/inexperience (+) Average length of haul (–) Carrier size (–) Carrier financial strength (–) Carrier age (+/–) Private carriage (–) Commodity operations (+/–)	Commuter (versus certificated) airline (+) Profitability(–)
Policy factors	Vehicle inspection (–) Seat belt laws (+/–) Minimum legal drinking age (–)	Roadside inspection (–)	
Other factors	Accident cost (–)	Trucking deregulation (–)	Airline deregulation (–)

194

Determinant Category[a]	Recreational Boating	Commercial Vessel	Railroad
Driver factors	Alcohol involvement (+) Operator age (+) Operator inexperience (+)		Income (+/–) Fuel price (+/–) Economic activity (+) Hospital access (–)

Vehicle factors	Horsepower (–)	Age of vessel (+)
		Size of vessel:
		  Tankship (–)
		  Oil barge (+)	

Way/travel/environmental factors	Drifting (versus cruising) (+)
	Choppy (versus calm) waters (–)
	Strong current (versus calm waters) (+)
		Coastal (versus ocean) waterway (–)
		Inland (versus ocean) waterway (–)
		Adrift (versus docked or moored):
		  Tankship (+)
		  Oil barge (–)
		Underway (versus docked or moored) (–)
		Night (versus day):
		  Tankship (–)
		  Oil barge (+)	

Table 9.1, continued

Determinant Category[a]	Recreational Boating	Commercial Vessel	Railroad
Firm characteristics			Profitability (+/−)
Other factors	Capsizing (versus victim-falls-overboard) accident (−) Swamping (versus victim-falls-overboard) accident (−) Collision (versus victim-falls-overboard) accident (−)	Collision accident (versus grounding) (+) Fire explosion accident (versus grounding) (+) Material-equipment failure accident (versus grounding) (+)	Number of firemen (−) Rail deregulation (−)

[a]In parentheses to the right of a determinant, a "+" ("−") indicates that the factor was found to have a significant direct (inverse) relationship with a measure of accidents, accident risk, or accident severity in at least one statistical study.

[b]For trucks, the figure in square brackets to the right of a determinant indicates the percentage of cases the determinant was a causal or contributing factor in 182 driver-fatal large truck accidents investigated by the NTSB between October 1, 1987, and September 30, 1988. Computed from information provided in NTSB (1990).

[c]For air carriers, the figure in square brackets to the right of a determinant indicates the percentage of cases in which the determinant was a contributing factor in 59 fatal accidents of U.S. certificated airlines investigated by the NTSB during 1965–86. Computed from information provided in Morrison and Winston (1988).

Source: Compiled by the authors.

cases investigated by the NTSB in which the determinant was present. The NTSB investigation results reported here pertain to trucks and aircraft. Results for trucks, drawn from NTSB (1990), correspond to investigations of 182 driver-fatal medium/heavy truck accidents in the United States between October 1, 1987, and September 30, 1988. Investigation findings on aircraft, drawn from Morrison and Winston (1988), correspond to 59 fatal accidents of U.S. certificated airlines during 1965–86.

Driver Factors

Gender

The percentage of licensed drivers who are male has been found to have a significant direct relationship with motor vehicle death measures. This finding may be attributable to gender-based differences in the circumstances, time, and location of driving. However, it may also reflect greater risk taking on the part of male drivers.

Age

With some exceptions, proxies for youthful and elderly driving have been reported to have significant direct linkages with motor vehicle death measures. Furthermore, exposure-based accident rates indicate that both young and elderly motorists are overinvolved in intersection accidents of motor vehicles. Greater inclination to take risks may partly account for the results for young drivers. Deterioration in eyesight, reflexes, and other factors that directly affect driving performance is a likely reason for elderly drivers' overinvolvement in accidents.

As in motor vehicle crashes, driver age is an important factor in accidents involving aircraft and recreational boats. Pilot and operator ages have been found to have significant direct relationships with the severity of aircraft damage and the probability that a boating accident will be fatal (versus non-fatal), respectively.

Alcohol and Drug Use

There is strong evidence that alcohol use is a cause of motor vehicle and boating accidents. Proxies for driver intoxication have been found to have significant positive associations with highway fatality measures. Impairment due to alcohol was a factor in nearly 12 percent of the truck accidents investigated by the NTSB. It has been reported that alcohol involvement significantly increases the likelihood that a boating accident will result in fatalities.

Drug use is a contributing factor in truck accidents. Impairment due to drugs was cited in more that one-fifth of the truck accidents investigated by the NTSB.

Fatigue

Apparently, operator fatigue is a major cause of truck crashes, and it influences the extent of aircraft accident damage. Impairment due to fatigue was found in more than 30 percent of the NTSB truck accident investigations. Also, other estimates indicate that the likelihood of a truck accident increases with driving time. Pilot utilization — measured by landings by a pilot during the last 90 days — has been found to have a significant positive relationship with the severity of aircraft accident damage.

Experience

Evidence pertaining to accidents involving trucks, aircraft, and boats indicate that driver experience has a beneficial impact on travel safety. Driver inexperience was identified as a causal or contributing factor in about 5 percent of the truck accidents investigated by the NTSB. Pilot experience has been found to have a significant negative linkage with the severity of aircraft accident damage. A significant direct relationship has been reported between operator inexperience and the probability that a recreational boating accident is fatal (versus non-fatal).

Health

Driver health problems can be a causal or contributing factor in trucking accidents. The NTSB found evidence of physical incapacitation in more than 10 percent of the truck crashes it investigated.

Speed and Speed Variance

Evidence suggests that speed and speed variance are factors in motor vehicle accidents. Measures of both have been found to have significant direct relationships with motor vehicle fatality measures and truck accident rates.

Driver Error

Operator error can lead to transportation accidents. The NTSB documented several trucker mistakes committed in the truck accidents it investigated: misjudgment of safe speed (present in 13.5 percent of the cases); failure to yield, perceive, observe (7.0 percent); unsafe movement (5.9 percent); and disregard of warnings or signs (2.7 percent). In the certificated-airline accidents that it studied, the NTSB found that pilot error was the most frequent causal factor (in 77.2 percent of the cases).

Vehicle Factors

Size

Evidence for some modes suggests that, on balance, greater vehicle size has a lifesaving effect. For example, studies have found a significant negative association between size — approximated by weight — and various motor vehicle fatality measures. Also, for recreational boating a significant negative relationship has been reported between horsepower and the probability of a fatal (versus a non-fatal) accident.

In commercial vessel accidents, the relationship between size and the extent of damage varies by vessel type. Findings indicate a significant negative relationship between vessel size and tankship damage severity, but they reveal a significant positive linkage between size and oil barge damage severity.

Age

There is evidence that older vehicles are less safe than newer ones. Studies have found that vehicle age has a significant direct association with various motor vehicle death rates. The extent of vehicle accident damage also appears to depend on age. It has been reported that age of vessel has a significant positive relationship with damage severity for both tankships and oil barges.

Mechanical Defects

Accident investigations have identified that mechanical problems sometimes exist in both trucks and planes that crash. The NTSB found mechanical or maintenance problems in 5.9 percent of the cases and brake problems in 4.3 percent among the truck accidents examined. It discovered that equipment failure and maintenance were contributing factors in 19.3 percent and 5.3 percent, respectively, of the fatal accidents of certificated airlines that were investigated. Other research on trucking firms has found that the percent of accidents resulting from defective equipment has a significant direct relationship with accident rate.

Safety Features

There is evidence that certain vehicle safety features have enhanced transportation safety. For example, the consensus among statistical studies is that federally mandated automobile safety features have had a net lifesaving effect. Also, the installation of stall warning systems has been found to have a significant negative relationship with the severity of aircraft damage in accidents and incidents involving certificated and commuter airlines. The NTSB found that occupant protection (for example, seat belts and crashworthiness of truck cabs) was the factor most often present (36.8 percent of the time) in the truck accidents it investigated. This factor was not identified as a cause of these accidents. Rather, it was found to have a bearing on accident survivability.

Other Vehicle Factors

The NTSB noted that additional vehicle-related factors were sometimes present in the truck accidents it investigated. These included conspicuity (a factor in 4.9 percent of the crashes) and load/load shift/center of gravity (2.7 percent).

The mix of vehicles is a consideration in highway safety. A number of studies have found a significant direct relationship between truck activity and highway death measures. Type of truck is another relevant factor suggested by the finding that truck-tractors with no trailer (bobtails) have significantly higher accident rates than tractors pulling either one trailer (singles) or two trailers (doubles).

Way/Travel/Environmental Factors

Type of Way

Evidence suggests that interstate highways are safer than other types of roadways. Studies have reported that the relative amount of travel on interstate highways has a significant negative relationship with measures of total or vehicle-occupant deaths. This is probably attributable to special design features (for example, wide shoulders, limited access, divided highways) of interstate roadways. Consistent with the findings on the relative safety of interstates, it has been reported that the accident risk of truck-tractors is significantly lower on limited access highways than on major arteries and other roads.

Location of Way

Location is a distinguishing characteristic in highway travel safety. Studies have reported that the proportion of travel on urban highways has significant inverse associations with total and occupant motor vehicle fatality measures and a significant direct linkage with nonoccupant deaths. The lower total and occupant death rates on urban roadways are due at least partly to differences in urban and rural travel. For example, there are typically lower speeds and more commuter travel on urban highways than on rural highways. More nonoccupants are killed in urban settings because of the greater concentration of such individuals in these locations. Urban roads are apparently safer than rural roads for truck-tractors because the accident risk for these trucks has been estimated to be significantly higher in rural rather than in urban settings.

Location also appears to be a factor in the severity of water vessel accidents. Tankship damage severity has been found to be significantly less on both coastal and inland waterways than on the ocean.

Craft/Way Movement Characteristics

Movement characteristics of the craft or way appear to affect the safety of water travel. For example, drifting (versus cruising) has been found to have a significant positive relationship with the probability of a recreational boating accident being fatal (versus non-fatal). In addition, this probability has been found to be directly related to the presence of strong current (versus calm current) waters.

It has been reported that being adrift (versus docked or moored) has a significant positive relationship with tankship damage severity and a significant negative association with oil barge damage severity. Being underway (versus docked or moored) has been found to have a significant negative linkage with oil barge damage severity.

Traffic Density

Researchers have analyzed the relationship between traffic density and motor vehicle accident measures. Overall density has been found to have both positive and negative significant associations with total motor vehicle deaths. It has been reported as having a significant direct linkage with truck accident rates. Analysis of locational congestion measures has revealed that urban and rural driving densities have significant positive and negative relationships, respectively, with total highway deaths.

Volume of Traffic

Evidence for one mode indicates a direct association between accident-related outcomes and the amount of travel. Many studies have reported significant positive linkages between proxies for travel volume and measures of motor vehicle deaths.

Traffic Supervision

There is evidence for various modes that traffic supervision activities can enhance transportation safety. For example, a measure of police enforcement has been found to have a significant negative relationship with truck accident rates. The NTSB found that air traffic control problems were contributing factors in nearly one-fourth of the fatal certificated airline crashes investigated. Consistent with this latter finding, it has been reported that the number of air traffic controllers has a significant inverse association with certificated airline accidents.

Weather

There is evidence that unfavorable weather conditions (for example, precipitation and colder temperatures) have lifesaving effects on highways, possibly by discouraging travel. Motor vehicle death rates have been found to have significant inverse associations with both snowfall and precipitation. In addition, they have been reported as having a significant positive linkage with average temperature. Snowfall has also been reported to be negatively related to truck accident rates, although rain has been found to have a direct linkage with these rates.

Unfavorable weather also appears to have a beneficial impact in terms of the severity of boating accidents. The existence of choppy (versus calm) waters has been found to have a significant inverse relationship with the probability that a boating accident is fatal versus non-fatal.

While adverse weather is an apparent deterrent of accidents or accident severity for motor vehicles and boats, it is a major causal factor in aircraft accidents. The NTSB found weather to be a contributing factor in nearly half of the fatal accidents of certificated carriers it investigated.

Lighting/Visibility

Better lighting or visibility conditions appear to enhance truck and air travel safety, but their impact on commercial vessel accident damage severity varies with the type of craft. Truck-tractor accident risk has been found to be significantly higher at night than during the day. For accidents and incidents involving certificated and commuter airlines, a significant positive relationship has been reported between occurrence at night and severity of aircraft damage. In addition, the extent of aircraft damage has been found to have a significant negative association with the existence of visual flying conditions. For commercial vessel accidents, it has been reported that occurrence at night has a significant negative linkage with tankship damage severity and a significant positive relationship with oil barge damage severity.

Altitude

Altitude is a consideration in highway safety. Its interaction with alcohol consumption has been found to have a significant direct association with motor vehicle fatalities.

Firm Characteristics

The relationship of accident-related measures to firm characteristics has been studied for trucks, aircraft, and railroads. Certain trucking firm practices appear to adversely affect safety. For example, accident rates for trucking firms have been found to have significant direct associations with owner-operator use, driver turnover, and carriage of certain commodities (for example, general freight and hazardous materials). Other carrier practices in trucking apparently enhance safety. For instance, accident rates have been significantly and negatively linked to average length of haul, carrier financial strength, private carriage, and carriage of certain commodities (for example, agricultural goods). There are mixed results regarding the safety impact of some trucking firm practices. Safety management practices and carrier age have been found to have significant direct and inverse relationships with carrier accident rates.

Type of carrier is an important consideration in aircraft accidents. The severity of aircraft accidents, both in terms of passenger and crew injuries and aircraft damage, has been found to be significantly higher for commuter airlines than for certificated airlines. Regarding the role of carrier financial strength in air safety, there have been findings of a significant negative association between profitability and airline accident rates.

Evidence on the relationship between accident rates and profitability for railroads is mixed. Statistically significant positive and negative linkages have been reported.

Policy Factors

Programs and laws have been implemented with the intent of improving transportation safety. Evidence suggests that some have been successful in accomplishing this objective. For example, although there are some exceptions, several findings indicate that motor vehicle inspection programs and seat belt laws have led to significant reductions in motor vehicle deaths and injuries. Evidence of a significant negative relationship between roadside inspections and trucking accidents has also been reported.

Evidence on the safety benefits of some policies is inconsistent. For example, while some studies have found that raising the Minimum Legal Drinking Age has contributed to significant reductions in motor vehicle fatality rates, other research findings suggest that experience with alcohol may have a more important impact on these rates. The latter results lead some to conclude that imposing a higher Minimum Legal Drinking Age merely postpones accidents to an older age profile of drivers. Another policy of questionable safety effects is the program of increased safety audits of trucking firms, which began in 1986. One study has concluded that this program has not led to lower accident rates in the trucking industry.

Other Factors

Factors besides those just discussed have been found to have statistically significant relationships with accident-related measures. For example, accident cost, long-run income, and hospital access are inversely linked to motor vehicle death measures; short-run income and the level of economic activity are directly related to measures of highway fatalities; the association between fuel price and motor vehicle death measures is positive in some studies and negative in others; the number of firemen has a negative association with rail collisions; type of water accident has a bearing on accident severity. Regarding the latter, victim-falls-overboard is more severe than the other types of recreational boating accidents; accident types besides grounding have more severe tankship and oil barge damage.

THE DEREGULATION-SAFETY RELATIONSHIP

In the United States, airlines were deregulated with passage of the Airline Deregulation Act of 1978; railroads were deregulated with passage of the Railroad Revitalization and Regulatory Reform Act of 1976 and the Staggers Rail Act of 1980; truck carriers were deregulated with passage of the Motor Carrier Act of 1980; ocean carriers were deregulated with passage of the Shipping Act of 1984. There has been public concern that economic deregulation might result in a deterioration in transportation safety. Findings reported in this book suggest that there has not been a decline in safety under deregulation. In fact, it appears that the opposite has occurred. For trucks, aircraft, and railroads, there have been statistically significant declines in accident-related measures under deregulation. While these results do not necessarily imply that deregulation caused an improvement in safety, at a minimum, they suggest that the removal of economic restrictions has not completely offset the forces responsible for safety improvements. However, the possibility that safety may have meliorated even more without deregulation cannot be dismissed. Additional statistical analysis is needed to determine whether the overall level of safety would be greater with or without deregulation.

CROSS-MODAL POLICY CONSIDERATIONS

Should a policy that enhances safety in one transportation mode be adopted in other modes as well? Two important considerations in responding to this question are effectiveness and cost. Particular safety policies may not be equally effective across modes. Policies that may be highly effective in various modes might be unwarranted in some instances because of prohibitively high costs.

The importance of effectiveness in cross-modal safety policies is demonstrated by the issue of operator use of alcohol. It is well documented that alcohol consumption impairs operator performance. One would expect that policies that reduce operator use of alcohol would be safety enhancing. However, strategies that effectively accomplish this in some modes might be considerably less successful in others. For example, strict drunk-driving laws or wide promotion and use of designated drivers who agree to remain sober may effectively reduce alcohol-related motor vehicle accidents and fatalities. Such strategies might also cause recreational boat operators to abstain from alcohol use. However, they may not be as effective in reducing accidents on this latter mode as in motor vehicles, because recreational boat passengers still risk falling overboard when they become intoxicated. Thus, the effectiveness of a particular strategy in achieving greater safety may vary greatly across modes.

The importance of cost considerations in deciding whether to adapt a successful safety program in one mode to another mode is demonstrated by the policy of vehicle inspection. Evidence cited in this book suggests that automobile and truck inspection programs reduce accidents. Implementing similar programs in other modes, such as recreational boating, may enhance safety in those modes as well. However, it would need to be determined whether the programs are cost effective (that is, whether the benefits of such programs exceed the costs, both direct and indirect). Such a determination could be provided by statistical and economic studies. A lack of cost effectiveness provides a strong rationale for not adopting a policy.

To help identify potential cross-modal safety policies, it is informative to note accident determinants that have similar effects across modes. Operator experience with a given mode appears to be one such factor. Driver experience has been found to have a beneficial impact on travel safety in the truck, aircraft, and recreational boating modes. Policy measures requiring training, perhaps using computer simulations, may serve as an effective method to enhance driver experience.

Driver experience with alcohol has been suggested to have an important effect on motor vehicle accidents. Such a phenomenon has not been studied in the other modes but might be a relevant consideration there as well. In any case, educating operators on alcohol's effect on driving skills may mitigate the impact of inexperience with the use of alcohol.

Evidence reported in this book suggests that operator fatigue is a major factor in truck and aircraft crashes. We would anticipate that operator fatigue plays a similar role in accidents of other modes. Drivers of large trucks and pilots of commercial aircraft are already subject to certain restrictions on the duration of operating time. However, verification that such restrictions are adhered to may be problematic. Technological improvements (for example, smaller computers) might aid in monitoring for compliance with these regulations.

In conclusion, a policy that enhances safety in one mode becomes a candidate for adaptation in other modes. Before the policy is applied to other modes, its potential effectiveness in the new settings must be determined. This requires determination of whether the factors of concern operate similarly across modes. The costs associated with the policy must also be estimated and compared to the projected benefits. These concerns suggest the basis for future investigation.

NOTE

1.   Naturally, alternative criteria can be used in identifying the importance of factors (for example, weighting the results of various studies). However, such evaluations are beyond the scope of this book.

REFERENCES

Morrison, S. A., and C. Winston. (1988). "Air Safety, Deregulation, and Public Policy." *The Brookings Review* 6: 10–15.

National Transportation Safety Board. (1990). *Safety Study: Fatigue, Alcohol, Other Drugs, and Medical Factors in Fatal-to-the-Driver Heavy Truck Crashes* (Vol. I). NTSB/SS-90/01. Washington, DC: National Transportation Safety Board.

Subject Index

accident(s): approaches in investigating determinants of, 7; causes of, 6, 192; definition of, 3; deterrents of, 6, 192; by mode, 2–3, 4–5. *See also* type of accident

accident cost: for air accidents, 139–41; for motor vehicle accidents, 17–18, 204

accident statistics: for air accidents, 130–33; for commercial vessels, 169–72; for motor vehicles, 9–13; for railroads, 179–82; for recreational boating, 153–57; for trucks, 86, 87

age as factor: in motor vehicle accidents, 23–25, 197; in transportation accidents, 197; in truck accidents, 91

agricultural carriers, accident risk for, 111

air accidents, 127–49; analytical perspective on determinants of, 144–46; costs of, 139–41; and deregulation, 36, 130–39; driver factors in, 193, 197; firm characteristics in, 194; inspection perspective on determinants of, 142–44; measures of unsafe air travel, 127–30; safety of commuter versus certificated airlines, 145–46; severity of unsafe air occurrences, 146–47; vehicle factors in, 193; way/travel/environmental factors in, 194

aircraft accident, definition of, 128

aircraft damage: categories of, 146; factors relating to, 147

aircraft incident, 128

aircraft manufacturers, stock market value of, and aircraft accidents, 141

airline demand, 140

airline deregulation: impact on motor vehicle accidents/fatalities, 36; market forces and safety, 133–37; new entrants, congestion, and safety, 137–39; safety statistics under, 130

Airline Deregulation Act (1978), 1, 130, 204

airlines, costs to, for air accidents, 139–41

airport congestion, and airline deregulation, 138–39

air taxi carriers: accident rates for, 132; definition of, 149n

alcohol consumption: and boating accidents, 158–60, 162–65, 205; and minimum legal drinking age, 60–65, 204; and motor vehicle accidents,

Name Index

ABOUT THE AUTHORS

Peter D. Loeb is a professor of economics at Rutgers University, Newark. Dr. Loeb has published extensively on transportation safety issues and applied econometrics. He has authored and co-authored articles that appeared in various journals including *The American Economic Review*, the *Journal of Transport Economics and Policy*, *Econometrica, Accident Analysis and Prevention*, and the *Southern Economic Journal*. He is also co-author of *The Stat Tutor* and co-editor of *Essays in Regional Economic Studies*.

Wayne K. Talley is a professor of economics, holding the designation of Eminent Scholar, at Old Dominion University. Dr. Talley has written extensively on a number of transportation issues and is the author or co-author of *Introduction to Transportation, Transport Carrier Costing*, and *Ocean Container Transportation: An Operational Perspective*.

Thomas J. Zlatoper is an associate professor of economics at John Carroll University and a research associate at the Center for Regional Economic Issues, Case Western Reserve University. He has authored articles on transportation safety issues that appeared in various journals including the *Journal of Transport Economics and Policy*, the *Quarterly Review of Economics and Business, Accident Analysis and Prevention*, and *Applied Economics*.

ISBN 0-89930-806-6

90000>

EAN

9 780899 308067

HARDCOVER BAR CODE